Lecture Notes in Computer Science　　10379

Commenced Publication in 1973
Founding and Former Series Editors:
Gerhard Goos, Juris Hartmanis, and Jan van Leeuwen

More information about this series at http://www.springer.com/series/7410

Eric Bodden · Mathias Payer
Elias Athanasopoulos (Eds.)

Engineering Secure Software and Systems

9th International Symposium, ESSoS 2017
Bonn, Germany, July 3–5, 2017
Proceedings

 Springer

Editors
Eric Bodden
University of Paderborn
Paderborn
Germany

Elias Athanasopoulos
University of Cyprus
Nicosia
Cyprus

Mathias Payer
Purdue University
West Lafayette
USA

ISSN 0302-9743   ISSN 1611-3349 (electronic)
Lecture Notes in Computer Science
ISBN 978-3-319-62104-3   ISBN 978-3-319-62105-0 (eBook)
DOI 10.1007/978-3-319-62105-0

Library of Congress Control Number: 2017944218

LNCS Sublibrary: SL4 – Security and Cryptology

Printed on acid-free paper

This Springer imprint is published by Springer Nature
The registered company is Springer International Publishing AG
The registered company address is: Gewerbestrasse 11, 6330 Cham, Switzerland

Preface

It is our pleasure to welcome you to the proceedings of the 9th International Symposium on Engineering Secure Software and Systems (ESSoS 2017), co-located with the conference on Detection of Intrusions and Malware and Vulnerability Assessment (DIMVA 2017). ESSoS is part of a maturing series of symposia that attempts to bridge the gap between the software engineering and security communities with the goal of supporting secure software development. The parallel technical sponsorship from ACM SIGSAC (the ACM interest group in security) and ACM SIGSOFT (the ACM interest group in software engineering) demonstrates the support from both communities and the need for providing such a bridge.

Security mechanisms and the act of software development usually go hand in hand. It is generally not enough to ensure correct functioning of the security mechanisms used. They cannot be blindly inserted into a security-critical system, but the overall system development must take security aspects into account in a coherent way. Building trustworthy components does not suffice, since the interconnections and interactions of components play a significant role in trustworthiness. Lastly, while functional requirements are generally analyzed carefully in systems development, security considerations often arise after the fact. Adding security as an afterthought, however, often leads to problems. Ad hoc development can lead to the deployment of systems that do not satisfy important security requirements. Thus, a sound methodology supporting secure systems development is needed. The presentations and associated publications at ESSoS 2017 contributed to this goal in several directions: first, by improving methodologies for secure software engineering (such as flow analysis and policy compliance). Second, with results for the detection and analysis of software vulnerabilities and the attacks they enable. Finally, for securing software for specific application domains (such as mobile devices and access control).

The conference program featured two keynotes by Konrad Rieck (TU Braunschweig) and Cristiano Giuffrida (VU Amsterdam), as well as research and idea papers. In response to the call for papers, 32 papers were submitted. The Program Committee selected 12 full-paper contributions, presenting new research results on engineering secure software and systems. In addition, three idea papers were selected, giving a concise account of new ideas in the early stages of research. Many individuals and organizations contributed to the success of this event. First of all, we would like to express our appreciation to the authors of the submitted papers and to the Program Committee members and external reviewers, who provided timely and relevant reviews. Many thanks go to the Steering Committee for supporting this series of symposia, and to all the members of the Organizing Committee for their tremendous work and for excelling in their respective tasks. We owe gratitude to ACM SIGSAC/SIGSOFT and LNCS for continuing to support us in this series of symposia.

Finally, we thank the sponsors ERNW, genua, Huawei, Rohde & Schwarz Cybersecurity, and VMRay for generously supporting the ESSoS and DIMVA conferences this year.

May 2017   Eric Bodden
                                                         Mathias Payer
                                               Elias Athanasopoulos

Organization

Program Committee

David Aspinall	University of Edinburgh, UK
Domagoj Babic	Google Inc., USA
Alexandre Bartel	University of Luxembourg, Luxembourg
Amel Bennaceur	The Open University, UK
Stefan Brunthaler	Paderborn University, Germany
Will Enck	NC State University, USA
Michael Franz	University of California, Irvine, USA
Christian Hammer	University of Potsdam, Germany
Michael Hicks	University of Maryland, USA
Trent Jaeger	The Pennsylvania State University, USA
Vassilis P. Kemerlis	Brown University, USA
Johannes Kinder	University of London, UK
Byoungyoung Lee	Purdue University, USA
Yang Liu	University of Oxford, UK
Ben Livshits	Imperial College London, UK
Clémentine Maurice	Technical University Graz, Austria
Andy Meneely	Rochester Institute of Technology, USA
Mira Mezini	Technical University Darmstadt, Germany
Alessandro Orso	Georgia Tech, USA
Christina Pöpper	New York University Abu Dhabi, UAE
Awais Rashid	Lancaster University, UK
Kaveh Razavi	Vrije Universiteit Amsterdam, The Netherlands
Tamara Rezk	Inria, France
Angela Sasse	University College London, UK
Zhendong Su	University of California, Davis, USA
Melanie Volkamer	Karlstad University, Sweden
Xiangyu Zhang	Purdue University, USA

Contents

SEQUOIA: Scalable Policy-Based Access Control for Search Operations
in Data-Driven Applications   1
   Jasper Bogaerts, Bert Lagaisse, and Wouter Joosen

A Voucher-Based Security Middleware for Secure Business Process
Outsourcing   19
   Emad Heydari Beni, Bert Lagaisse, Ren Zhang, Danny De Cock,
   Filipe Beato, and Wouter Joosen

LASARUS: Lightweight Attack Surface Reduction for Legacy
Industrial Control Systems   36
   Anhtuan Le, Utz Roedig, and Awais Rashid

Exploring the Relationship Between Architecture Coupling
and Software Vulnerabilities   53
   Robert Lagerström, Carliss Baldwin, Alan MacCormack,
   Dan Sturtevant, and Lee Doolan

Natural Language Insights from Code Reviews that Missed a Vulnerability:
A Large Scale Study of Chromium   70
   Nuthan Munaiah, Benjamin S. Meyers, Cecilia O. Alm, Andrew Meneely,
   Pradeep K. Murukannaiah, Emily Prud'hommeaux,
   Josephine Wolff, and Yang Yu

Idea: Optimized Automatic Sanitizer Placement   87
   Gebrehiwet Biyane Welearegai and Christian Hammer

FPRandom: Randomizing Core Browser Objects to Break Advanced
Device Fingerprinting Techniques   97
   Pierre Laperdrix, Benoit Baudry, and Vikas Mishra

Control What You Include!: Server-Side Protection Against
Third Party Web Tracking   115
   Dolière Francis Somé, Nataliia Bielova, and Tamara Rezk

Idea-Caution Before Exploitation: The Use of Cybersecurity Domain
Knowledge to Educate Software Engineers Against Software
Vulnerabilities   133
   Tayyaba Nafees, Natalie Coull, Robert Ian Ferguson,
   and Adam Sampson

Defeating Zombie Gadgets by Re-randomizing Code upon Disclosure   143
  Micah Morton, Hyungjoon Koo, Forrest Li, Kevin Z. Snow,
  Michalis Polychronakis, and Fabian Monrose

KASLR is Dead: Long Live KASLR   161
  Daniel Gruss, Moritz Lipp, Michael Schwarz, Richard Fellner,
  Clémentine Maurice, and Stefan Mangard

JTR: A Binary Solution for Switch-Case Recovery   177
  Lucian Cojocar, Taddeus Kroes, and Herbert Bos

A Formal Approach to Exploiting Multi-stage Attacks Based
on File-System Vulnerabilities of Web Applications   196
  Federico De Meo and Luca Viganò

A Systematic Study of Cache Side Channels Across AES
Implementations   213
  Heiko Mantel, Alexandra Weber, and Boris Köpf

Idea: A Unifying Theory for Evaluation Systems   231
  Giampaolo Bella and Rosario Giustolisi

Author Index   241

SEQUOIA: Scalable Policy-Based Access Control for Search Operations in Data-Driven Applications

Jasper Bogaerts[(✉)], Bert Lagaisse, and Wouter Joosen

imec-DistriNet, KU Leuven, 3001 Leuven, Belgium
{jasper.bogaerts,bert.lagaisse,wouter.joosen}@cs.kuleuven.be

Abstract. Policy-based access control is a technology that achieves separation of concerns through evaluating an externalized policy at each access attempt. While this approach has been well-established for request-response applications, it is not supported for database queries of data-driven applications, especially for attribute-based policies. In particular, search operations for such applications involve poor scalability with regard to the data set size for this approach, because they are influenced by dynamic runtime conditions. This paper proposes a scalable application-level middleware solution that performs runtime injection of the appropriate rules into the original search query, so that the result set of the search includes only items to which the subject is entitled. Our evaluation shows that our method scales far better than current state of practice approach that supports policy-based access control.

1 Introduction

Access control is a crucial security measure constraining actions that subjects (e.g., users) can perform on resources. To manage this, several requirements must be taken into account. These include the ability to specify fine-grained rules and support for separation of concerns [6], which enables application developers to delegate security management responsibilities.

A combination of policy-based and attribute-based access control satisfies these requirements. Policy-based access control externalizes access control from the application code and has a policy engine evaluation at each access attempt [21]. This technology provides separation of concerns and increases application modularity. Attribute-based access control supports attributes to be assigned to subjects, actions, resources and the environment. These attributes are compared to each other and to concrete values to determine if access is permitted [11]. This supports specification of fine-grained rules such as *"a document can be read by its creator at any time, and by members of the IT department during working hours"*. XACML [14] is considered the de-facto standard policy language for policy-based, attribute-based access control, with characteristics such as policy trees and multi-valued logic.

Because databases hold a crucial position within IT infrastructures, support for properties such as the ability to enforce fine-grained rules and separation

© Springer International Publishing AG 2017
E. Bodden et al. (Eds.): ESSoS 2017, LNCS 10379, pp. 1–18, 2017.
DOI: 10.1007/978-3-319-62105-0_1

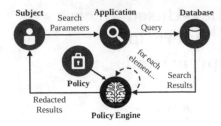

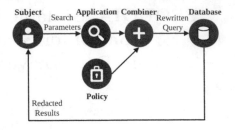

Fig. 1. The a posteriori filter approach evaluates an externalized policy
for each item of the result set.

Fig. 2. The rewriting approach takes
into the access control policy as part of
the query.

of concerns is essential for database operations performed by data-driven applications as well. However, existing approaches generally scale insufficiently with
regard to the database size.

Access control techniques integrated in **database systems** fall short for
three reasons. First, they require database administrators to be involved in the
specification of the policies, thereby violating the separation of concerns. Second,
contemporary applications are designed according to a multi-tier architecture.
This results in applications that perform queries on behalf of the subject without
the latter being identified to the database, which only supports access to be
constrained for individual applications instead of for subjects [20]. Third, in
large scale deployments such as cloud applications, subjects are managed at the
application level and not by the identity management system of the database.

In contrast, access control techniques in the **application**, such as an *a posteriori filter* approach can support externalized policies, but evaluate them for each
item that is part of the search result (i.e., the *resources*). This approach filters
out any item to which the subject is not entitled based on a policy evaluation,
as illustrated in Fig. 1. While this approach supports separation of concerns, as
security administrators can manage policies independently from the application,
it does not scale with an increasing result set. This is true especially for large
attribute-based policies [22].

This paper takes an alternative approach that performs runtime injection of
the appropriate access rules into the search query based on the context in which
subjects perform the search operation. It is illustrated in Fig. 2. The approach
leverages the filtering system of the underlying database to select only items
to which the subject is entitled. Using this approach, we support separation
of concerns, the ability to specify attribute-based policies, and can scale with
regard to the database size. This paper presents the following contributions:

- A set of well-defined transformation rules that rewrites STAPL policies [2],
  which are similar to XACML [14], into search queries for RDBMSes.
- An architecture and evaluation of Sequoia, an application-level middleware
  that transforms and executes search queries for data-driven applications.

This paper is organized as follows: Sect. 2 describes supporting technologies and discusses the state of the art. Section 3 elaborates on the architecture of Sequoia that enables query rewriting. Section 4 discusses how STAPL policies can be transformed to a query expression. Section 5 provides an evaluation of a prototype of Sequoia. Section 6 concludes the paper.

2 Background and Related Work

This section discusses the background that serves as a basis for the remainder of the paper. First, it discusses the supporting technologies, such as XACML and STAPL, and provides further analysis of the problem. Next, it elaborates on related database access control technologies.

Supporting technologies. Access control policies can be externalized from the application into a separate artifact that is evaluated by a specialized engine at each access attempt [21]. As opposed to in-code access control, this approach, called *policy-based access control*, increases modularity, avoids application redeployment when a policy is modified, and provides separation of concerns.

XACML [14] is a framework and policy language that supports policy-based access control. It also supports the specification of *attribute-based policies*, which enables fine-grained rule specification. Attribute-based policies support attributes assigned to subjects, resources, actions and the environment that are compared to each other and to concrete values in *expressions*. Attributes are substituted by concrete values at each access attempt to determine if access is permitted.

The basic elements of a XACML policy are *policy components* and *rules*[1]. Rules have a *condition* expression, and policy components have a *target* expression[2]. An expression evaluates to `true`, `false`, or leads to an error (e.g., when an attribute could not be retrieved). Expressions compare attributes or combine other expressions with logical operators (i.e., and, or, not). Whenever an expression evaluates to `false` for a rule or policy component, that element is *not applicable*. Elements that are not applicable are not taken into account in the evaluation decision. For example, rule r_1 of Fig. 3 is not applicable for a subject with `org=bankA` that performs a `view` action on a resource with `is_private=true` and `destination_org=bankB`. However, the targets of p_1 and p_2 are applicable for this access attempt.

Besides a condition, rules also specify an effect (i.e., `permit` or `deny`) that is taken into account when the condition of the rule is applicable. As a result, policy elements evaluate to permit, deny, not applicable or an error (called indeterminate in XACML).

---

[1] XACML differentiates between policy *sets* and policies, but for brevity we make no distinction in this paper.

[2] Rules can also have targets, but a conjunction with their condition is semantically equivalent, so we disregard this.

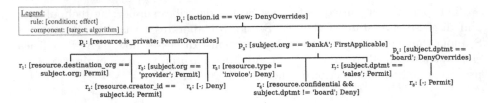

Fig. 3. Example of a XACML-like policy. Policy component p_1 has a deny overrides combining algorithm and a target expression that specifies its children are only relevant for *view* actions. Components p_2 and p_3 have a permit overrides and first applicable combining algorithm, respectively, and child rules. Dashes indicate empty expressions.

A policy component evaluation can yield multiple, possibly conflicting decisions (e.g., when multiple rules are applicable). This is resolved by using *combining algorithms*. This paper focuses on permit overrides (in which a permit decision overrides other decisions of direct children in the component), deny overrides and first applicable (in which the first applicable rule determines the final decision). For example, p_1 in Fig. 3 has a deny overrides algorithm, meaning that if p_3 evaluates to deny, then p_1 evaluates to deny regardless of the decision of p_2 or p_4. Policy components have either rules or other policy components as children, thus forming *policy trees*. When their target expressions are applicable, their child elements are also evaluated to come to a policy decision.

This paper uses STAPL [2] policies as a basis for transformation. STAPL is a framework and policy language that closely resembles XACML, but which offers more ease of use and a slightly better evaluation performance. Any XACML policy can generally be converted to a STAPL policy, and STAPL policies can similarly be expressed in XACML. Hence, the transformation process applied in this paper is also applicable for XACML policies.

Figure 3 illustrates a small example policy of an industry case study that motivated this work [7]. Here, if the action that is performed is *"view"* (e.g., as is the case in a search operation), subjects can access documents depending on their department, whether they have created it or were addressed, and so on. For example, a subject of the sales department can view invoices if the organization to which he/she belongs was addressed (rules 1, 5 and 7), unless it involves a confidential invoice (rule 6).

While both XACML and STAPL support fine-grained specification of access rules, their policy evaluation process also involves a considerable overhead [22]. For traditional request-response applications, this overhead is in many cases acceptable. When the policy is evaluated for a large set of resources such as for search operations on a database, however, this can become an impeding factor.

Related work. Because of its importance, a lot of prior research has focused on database security [3]. This paper focuses on row-level access control [3] that follows the Truman model[3] [19]. In this regard, there generally exist three approaches to provide scalable search queries on databases.

---

[3] In a Truman model, queries are transparently modified to restrict access of a subject to database items.

The first approach involves techniques generally classified under the term *"Fine-Grained Access Control (FGAC)"* [19]. FGAC uses query rewriting techniques [1,5,8,10,15,19] to provide database security. This is typically performed using rules that are specified in the native query language of the target database and may be realized through the creation of *views*. While this approach scales with regard to the size of the result set, it also has some issues. In particular, since rules are specified in the native query language, they at least partly violate the principle of separation of concerns [6], because the database administrator must help specify the policies. Worse, this approach generally assumes a two-tier architecture in which subjects directly query the database and can be identified accordingly. Contemporary applications are typically designed according to a multi-tier architecture, and generally perform queries on behalf of the subject without identifying them to the database [20]. This only supports access control to filter based on accessing applications. Moreover, in large-scale deployments such as cloud applications, subjects are typically managed at the application level, and not by the identity management system of the database. Our approach does not suffer these issues due to substitution of subject properties in the query and the support for externalized policies that are rewritten.

A second approach involves configuring the access control component that is used by the database based on an external policy. Compared to the previous approach, this does support separation of concerns. Notable examples for this approach are MyABDAC [12] and a recent system proposed by Mutti et al [13]. MyABDAC uses XACML policies to generate access control lists for the underlying database system. These can then be employed to constrain access. While this approach maintains separation of concerns, it also assumes a two-tier architecture and hence suffers the same issues as the first approach. Moreover, it does not scale well with regard to the size of the database. Mutti et al. introduce a system that extends SQLite for SELinux support. While this system scales, it requires specification of database hooks and supports only lattice-based policies, which are not as fine-grained as XACML policies supported by our approach.

A third approach involves evaluating the access control policy for each of the items in the result set of a search query. Bouncer [16] takes this approach for the CPOL trust management system. While this approach supports separation of concerns and the specification of fine-grained policies, it can also introduce a considerable overhead when the size of the search result set increases. This is especially true for fine-grained rules, typically included in attribute-based policies [22]. Our approach does not suffer from this problem.

This paper pursues an approach that uses query rewriting by using an externalized policy that is injected at runtime as part of the search query. This approach scales with regard of the result set and regards the separation of concerns principle. Also, it does not require DBMS modification. This approach has also been explored by Axiomatics Data Access Filter [18]. Compared to them, this work focuses on the transformation process, including conversion of XACML concepts such as policy trees, combining algorithms and multi-valued logic to a database query. Moreover, we present a thorough evaluation of the approach.

Besides access control techniques, several other security measures can secure search queries on database systems. In particular, secure query processing [24] and homomorphic encryption [9] aim at supporting queries on an encrypted data set. While these measures have several issues such as performance and fine-grainedness of the data set, they can be used complementary to our approach.

Lastly, this research was also influenced by related work done in the enforcement of usage control. In particular, Pretschner et al. [17] have presented an architecture that enforces usage control policies in a distributed system, with an emphasis of reducing policy enforcement overhead. In contrast, our approach does not focus on distributed evaluation for enforcing policies.

3   Sequoia Architecture

This section describes an application-level solution that supports access control on database search operations in data-driven applications. The solution provides scalability, expressiveness and separation of concerns. In order to comply with these requirements, we employ a policy-based, attribute-based access control system as a basis for the access control rules that must be supported. Since XACML is considered the de-facto standard for such access control systems, we use its language model as a basis for the transformation. We use a rewriting approach that involves transforming the policy to a query. The transformation process must cope with fundamental issues to support STAPL policy conversion. In particular, characteristics such as policy trees, multi-valued logic and combining algorithms must be translated to a semantically equivalent query expression.

Scope. This paper analyzes the query rewriting approach for relational databases. We expect resources to be represented as the *rows* of (one or more) tables and their corresponding attributes as the *columns* of these tables. These resources are referred to as *items*. We assume that all attributes of the resources referred to in the policy are stored in the database. In addition, the database schema is expected to provide proper mapping of the attributes onto columns.

Overview. Figure 4 provides an overview of the architecture. The Sequoia middleware operates between the application layer and the database. Whenever the

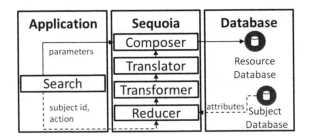

Fig. 4. The rewriting approach reduces, transforms and translates the policy and combines it with the original search parameters into a query.

application queries the database, the middleware intercepts the query and performs run-time injection of the appropriate access rules that are combined with the original search parameters in a query. The composed query reflects only relevant rules for the subject and ensures that only the items to which the subject is entitled (i.e., those permitted if the policy is evaluated for each item of the original search result) are returned.

The policy semantics are preserved throughout the transformation process. The result set for executing the transformed query is equivalent to the set of items permitted when performing a policy evaluation on each item resulting from the original query. To support this, the middleware uses four components: the reducer, transformer, translator and composer.

Reducer. This component obtains the relevant attribute values associated with the acting subject, action and environment. Next, similar to [18], it performs a partial substitution and evaluation of all expressions in the policy that do not refer to any resource attributes (which will be queried in the database). This enables pruning of the policy for rules and policy components that always evaluate to true or false. The reduction minimizes the query that is generated and eliminates the need for subject attributes to be stored in the same database as the resources that are searched. For example, consider the policy in Fig. 3 reduced for the `view` action and a subject with `id=51, dptmt=sales` and `org=bankA`. This is shown in Fig. 5. The policy is significantly smaller, which avoids redundant checks and simplifies the final query.

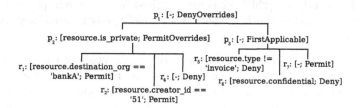

Fig. 5. Reduction of Fig. 3 for a subject with `id=51, dptmt=sales` and `org=bankA`.

Transformer. This component transforms the policy to a boolean expression that can be translated to the query language and combined with search parameters at a later stage. Due to policy reduction, no attributes associated with the subject, action or environment should be left in the policy as they were substituted with the relevant values.

The transformation must be equivalent for **permit** decisions. This means that whenever a policy evaluation leads to a **permit** decision for a certain item, the corresponding boolean expression evaluation must also be **true**. In contrast, if the evaluation of a policy leads to a **not applicable** or **deny** decision, its corresponding expression must evaluate to **false**. This also filters out any items for which the evaluation is indecisive. If an error occurs during the evaluation of the boolean expression, the search query must be aborted altogether[4].

For example, consider again Fig. 5 the reduced policy. The transformation of this policy for the acting subject results in boolean expression $[resource.is\_private \land (resource.destination\_org == `bankA' \lor resource.creator\_id == `51')] \land [resource.type == `invoice' \land \neg resource.confidential]$. This expression is only satisfied for items to which the subject is entitled.

Transformation of STAPL policies is not trivial. In particular, we need to take into account policy trees, multi-valued logic and combining algorithms when a policy is transformed to a single expression. For this reason, we elaborate on this in more detail in Sect. 4.

Translator. This component translates the expression that resulted from the transformation to the query language of the database to which it is submitted. This involves two tasks. First, the syntax of the expression is translated to the syntax of the query language for the target database. Second, all attributes referenced in the expression are translated to column references in the database.

While the first task is generally straightforward because SQL supports boolean expressions equivalent to the ones to which we transformed, an attribute-to-schema mapping is required for the second task. This mapping describes how attributes are mapped onto the columns corresponding to tables in the database. In some cases, some of the attributes associated with the resource could be stored in a different table than the one that is queried. As a consequence, the mapping enables the translator to cope with the complexity of the database schema and can indicate which joins are required in the search query. The table that is being queried is the *base table* from which joins to auxiliary tables are accommodated.

Composer. This component combines search parameters of the original query with the translated access rules. For example, the transformation of the policy of Fig. 5 was previously translated to database-specific syntax. This is now combined with the query using an *and*-operator. Also, any required join operations are injected in the search query.

4   Transformation

This section addresses the second step in the approach outlined in the previous section. It performs the transformation of characteristics such as policy trees, multi-valued logic and combining algorithms to a boolean expression. To achieve a boolean expression, we iterate over two steps until the policy consists of a single policy component with a permit overrides algorithm, no target and only rules as children. We call this a *flat component*. Figure 6 shows an overview of the process. Figure 7 illustrates an example.

---

[4] In this transformation, we do not consider extended indeterminate decisions that are defined in XACML 3.0. Contrary to request-response applications, errors can not always be gracefully handled for individual data rows.

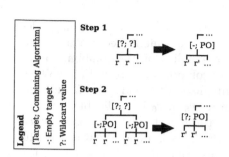

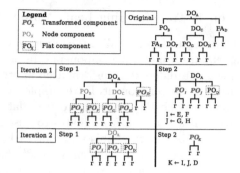

Fig. 6. Transformation process overview

Fig. 7. Policy transformation example

As a **first step**, we transform every component in the policy tree that has only rules as children (i.e., a *leaf component*) to an equivalent flat component. Also, we conjunct the target expression of each transformed policy component with the condition expressions of all of its child rules. For this, the original combining algorithm determines how the transformation is performed to retain semantic equivalence. As a **second step**, we regard every *node component*, i.e. components with only flat components as children. We pull up all rules of the children of these node components and transform them to a policy component with a permit overrides algorithm. Similar to the first step, semantic equivalence is retained through transformation methods that differ for each combining algorithm. By iterating over these steps, the policy tree is gradually flattened to result in a single, flat component containing only rules. A boolean expression is then created as disjunction of the conditions of all permit rule children. Figure 7 illustrates the transformation process applied on a policy. As the figure shows, the policy is gradually transformed to a single component in bottom-up fashion.

The boolean expression is semantically equivalent to the original with regard to the permit decision. In other words, if the policy evaluates to `permit`, the boolean expression evaluates to `true`. For `not applicable` and `deny` decisions in the policy, the boolean expression evaluates to `false`. If an error occurs (e.g., an attribute value could not be retrieved), the search query will be aborted. We have developed a formal proof that the transformation process maintains the semantics of the policy when these equivalence rules are taken into account [4]. Note that Turkmen et al. [23] also developed a flattening process for policies, but focus on policy analysis, while our approach is optimized for database queries.

In the remainder of this section, we elaborate on the two steps that are iterated over during the transformation process. Section 5 evaluates a Sequoia prototype that employs this process for generating queries from STAPL policies.

Step 1: Transforming Leaf Components

This step transforms all *leaf components* (i.e., policy components with only rules as children) into flat components. In order to retain semantic equivalence, this requires a different transformation approach depending on the combining algorithm of the component. For example, consider component p_3 from Fig. 5. When this component is transformed to a flat component, the condition of rule r_7 is transformed so that it evaluates to false if either r_5 or r_6 is applicable.

As a first part of this step, for each rule, the target expression is included in conjunction with the condition of that rule. This is done regardless of the combining algorithm. Next, we perform a transformation that depends on the combining algorithm of the component[5].

For **first applicable** components, a permit rule is applicable only if none of the deny rules that *precede* it are applicable. Consequently, we can transform a permit rule by conjunction of its original condition with the negation of conditions of its preceding deny rules. The deny rules of the original component can then be included without modification. More formally, the condition of each permit rule r_i of the original leaf component P is transformed as follows:

$$cond(r_i) \wedge \bigwedge_{r_j \in pre(r_i, P)} \neg cond(r_j)$$

In which cond indicates the condition of a rule, and pre the set of all preceding deny rules in the same component P.

For **deny overrides** components any applicable deny rule overrides other decisions. Consequently, the transformation of a permit rule conjuncts the original condition with the negation of *all* of the deny rule conditions of the original component. Similar to the first applicable transformation approach, deny rules are included without modification. More formally, the condition of each permit rule r_i of the original leaf component P is transformed as follows:

$$cond(r_i) \wedge \bigwedge_{r_j \in deny(P)} \neg cond(r_j)$$

With deny the set of all deny rules in the same component P as the given rule.

For **permit overrides** components, no further transformation is required as it already is a flat component after conjunction of conditions with the target.

Consider components p_2 and p_3 from Fig. 5 as an example of the approach. In this example, rules r_1, r_2 and r_4 are rewritten to conjunct target *"resource.is_private"* as an additional constraint for their conditions. For p_3, on the other hand, r_7 is transformed to contain a negation of conditions of r_5 and r_6. Also, r_5 and r_6 are included in the result without modification. This results in a permit overrides component with permit rule *"resource.type == 'invoice'* $\wedge$ $\neg$ *resource.confidential"* and original deny rules r_5 and r_6.

---

[5] For brevity, we do not elaborate on approaches for minimizing the generated expression in this paper.

Step 2: Pulling Up Flat Components Rules

This step involves all policy components that only have flat components as children. The policy components for which all child components satisfy these requirements are called *node components*. In this step, we transform the rules of all child components, and include them as direct children of the node component. We also change the node component combining algorithm to permit overrides.

The transformation approach for pulling up flat component rules to be combined at a higher level in the policy tree differs from the one introduced in step 1. In particular, it takes into account how rules of one child component affect the decision process at the level of the node component. For example, consider p_1 in Fig. 5. A deny rule such as r_5 can affect the decision process even if r_1 is applicable, because the deny decision that may stem from r_5 overrides any permit decision due to the deny overrides of p_1.

In order to pull up the rules associated with flat components, the transformation method needs to ensure that the result has the same semantics as the original policy component. Hence, the transformed rules must take into account their original condition, but may also include conditions of rules from other child components of the node component.

If the node component has a **first applicable** algorithm, all of the deny rules of preceding child components are taken into account when a permit rule of a certain child component is transformed. Consequently, the generated rule cannot be applicable if a deny rule of a preceding child component was applicable. This is done by generating a permit rule that has the condition of the original permit rule in conjunction with the negation for each deny rule of preceding components. Similar to the previous step, the deny rules are included without modification. More formally, the condition of each permit rule r_i of a child component is transformed as follows:

$$cond(r_i) \wedge \bigwedge_{r_j \in preco(r_i)} \neg cond(r_j)$$

In which **preco** reflects all deny rules from policy components of the given rule's ancestor that precede its parent. Deny rules are included in the result without modification. Note that if a deny rule of **preco** is applicable, it can still be overridden by a permit rule condition of its own component.

If the node component has a **deny overrides** algorithm, the permit rules of all child components are combined in a single, *unified* permit rule. All deny rules are again included without modification. The unified rule must ensure two properties. First, at least one permit rule of the child components must be applicable in order for the unified rule to be applicable. Second, for each child component, if no permit rule is applicable in that child, then its deny rules must not be applicable. Otherwise, the unified rule is also not applicable. The first property ensures that the *not applicable* decision is propagated during the flattening of the policy tree. The second property ensures that if a child component leads to a deny decision, then the evaluation of its parent component will also lead to a deny decision because of the deny overrides algorithm of the node component. In this case, the unified rule can not be applicable, while a deny rule is. The unified permit rule has a condition that is a conjunction of a clause of all permit rule conditions `appl`, and all *component clauses* `comp`. Here, `appl` ensures the first property and the component clauses ensure the second property of the unified rule. More formally, we describe this as

$$appl(P) := \bigvee_{r_i \in permits(P)} cond(r_i)$$

In which `permits` retrieves all permit rules of the given policy component and all its children. Similarly, `denies` fetches deny rules of a component and its children. For each child component P_C, component clause `comp` is constructed as

$$comp(P_C) := (\bigvee_{r_i \in permits(P_C)} cond(r_i)) \vee \bigwedge_{r_i \in denies(P_C)} \neg cond(r_i)$$

If a node component has a **permit overrides** algorithm, all rules of its children are included without modification.

For example, consider again component p_1 from Fig. 5. In order to be permitted, the following expression must be satisfied for a evaluation request: "$[resource.is\_private \wedge (resource.destination\_org == 'bank\,A' \vee resource.creator\_id == '51')] \wedge [resource.type == invoice \wedge \neg resource.confidential]$". Here, the unified rule was simplified by applying common logical reduction techniques.

Flat Component to Boolean Expression

The transformation steps are repeated until a single, flat component is resulted. Finally, the flat policy component is converted to a boolean expression by constructing a disjunction of all permit rule conditions of the flat policy component. If none of the permit rule conditions are applicable, the boolean expression will evaluate to false, and the database item for which the expression was evaluated will not be included in the result set. This maintains the original policy semantics because each transformation step ensures that a permit rule of the transformation is only applicable if it was not overridden by a deny decision. A formal equivalence proof is given in [4].

5   Performance Evaluation

As discussed earlier in this paper, the a posteriori filter approach for supporting policy-based access control for search operations on databases becomes prohibitive with regard to performance when the size of the search result set is large. To resolve this, we have presented an alternative approach that uses query rewriting to reduce the overhead of access control. This section evaluates an implementation of the rewriting approach discussed in Sects. 3 and 4 for transformations from STAPL [2] policies to relational databases, and compares it to the a posteriori filter approach that was illustrated in Fig. 1.

We evaluate five aspects. First, we discuss scalability of the rewriting approach compared to the a posteriori filter. Second, we evaluate the overhead introduced by the rewriting approach. Third, we discuss the impact of policy size for different combining algorithms. Fourth, we inspect the performance impact of the amount of evaluated attributes. Fifth, we also determine the impact of the proportion of permitted items on performance.

Setup. The evaluation was performed on a Dell OptiPlex 755 computer with Intel Core 2 Duo 3 GHz processor and 4 GB internal memory using Ubuntu 15.10 as an operating system and performing all database requests using JDBC to a MariaDB[6] database with caching disabled as much as possible. All queries were performed locally (i.e., no network traffic was involved). We repeated all tests 10000 times after 100 warmups and took the mean values for processing times.

Scalability. As a first part of the evaluation, we have assessed the scalability of the rewriting approach with regard to the size of the search result set. To do this, we have compared how the approach performs with regard to a posteriori filter, which was illustrated in Fig. 1. The test evaluated the total processing time required to perform the search query together with determining what items must be part of the result set. We did this based on an extensive policy that was inspired by an industry case study [7] that motivated this work and that contains 32 policy components and 63 rules that regard 33 attributes[7].

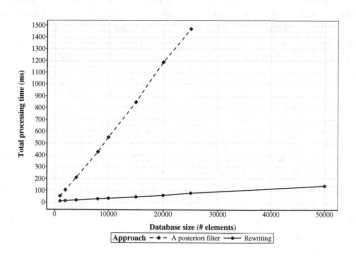

Fig. 8. Comparison of processing times for an increasing data set size. Lower is better.

The results are shown in Fig. 8. They demonstrate the processing times involved with both approaches for a subject that is entitled to about 40% of

---

[6] https://mariadb.org/.

[7] This policy can be found at https://github.com/stapl-dsl/stapl-examples/blob/master/src/main/scala/stapl/examples/policies/EdocsPolicy.scala.

the items. As the figure shows, the rewriting approach performs far better than
the a posteriori filter. We only performed evaluation for the latter for up to 25000
items, because measuring it involved too much processing time for repeated tests.
In contrast, the rewriting approach requires considerably less processing time
with regard to the database size. For example, the same test for a data set of a
million items had a processing time of 4037 ms. This included the serialization
of the items in the result set in Java data structures, which amounted to 67% of
the query processing time on average. Consequently, we can conclude that the
rewriting approach scales well with an increasing data set.

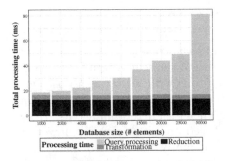
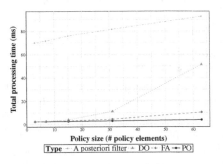

Fig. 9. Transformation overhead
analysis. The processing times for
reduction and transformation steps
remain constant, whereas query
processing times increase with the
amount of data items.

Fig. 10. The processing time in function of the policy depth for first
applicable (FA), deny overrides (DO),
permit overrides (PO) policies and the
a posteriori filter. Lower is better.

Overhead. As a second part of the evaluation, we inspected the overhead
involved with the different steps of the rewriting process. We have done this
for an increasing search result size in a same test setup as the scalability test.

Figure 9 shows the overhead of different transformation steps in the rewriting
approach. The figure shows that the policy reduction and transformation steps
remain constant and are dominated by the query processing for larger result
sets. The overhead for the policy reduction and transformation steps depends on
the subject. For some subjects, for example, the transformation step amounts to
less than 1 ms.

Because overhead of the transformation steps remain constant, the query
processing time becomes the dominant factor in the total processing time as
the size of the database increases. In the a posteriori filter approach, the time
required for policy evaluation on each element is the dominating factor for the
processing time. Also, note that the result of the transformation can be cached for
each subject, which reduces the overall processing time for subsequent searches.

Policy size impact. As a third part of the evaluation, we have assessed the
impact of the size of the policy on the processing time of the rewriting approach.

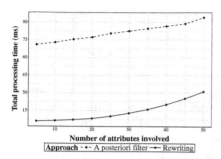

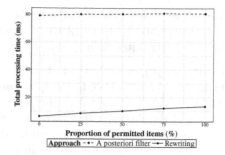

Fig. 11. Processing time in function of the number of involved attributes. Lower is better.

Fig. 12. Impact of the proportion of permitted items on processing times. Lower is better.

We evaluate this for the deny overrides, permit overrides and first applicable combining algorithms.

The test generated policies for varying policy *depths*, i.e., numbers of nodes on the path from the root policy component to the leaf-level components. For each depth, the policy contains $2^{d+1} - 1$ policy elements, 2^d of which are rules. Each component has two children and the same combining algorithm. Leaf components all have one permit and one deny rule. The test was performed on 1000 elements.

Figure 10 shows the processing time for the rewriting approach for different combining algorithms and the a posteriori filter when the depth of the policy tree increases. For the a posteriori filter, we have plotted the mean evaluation time for the three policy types, as they had similar processing times. As expected, total processing times increase due to an increasing number of policy elements. The deny overrides algorithm performs worst for the rewriting approach. This is because the transformation introduces inevitable redundancy in the query to maintain original semantics. This test, however, involves the worst-case scenario for a large policy. Moreover, a posteriori filtering still exceeds the query rewriting approach for an extensive policy. The largest proportion of the overhead is due to policy transformation, which amounts to about 85% of the total time for deny overrides components in the rewriting approach.

The permit overrides transformations, on the other hand, perform best because the transformation does not need to take into account the conditions of any deny rules.

Attribute impact. As a fourth part of the evaluation, we investigated the impact that the amount of attributes involved in the evaluation had on the processing time of the secured search query. To determine this, we generated several policies that require n resource attributes to be evaluated prior to resorting to a decision, with n ranging from 5 up to 50 attributes. The test was performed on a data set of 1000 items, from which 50% are part of the final result.

Figure 11 shows that the rewriting approach performs better than the a posteriori filter, while difference in processing times is fairly constant. The a posteriori filter has higher overhead because all items are fetched and evaluated. For the rewriting approach, the curve is explained due to the time required to perform the transformation (up to 78% of the total time) and the overall impact of the amount of attributes seems limited for the amount of attributes involved.

Result size impact. As the last part of the evaluation, we measured the impact on the processing time of the proportion of items that are part of the permitted result set. This test considers the processing time for an increasing percentage of items of the data set to which the subject is entitled. For this test, we used the same setup as for the attribute impact evaluation.

Figure 12 demonstrates that the processing time for the a posteriori filter approach remains fairly constant, because it needs to evaluate all items regardless of the proportion of permitted items. In contrast, the rewriting approach has a processing time that is directly proportional to the amount of items that are permitted. In other words, if a subject is entitled to a smaller proportion of the data set, the rewriting approach will perform better than if he/she is entitled to a large proportion. For example, if a subject is entitled to 25% of the items, the processing time will be smaller than if he/she is entitled to 75% of the items. In all cases however, the rewriting approach performs significantly better than the a posteriori filter.

Summary. The evaluation indicates that the rewriting approach performs far better than the a posteriori filter, because it scales well with regard to the result set size and the number of attributes evaluated. Moreover, the approach performs even better when a subject is entitled to a smaller proportion of the data set, which is common in contemporary applications.

6   Conclusion

This paper presented an application-level middleware that supports scalable policy-based access control for search queries on relational databases. It does this in a manner that also supports expressive policies and separation of concerns. Because the de-facto standard for policy-based, attribute-based languages is XACML, this paper also elaborated on a method that transforms policies with a similar model to a boolean query expression that can be translated and combined with the search parameters. The evaluation shows that our approach performs far better than the current state of practice. As a result, we can conclude that this work constitutes an important step for maturation of both policy-based access control and database access control using application-level middleware.

References

1. Oracle Virtual Private Database (VPD). http://docs.oracle.com/cd/B28359_01/network.111/b28531/vpd.htm. Accessed 9 Sept 2016
2. Simple Tree-structured Attribute-based Policy Language (STAPL), June 2016. https://github.com/stapl-dsl. Accessed 26 Sept 2016

3. Bertino, E., Sandhu, R.: Database security-concepts, approaches, and challenges. IEEE Trans. Dependable Secur. Comput. **2**(1), 2–19 (2005)
4. Bogaerts, J., Lagaisse, B., Joosen, W.: Transforming XACML policies into database search queries. Technical report, KU Leuven (2017)
5. Carminati, B., Ferrari, E., Cao, J., Tan, K.L.: A framework to enforce access control over data streams. ACM TISSEC (2010)
6. De Win, B., Piessens, F., Joosen, W., Verhanneman, T.: On the importance of the separation-of-concerns principle in secure software engineering. In: Application of Engineering Principles to System Security Design (2002)
7. Decat, M., Bogaerts, J., Lagaisse, B., Joosen, W.: The e-document case study: functional analysis and access control requirements. Technical report, KU Leuven (2014)
8. Franzoni, S., Mazzoleni, P., Valtolina, S., Bertino, E.: Towards a fine-grained access control model and mechanisms for semantic databases. In: IEEE International Conference on Web Services, ICWS 2007, pp. 993–1000. IEEE (2007)
9. Gentry, C.: Fully homomorphic encryption using ideal lattices. In: STOC, vol. 9, pp. 169–178 (2009)
10. Grummt, E., Müller, M.: Fine-grained access control for EPC information services. In: Floerkemeier, C., Langheinrich, M., Fleisch, E., Mattern, F., Sarma, S.E. (eds.) IOT 2008. LNCS, vol. 4952, pp. 35–49. Springer, Heidelberg (2008). doi:10.1007/978-3-540-78731-0_3
11. Hu, V.C., Ferraiolo, D., Kuhn, R., Schnitzer, A., Sandlin, K., Miller, R., Scarfone, K.: Guide to Attribute Based Access Control (ABAC) Definition and Considerations. NIST Special Publication (2014)
12. Jahid, S., Gunter, C.A., Hoque, I., Okhravi, H.: MyABDAC: compiling XACML policies for attribute-based database access control. In: Proceedings of the First ACM Conference on Data and Application Security and Privacy, pp. 97–108. ACM (2011)
13. Mutti, S., Bacis, E., Paraboschi, S.: SeSQLite: security enhanced SQLite: mandatory access control for android databases. In: Proceedings of the 31st Annual Computer Security Applications Conference, pp. 411–420. ACM (2015)
14. OASIS: eXtensible Access Control Markup Language (XACML) Standard, Version 3.0 (2013). http://docs.oasis-open.org/xacml/3.0/xacml-3.0-core-spec-os-en.pdf
15. Olson, L.E., Gunter, C.A., Cook, W.R., Winslett, M.: Implementing reflective access control in SQL. In: Gudes, E., Vaidya, J. (eds.) DBSec 2009. LNCS, vol. 5645, pp. 17–32. Springer, Heidelberg (2009). doi:10.1007/978-3-642-03007-9_2
16. Opyrchal, L., Cooper, J., Poyar, R., Lenahan, B., Zeinner, D.: Bouncer: policy-based fine grained access control in large databases. Int. J. Secur. Appl. **5**, 1–16 (2011)
17. Pretschner, A., Hilty, M., Basin, D.: Distributed usage control. Commun. ACM **49**, 39–44 (2006)
18. Rissanen, E.: Fine-grained relational database access-control policy enforcement using reverse queries. US Patent 9,037,610, 19 May 2015
19. Rizvi, S., Mendelzon, A., Sudarshan, S., Roy, P.: Extending query rewriting techniques for fine-grained access control. In: SIGMOD. ACM (2004)
20. Roichman, A., Gudes, E.: Fine-grained access control to web databases. In: Symposium on Access Control Models and Technologies. ACM (2007)
21. Samarati, P., Vimercati, S.C.: Access control: policies, models, and mechanisms. In: Focardi, R., Gorrieri, R. (eds.) FOSAD 2000. LNCS, vol. 2171, pp. 137–196. Springer, Heidelberg (2001). doi:10.1007/3-540-45608-2_3

22. Turkmen, F., Crispo, B.: Performance evaluation of XACML PDP implementations. In: Proceedings of the 2008 ACM Workshop on Secure Web Services (2008)
23. Turkmen, F., Hartog, J., Ranise, S., Zannone, N.: Analysis of XACML policies with SMT. In: Focardi, R., Myers, A. (eds.) POST 2015. LNCS, vol. 9036, pp. 115–134. Springer, Heidelberg (2015). doi:10.1007/978-3-662-46666-7_7
24. Wang, S., Agrawal, D., Abbadi, A.: A comprehensive framework for secure query processing on relational data in the cloud. In: Jonker, W., Petković, M. (eds.) SDM 2011. LNCS, vol. 6933, pp. 52–69. Springer, Heidelberg (2011). doi:10.1007/978-3-642-23556-6_4

A Voucher-Based Security Middleware for Secure Business Process Outsourcing

Emad Heydari Beni[1]([⊠]), Bert Lagaisse[1], Ren Zhang[2], Danny De Cock[2],
Filipe Beato[2], and Wouter Joosen[1]

[1] imec-Distrinet, KU Leuven, Leuven, Belgium
{emad.heydaribeni,bert.lagaisse,wouter.joosen}@cs.kuleuven.be
[2] imec-COSIC, KU Leuven, Leuven, Belgium
{ren.zhang,danny.decock,filipe.beato}@esat.kuleuven.be

Abstract. Business Process Outsourcing (BPO) enables the delegation of entire business processes to third party providers. Such scenarios involve communication between federated and heterogeneous workflow engines. However, state-of-the-art workflow engines fall short of a distributed authorisation mechanism for this heterogeneous, federated BPO setting.

In a cross-organisational context, the security requirements involve (i) delegation and verification of privileges in a confidential manner, (ii) secure asynchronous operations during the long-term workflows even when the users are logged-off, and (iii) controlling access to interfaces of the different workflow engines involved.

To address these challenges, we present a voucher-based authorisation architecture and middleware. We extended the WF-Interop [2] middleware with a security module to support this authorisation architecture. We further validated our contributions by prototyping a billing workflow case study on top of the extended WF-Interop middleware and evaluated the performance overhead of the security extensions to the middleware.

Keywords: Security middleware · Authorization · Business process

1 Introduction

Software service providers are evolving towards a Business Process Outsourcing (BPO) model. BPO refers to delegation of entire business processes to third party providers. Providers take over the complete business functions and are free to choose the implementations; consumers only receive the results of processes [2, 6,11,25].

For example, accounting departments of many companies outsource their billing processes to external service providers. These processes comprise activities such as documenting, shipment and payment. For instance, (1) an accounting manager submits an order to send some bills by the end of the month. (2) The billing process gets started at the provider's side by the accounting department. The service provider takes over the entire process. (3) They print and package

E. Bodden et al. (Eds.): ESSoS 2017, LNCS 10379, pp. 19–35, 2017.
DOI: 10.1007/978-3-319-62105-0_2

the bills. Afterwards, (4) they start a delivery process at a shipping company. The accounting department periodically inspects the running processes at the provider for progress updates to know the current status of the bills (e.g. sent, resent, paid, etc.).

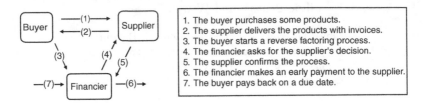

Fig. 1. Reverse Factoring (RF)

Reverse Factoring (RF) in the FinTech sector is another example of such a process. Reverse Factoring enables companies to pay their bills on time with assistance of financiers (also called brokers), see Fig. 1. In brief, (1) a buyer purchases some products from a supplier; (2) the supplier sends a bill to the buyer with a due date; the buyer wants to pay the bill on time to ensure their business continuity; (3) they therefore request a financier to get financial assistance; (4, 5) the financier evaluates the request in first place; then they negotiate with the supplier for their decision. If all parties reach an agreement on this process, (6) the financier pays the buyer's bill before its due date; and instead, (7) the buyer will pay the bill to the financier with an extended due date, perhaps with interest. Buyer companies tend to employ BPO in order to outsource the entire process to a provider (a broker/financier) to be able to concentrate on their core business. The Reverse Factoring scenario is the running example in this section.

Each of the business processes gets executed over different workflow engines located in different companies. These heterogeneous workflow engines have their own business-specific security mechanisms to protect their sensitive data and control the access rights. The diversity of technologies used in workflow management systems across the BPO parties introduces interoperability issues with respect to service computing in general, and security in particular. Heydari et al. [2] outlines the common patterns among such BPO scenarios as follows.

- Multiple parties are involved in BPO model, resulting in federated, heterogeneous workflow engines.
- Outsourced processes are long running workflows, e.g. taking days or weeks to be completed.
- Occasionally, the client parties inspect the progress of outsourced processes.

On the one hand, most of the security mechanisms in workflow engines are used to meet the intra-organisational requirements, e.g. Role Based Access Control (RBAC) [9]. On the other hand, the federated, cross-organisational approaches in more general context (e.g. WS-Trust [19]) do not particularly take all of the process outsourcing characteristics into account. Such characteristics include hierarchical and iterative delegation of privileges, human-involvement, organisational confidentiality, long-running workflows or asynchronous operations without active sessions (see Fig. 2).

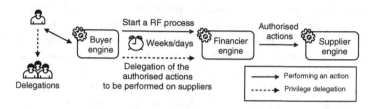

Fig. 2. Reverse Factoring (RF)

The scope and contribution of this paper is a security architecture and middleware that support following authorisation requirements and features in a BPO setting with federated, heterogeneous workflow engines.

1. *Delegation and validation of all or subsets of authorised privileges (access rights) to other involved people or executing, federated workflow engines.* For example, an accounting manager (buyer company) delegates the progress inspection privilege to an accountant; or an accounting workflow engine delegates a subset of its BPO functional rights (e.g. starting a process at a seller) to a financier engine.
2. *Secure asynchronous operations during long-term workflows even when the users are logged off.* For example, an accounting engine in a buyer company may require to perform an action (e.g. start/inspect a process) when the accountant is not logged in and there is no actual session available in the execution context of the engine. Therefore, there should be a way for the buyer's engine to authenticate against the financier's engine and perform the authorised actions.
3. *Controlling access to interfaces of workflow engines in the context of BPO.* For example, when an accounting manager `starts` a Reverse Factoring process, an accountant should not be able to `cancel` the process, but only inspect it. That constraint should be reflected to the accounting workflow engine by the application interface (API) of the financier's workflow engine.

To address these requirements, we present an access and enforcement mechanism as an integral part of the BPO model and middleware. This system works with *vouchers* (also called *tokens* or *assertions*), i.e. a digital representation of a claim or set of claims which has been certified by a particular entity [22]. Vouchers establish a decentralised authorisation management that aims to provide trust and security assurance to the involved parties in BPO scenarios.

To validate the voucher system, we implemented a security module for the *WF-Interop* middleware [2], i.e. a middleware interfacing heterogeneous and federated workflow engines in a unified RESTful architecture to support the BPO use cases. The security module enables BPO consumers and providers (1) to manage (i.e. produce or delegate) security vouchers and (2) to verify the privileges and integrity of vouchers for each service call.

Furthermore, WF-Interop has a *hypermedia-driven* application interface, meaning that it enables the service consumers to discover the capabilities of underlying workflow engines by offering pointers to the next possible actions upon each service invocation. For example, if a consumer, via WF-Interop, starts a workflow instance in a Ruote [17] engine, WF-Interop embeds hyperlinks of other related actions such as `pause` and `abort` in the response. The capability propositions are based on the underlying engine, the type, the state of the process, and most importantly, the access right of the entity identity. **Hence the security module securely controls the consumer-specific action propositions based on the voucher content.**

The rest of this paper is structured as follows. Section 2 describes the necessary background about business processes and BPO, as well as an overview of related work in the authorisation domain. Section 3 introduces a voucher-based architecture to achieve secure BPO. Section 4 validates the aforementioned concepts and the security extensions to the WF-Interop middleware by a billing workflow case study. Section 5 evaluates the WF-Interop extensions in terms of performance. Section 6 concludes this paper.

2   Background and Related Work

In this section, we present a brief overview of workflows[1] and Business Process Outsourcing (BPO). Afterwards, the WF-Interop [2] middleware is described, including the key interfaces and hypermedia-driven architecture. In addition, the related work in the domain of security protocols and frameworks for authentication and authorisation are presented.

2.1   Background on BPO and WF-Interop

A business process is a group of activities that, once completed, will accomplish an organisational goal. For example, when you purchase a product online, you start a business process of purchase. This business process contains activities such as order placement, bank transfer, inventory checks and shipment. Once all are completed, you receive the product (the main goal).

A *process definition* is a representation of what is intended to happen [5], described by a business process modelling language such as BPMN. It contains a sequence of activities showing the order, relationships and semantics of the business process. Workflow engines execute the activities of process definitions. For each round of execution, an instance of a definition is created, holding a set of context-specific variables. *Business Process Outsourcing (BPO)* refers to delegation of entire business process to third party providers. Process definitions get deployed, instantiated and then executed entirely by different workflow engines.

---

[1] In this paper, we use the terms *business process* and *workflow* interchangeably.

WF-Interop is a middleware interfacing heterogeneous and federated work-flow engines in a unified RESTful architecture aiming at facilitating BPO. Heydari et al. [2] describes WF-Interop, which has three interfaces: (i) *deployment*, i.e. enabling consumers to manage process definitions; (ii) *activation*, i.e. enabling consumers to activate process instances; (iii) *progress monitoring*, i.e., enabling them to monitor the progress of running instances. Accordingly, all workflow activities are delegated to the third parties and the level of communication of BPO clients is limited to coarse-grained interactions provided by the interfaces.

Hypermedia-driven interfaces in BPO. WF-Interop interfaces leverage well-known principles such as Hypermedia as the Engine of Application State (HATEOAS). In brief, when a BPO consumer calls a service function from one of the WF-Interop interfaces, WF-Interop embeds some navigational information (a set of links) in the response. For example, the Ruote workflow engine supports a set of functionalities on process instances such as `start`, `get`, `pause`, `resume` and `abort`. A BPO consumer calls the `start` functionality (from the `activation` interface) of WF-Interop. The WF-Interop middleware acts as a facade to several workflow engines and provides a uniform, coherent abstraction for consumers. Therefore, for this request it uses the built-in adapter for Ruote and starts a process. The process instantiation is an asynchronous service call, meaning that WF-Interop responds to the request initiator earlier than the complete process instantiation. In the body of the response, it embeds {`get`, `abort`} as the relevant navigational links. If the consumer calls the `get` function for that process instance after a while (when the process is instantiated), WF-Interop proposes {`get`, `abort`, `pause`} in the response. The capability propositions of WF-Interop are based on the underlying engine, the type, and the state of the process.

2.2   Related Work

Workflow engines support different access control models. Role-Based Access Control (RBAC) [9] is an access control mechanism that comprises users' roles and privileges. Attribute-Based Access Control (ABAC) [13] employs a more flexible paradigm by use of policies combining attributes and producing boolean logic outcomes. Business processes benefit from these mechanisms for authorisation of users' actions and restricting the access to resources in an intra-organisational context [3,23]. WS-HumanTask [10] has an emphasis on the human-involvement in business processes by providing roles illustrating actions that users can perform on tasks. Other approaches to access control for resources in a workflow context are studied in [18]. Considering the delegation of roles and access rights, some studies presented delegation models and frameworks for RBAC [24,26]; moreover, an extensive comparison of delegation models in a business context is provided in this review [21]. Most of these works did not take the cross-organisational characteristics of business process outsourcing into account.

WS-Trust [19] introduces a Security Token Service responsible for issuing tokens. It establishes a broker trust relationship among participants involved in distributed systems. Recently the state of practice has moved towards the OAuth 2.0 authorisation framework [12]. Through different flows, OAuth2 enables third party applications to have limited authorised access to services on behalf of the resource owners by providing access tokens. To harden the authorisation mechanism presented in OAuth2, OpenID Connect [20] adds an identity layer on top of the OAuth2 protocol in order to provide authentication.

Another improvement is to employ Macaroons [4] to structure each OAuth2 token. Macaroons embed caveats (i.e. that defines specific authorisation requirements), as well as attenuation and contextual confinement of authorisation requests. The proof-carrying characteristic of Macaroons is based on an HMAC-based construction inspired by Merkle-Damgård hash function.

In the public-key-based area, SPKI/SDSI [8] employs name and namespace certificates to define identities, and authorisation certificates (delegatable by subjects) to define what each principal is allowed to do. To perform an action on a secure api, a certificate chain needs to be provided by the subjects.

All of the given mechanisms focus on authorisation and authentication of parties in a generic context which can be applied to business processes in general and BPO in particular. But most of the mechanisms support some or none of the cross-organisational characteristics of a BPO context with federated workflow engines. For example, the lacking characteristics include hierarchical structure of authorisation, confidential assertions, long-running workflows with asynchronous operations, and secure proposition filtering of HATEOAS which is used in the BPO middleware.

3   Secure BPO

In this section, we describe a security architecture and middleware for the three requirements defined in Sect. 1:

1. Delegation and validation of access rights using a voucher-based approach.
2. Secure asynchronous operations by workflow engines when the executing user is logged-off.
3. Secure filtering of HATEOAS propositions in BPO APIs.

The features of this security architecture are implemented as extension to the WF-Interop middleware and are applied to the communication between heterogeneous and federated workflow engines. In Sect. 3.1, we present the voucher structure, as well as how it facilitates the delegation and verification of privileges. In Sect. 3.2, the secure asynchronous operations are described. The secure filtering of HATEOAS propositions is explained in Sect. 3.3.

3.1   Delegation and Validation of Access Rights

We present a voucher-based authentication and authorisation protocol that establishes an architecture aiming to provide delegation and validation of access rights in BPO scenarios. In this subsection, we describe (i) the structure of a voucher; (ii) the procedure of voucher delegations; (iii) the voucher verification steps; and lastly (iv) the renewal procedures.

Voucher Structure. *"A claim is a statement that something is the case, without being able to give proof"* [1]. A voucher (also called *token* or *assertion*) is a digital representation of a claim or set of claims which has been certified by a particular entity[2] [22]. In addition to the *non-repudiation*[3] characteristic common among similar works [15], our vouchers contribute a set of features:

- *Hierarchical structure.* A voucher owner can delegate a subset of his claims to a new subject by creating a new voucher with less or equal validity period. The parent vouchers are embedded within a child voucher. Therefore, the verifiable iteration of parents provides a chain of trust.
- *Confidentiality.* The subject cannot learn anything from the parent vouchers because all of the parent vouchers are protected by hybrid encryption[4].
- *Stateless.* The identity provider and servers store no information about sessions and delegations (parent vouchers).

According to the JSON web tokens (JWT) [15] representation, there are three types of claims: registered, public and private.

Listing 1.1. Voucher payload

```
{
    parent: Enc(parent vouchers),
    jti: a voucher unique identifier,
    iss: the issuer identity,
    sub: the subject identity,
    iat: the issuing time,
    exp: the expiration time
    wfi: the workflow identifier,
    wei: the engine identifier,
    actions: the list of allowed actions
}
```

The registered and public claims are predefined in the standard [15], e.g. `jti`, `iss`, `sub`, `iat` and `exp` (see Listing 1.1). We extended the representation by adding extra fields such as `parent`, `wfi`, `wei` and `actions` in the form of private claims. The `parent` field is the issuer's voucher encrypted using a hybrid encryption scheme with the public key of an identity provider (WF-Interop). The `wfi` and `wei` are the unique identifiers of the workflow and the responsible

---

[2] In BPO, entity can be a person, a group, a department or a workflow engine. Attributes of an entity can be an email address, a public key or a randomly generated value.

[3] Using cryptographic signatures the integrity of the voucher and the authenticity of the issuer are guaranteed.

[4] This scheme is a mix of a public-key cryptosystem with a symmetric-key crypto system, e.g. OpenPGP.

workflow engine. Lastly, the `actions` field is a list of permitted actions that the subject is able to execute.

The JWT representation [15] has three segments: a header, a payload and a signature. Listing 1.1 represents the payload of a voucher. The header describes the cryptographic operations applied to the JWT [14] token, e.g. the scheme used in signatures. The third segment is the cryptographic signature as the vouchers are secured.

In summary, we employed the JWT standard representation with extension of embedded parent vouchers and BPO related fields as private claims.

Voucher Delegations. In this subsection, we describe an approach for delegation of vouchers. The key differentiators are decentralised voucher generation, iterative delegations and user-owned cryptographic keys.

In our running example, we use fictional characters: Alice, Bob and Carol. Each of the actors owns a pair of public-key cryptographic keys[5] (pk, sk) for voucher-based functionalities and a secret for authentication against WF-Interop. WF-Interop is aware of the public keys (Pk's), the secrets, the workflow engines, and the workflows with all set of possible actions. The public keys of the users are known to WF-Interop, however the private keys are only known to the users. In addition, WF-Interop has its own pair of public and private keys. The public key is broadcasted to all actors. Figure 3 illustrates voucher creation, voucher usage and voucher delegation:

1. *Voucher creation.* Alice wants to create a voucher for Bob. (i) She creates a voucher V_{ab} by adding some claims including permitted actions (e.g. starting a payment process), and (ii) signs it using her Sk. (iii) Afterwards, she sends the voucher to Bob via WF-Interop over a secure channel. WF-Interop checks the identifier of the voucher because the voucher might have been revoked by the issuer. In other words, WF-Interop only stores the identifiers of revoked vouchers.

2. *Voucher usage.* Bob wants to perform an action on a secure workflow engine which is authorised by Alice using the voucher V_{ab}. (i) He sends the execution request to the engine via WF-Interop along with his secret and the voucher. Before execution, (ii) WF-Interop verifies the authenticity of V_{ab} and validates that whether Bob's claim to perform the action is available in the voucher (refer to Sect. 3.1). (iii) Then it executes the actual request.

3. *Voucher Delegation.* Bob wants to delegate a subset of the permitted actions from his voucher V_{ab} to Carol. (i) He creates a voucher V_{bc} and adds some of his claims to it. (ii) He encrypts the V_{ab} with the public key of WF-Interop using hybrid encryption and embeds it in the V_{bc} as the parent voucher. His *confidentiality* is protected as she is not able to see the complete set of his claims within V_{ab}. (iii) Afterwards, he sends V_{bc} to Carol via WF-Interop over a secure channel. The validity period of the vouchers are less than (or equal to) the validity of the parent vouchers.

---

[5] Using a public key (pk), one can either encrypt a message or verify a signature and with a private key (sk) one can either decrypt or sign a message.

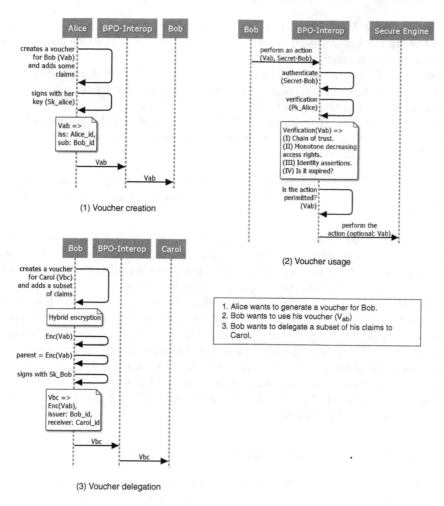

Fig. 3. Voucher creation, usage, and delegation

In a BPO context, iterative and hierarchical delegation of vouchers is unavoidable. For example, an accounting director may delegate her executive tasks to the other employees; or a BPO provider engine may need to again outsource some part of the process to another provider's engine for special services.

Voucher Verifications. The WF-Interop security component verifies the validity of the vouchers upon usage (e.g. see Fig. 3 when Bob wants to use his voucher). Obviously, a voucher must contain the claim to access a resource that the request initiator wants to have access to. Besides, the verification procedure encompasses three more criteria:

– *Chain of trust*. WF-Interop is able to decrypt the embedded parent vouchers and verify the signatures. The issuer of the child voucher must be the subject of the parent voucher.
– *Monotone decreasing access rights*. Every child voucher must contain less/equal claims than/to the chain of parents, meaning that there must be no unknown claim in the set of claims.
– *Identity assertions*. The identity of the issuer must be the subject of the parent voucher. Moreover, the provided secret adds a layer of authentication to the verification of the subject.

Ultimately if the verification process succeeds, the delegatee gains access to the requested resource on behalf of the delegator, e.g. starting an invoice delivery process by Carol.

Voucher Renewal. Vouchers have a validity period which is set by the issuer. A BPO provider's voucher may expire before completing the business process, e.g. a problem in the delivery of a bill may slow down a billing process. In such a case, the subject requests the issuer(s) to renew the voucher.

Assume that Carol wants her voucher (V_{bc}) to be renewed. V_{bc} is issued by Bob; and V_{ab}, as the parent of V_{bc}, is issued by Alice iteratively. (1) Carol sends a renewal request to WF-Interop along with V_{bc} and her secret; (2) WF-Interop authenticates Alice using the provided secret; (3) then it recursively checks the expiration time of the parents' vouchers (V_{ab}). If Bob's V_{ab}, as the first parent voucher, is still valid, it sends a renewal request to him. Otherwise, the request will be sent to Alice. (4) The responsible issuer creates a new voucher and sends it back to Carol via WF-Interop.

3.2   Secure Asynchronous Operations

Sometimes workflow engines perform BPO actions on external workflow engines when the responsible user is not logged in. For example, there might be a timer in the business process to start an instance at the service provider in the future; or the client process inspects the progress of the outsourced workflow periodically every 2 h; or the logged-in person is not the person with the right authority to continue the execution. That means that the subject has no authenticated session in the workflow engine at the time of a service invocation because the outsourced processes are typically long running; in other words, the client workflow engine cannot authenticate against the BPO provider engine to perform the authorised actions.

There are two options to address this issue using vouchers. (i) The workflow engine keeps the vouchers in the running process instance and impersonates the subject at the execution time. In a more restricted case, (ii) the responsible person may delegate a set of his access rights by creating a new child voucher to the executing workflow engine or a person in charge for a specific amount of time as described in Sect. 3.1.

3.3   Secure HATEOAS Filtering

As described in Sect. 2.1, WF-Interop comprises a set of hypermedia-driven interfaces which are based on a principle called *Hypermedia as the Engine of Application State (HATEOAS)* [2]. In brief, when a client accesses a resource at the
provider's workflow engine, WF-Interop proposes a set of related resources to the
request initiator based on the (1) underlying workflow engine, (2) the type and
(3) the state of the running process instance. For example, when an accounting
manager `starts` a Reverse Factoring process, the accounting workflow engine
receives navigational information of the related resources such as `pause`, `inspect`
and `cancel`. In this case, an accountant should only be able to `inspect` the
progress without being able to `cancel` the process.

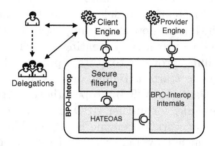

Fig. 4. Secure HATEOAS filtering

As illustrated in Fig. 4, the HATEOAS component retrieves the related
resources from the storage mechanism of WF-Interop upon each action execution
on the provider's workflow engine. Clients enable the secure filtering component
to filter out the unauthorised resources by passing along their vouchers to the
BPO interfaces of WF-Interop. In other words, a client only receives a set of permitted resources, which are securely included in the given voucher, as HATEOAS
propositions.

4   Validation and Illustration

As a validation of the principles and architecture of the voucher-based authentication and authorisation in a BPO context, we prototyped an accounting
workflow with an outsourced billing workflow on top of the WF-Interop middleware [2]. The goal of this validation is to illustrate a decentralised, cross-
organisational authorisation mechanism to support long-term remote interactions between heterogeneous workflow technologies.

To implement the accounting case study, we employed the jBPM workflow
engine for the accounting process and the Ruote workflow engine for the billing
process. They communicate via the WF-Interop middleware (see Fig. 6). Figure 5
illustrates a simplified accounting workflow responsible for starting a process at a

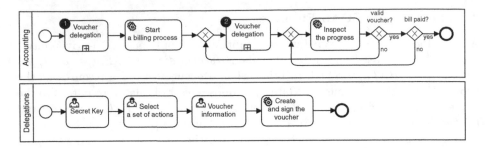

Fig. 5. Outsourcing a billing process in jBPM workflow engine.

billing provider (not shown in the figure) and inspecting the progress periodically, as well as a subprocess for creation or delegation of the vouchers.

The accountant is the business owner holding a voucher (V_a). (1) He delegates some privileges to the billing provider by creating a voucher (V_{ab}) (e.g. by adding a claim enabling the billing provider to start a process at his trusted package delivery service.). Then he starts a billing process at the billing provider by providing V_a and V_{ab}. Using V_a WF-Interop authorises the action and passes the V_{ab} to the billing provider for further BPO interactions in the future. (2) In the second stage, the client workflow engine is responsible to track the progress of the billing process which may take weeks. To start the periodic progress inspection, the workflow engine needs to have a voucher in order to be authorised against WF-Interop. Therefore, the accountant delegates the progress inspection privilege as a claim by creating a voucher V_{ae} for the responsible workflow engine. Then the workflow engine performs the inspection by passing V_{ae} to WF-Interop. As long as the voucher is still valid (not rejected by WF-Interop because of the validity period or voucher revocation), it inspects the progress. As soon as the voucher is expired, the voucher must be renewed by the accountant.

The main goal of this validation is to show (i) that the BPO client (accounting workflow) creates a voucher for delegation of a subset of their resources to the BPO provider for further usage; (ii) hierarchical, intra-organisational voucher delegations among entities (e.g. between the accountant and the workflow engine); (iii) secure asynchronous and impersonated operations when the business owner is offline (e.g. the periodic progress inspections by the workflow engine when the accountant is not logged in). (iv) The WF-Interop HATEOAS propositions within responses (not shown in the figure) are limited to the existing claims inside the vouchers (e.g. upon each invocation, the workflow engine is informed that it can only execute the progress inspection).

Furthermore, WF-Interop performs the verification procedure on the delegated actions based on the given vouchers. In other words, it stores no information about the access rights of the delegatees in order to be *stateless* and to respect organisational *confidentiality* according to the specific structure of the vouchers as described in Sect. 3.1.

5   Performance Evaluation

In this subsection, we evaluate the performance impact of vouchers with vary-ing number of delegations. More precisely, we evaluate the progress inspection requests on an outsourced process.

Set-up. To evaluate the performance overhead of vouchers, we implemented a security interceptor on top of the REST interfaces of the WF-Interop middle-ware. Since the voucher verification is the most recurring routine compared to the other activities, the progress inspection on the Ruote workflow engine is the target of this evaluation. Both the WF-Interop middleware and the security interceptor are written in Java using Spring Boot. The cryptographic schemes employed in the set-up for the hybrid encryption of parent vouchers are based on both RSA or Elliptic Curve (EC) cryptography in separate experiments, inte-grated with AES symmetric encryption algorithm. Voucher signatures are also implemented using RSA or EC[6].

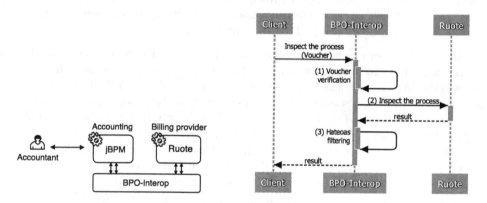

Fig. 6. Outsourcing a billing process.   **Fig. 7.** Performance evaluation set-up.

As illustrated in Fig. 7, a client sends a request to a Ruote workflow engine via the WF-Interop middleware to inspect the progress of a process. The procedure contains three sub-routines: (1) voucher verification, (2) process inspection and (3) HATEOAS filtering. We executed the procedure 500 times for different cases: using no voucher, as well as using vouchers with 1 to 6 delegations.

As illustrated in Fig. 8, the process inspection (baseline) has constant exe-cution time of 5.27 ms. The HATEOAS filtering has low impact of maximum 2.99 ms with six delegations. Therefore, the main performance overhead is on

---

[6] The RSA-based hybrid encryption is based on RSA/OAEP with AES/GCM, SHA-256 and MGF1 padding. The EC-based hybrid encryption is based on ECIES with AES/CBC, HMAC-SHA256, KDF2 and ECSVDP-DH (Elliptic Curve Secret Value Derivation Primitive [7,16]). The RSA-based signature algorithms are based on RS256 and RS512 and the EC-based ones are ES256, ES384 and ES512 [15].

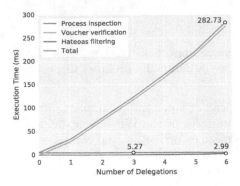
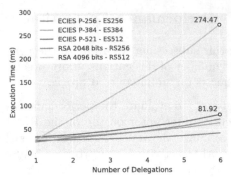

Fig. 8. The setup employs 4096 bits key size for RSA-based hybrid encryption and voucher signatures.

Fig. 9. Different setups employ various hybrid encryption and signature algorithms for voucher verification.

voucher verification. Considering a growing number of delegations, the signature verification of vouchers, as well as decryption and verification of parent vouchers are the main reasons for the performance overhead.

Results. The experiment results which are presented in Fig. 8 shows the worst-case scenario because we employed a set of strong encryption schemes with large key lengths. We also evaluated the overhead against the fastest WF-Interop function (namely process inspection). In a BPO context, these performance results can be considered low as the number of delegations rarely becomes six. The total response time of 282.73 ms is still acceptable in a BPO context.

We further evaluated the same experiments with different key lengths using RSA-based hybrid encryption, or Elliptic Curve integrated encryption scheme (ECIES) with various signature algorithms (see Fig. 9). The results show that the execution time of voucher verification is considerably improved from 274.47 ms to 81.92 ms in the case of 6 delegations. The detailed experiment results are provided in the appendix.

6   Conclusion and Future Work

In this paper, we presented a voucher-based authorisation architecture and middleware for BPO. Vouchers enable federated workflow systems to iteratively delegate all or subsets of claims to different entities. Nested vouchers protect the confidentiality of the parent issuers by using hybrid encryption, which is important in a cross-organisational context. Moreover, vouchers facilitate the asynchronous BPO operations in long-running workflows when the authorised subject has no active session in the workflow engine. We employed vouchers to filter the *Hypermedia as the Engine of Application State (HATEOAS)* propositions using an interceptor pattern in the WF-Interop middleware. We implemented a security module for the middleware and, on top of it, validated the architecture by prototyping a billing workflow case study. Furthermore, the evaluation showed that the measured performance overhead is acceptable in a BPO context.

The current centralised approach suffers from a single point of failure issue, but on the other hand, some of the important security controls such as voucher revocation and context-sensitive delegations can practically be employed in the current design. Our future work includes moving towards a decentralised architecture, and addressing potential limitations such as key management issues, context-sensitive and fine-grained controls on delegations by resource owners in that setting.

A   Appendix

See Tables 1 and 2.

Table 1. The setup employs 4096 bits key size for RSA-based hybrid encryption and voucher signatures. Execution times (ms) are as follows.

Number of delegations	0	1	2	3	4	5	6
Process inspection	5.27	5.27	5.27	5.27	5.27	5.27	5.27
Voucher verification	0	28.28	73.02	117.36	164.26	214.22	274.47
Hateoas filtering	0.27	0.27	0.27	0.39	0.99	1.16	2.99
Total	5.54	33.82	78.56	123.02	170.52	220.65	282.73

Table 2. Different setups employ various hybrid encryption and signature algorithms for voucher verification. Execution times (ms) are as follows.

Number of delegations	1	2	3	4	5	6
ECIES P-256 - ES256	27.63	28.89	30.31	32.87	36.79	42.68
ECIES P-384 - ES384	33.28	35.30	40.29	46.50	53.82	64.07
ECIES P-521 - ES512	35.19	39.30	46.77	56.21	66.26	81.92
RSA 2048 bits - RS256	24.48	32.61	39.02	47.13	57.45	72.30
RSA 4096 bits - RS512	28.28	73.02	117.36	164.26	214.22	274.47

References

1. ITU-T: Baseline identity management terms and definitions, X.1252 (2010)
2. Beni, E.H., Lagaisse, B., Joosen, W.: WF-Interop: adaptive and reflective rest interfaces for interoperability between workflow engines. In: Proceedings of the 14th International Workshop on Adaptive and Reflective Middleware, p. 1. ACM (2015)

3. Bertino, E., Ferrari, E., Atluri, V.: The specification and enforcement of authorization constraints in workflow management systems. ACM Trans. Inf. Syst. Secur. (TISSEC) **2**, 65–104 (1999)
4. Birgisson, A., Politz, J.G., Erlingsson, U., Taly, A., Vrable, M., Lentczner, M.: Macaroons: cookies with contextual caveats for decentralized authorization in the cloud (2014)
5. Coalition, W.M.: Terminology and glossary. WFMC Document WFMCTC-1011, Workflow Management Coalition, Avenue Marcel Thiry 204, 1200 (1996)
6. Dayasindhu, N.: Information technology enabled process outsourcing and reengineering: case study of a mortgage bank. In: AMCIS 2004 Proceedings, p. 437 (2004)
7. Diffie, W., Hellman, M.: New directions in cryptography. IEEE Trans. Inf. Theor. **22**(6), 644–654 (1976)
8. Ellison, C., Frantz, B., Lampson, B., Rivest, R., Thomas, B., Ylonen, T.: SPKI certificate theory (IETF RFC 2693) (1999)
9. Ferraiolo, D., Cugini, J., Kuhn, D.R.: Role-based access control (RBAC): Features and motivations. In: Proceedings of 11th Annual Computer Security Application Conference, pp. 241–48 (1995)
10. Ford, M., Endpoints, A., Keller, C., Kloppmann, M., König, D., Leymann, F., Müller, R., Pfau, O.G.: Web services human task (WS-HumanTask), v1.0 (2007)
11. Halvey, J.K., Melby, B.M.: Business Process Outsourcing: Process, Strategies, and Contracts. Wiley, New York (2007)
12. Hardt, D.: The OAuth2 authorization framework (2012)
13. Hu, V.C., Ferraiolo, D., et al.: Guide to attribute based access control (ABAC) definition and considerations (draft). NIST Special Publication 800(162) (2013)
14. Jones, M., Bradley, J., Sakimura, N.: JSON web signature (JWS). Technical report (2015)
15. Jones, M., Bradley, J., Sakimura, N.: JSON web token (JWT). Technical report (2015)
16. Koblitz, N.: Elliptic curve cryptosystems. Math. Comput. **48**(177), 203–209 (1987)
17. Mettraux, J., Kalmer, K., Meyers, R., de Mik, H., Kohlbecker, A., et al.: Ruote-a ruby workflow engine
18. Muller, J., Mulle, J., von Stackelberg, S., Bohm, K.: Secure business processes in service-oriented architectures-a requirements analysis. In: 2010 IEEE 8th European Conference on Web Services (ECOWS), pp. 35–42. IEEE (2010)
19. Nadalin, A., Goodner, M., Gudgin, M., Barbir, A., Granqvist, H.: Oasis WS-Trust 1.4. Specification Version 1, pp. 41–45 (2008)
20. Sakimura, N., Bradley, J., Jones, M., de Medeiros, B., Mortimore, C.: Openid connect core 1.0. The OpenID Foundation, p. S3 (2014)
21. Schefer-Wenzl, S., Bukvova, H., Strembeck, M.: A review of delegation and break-glass models for flexible access control management. In: Abramowicz, W., Kokkinaki, A. (eds.) BIS 2014. LNBIP, vol. 183, pp. 93–104. Springer, Cham (2014). doi:10.1007/978-3-319-11460-6_9
22. Van Alsenoy, B., De Cock, D., Simoens, K., Dumortier, J., Preneel, B.: Delegation and digital mandates: legal requirements and security objectives. Comput. Law Secur. Rev. **25**(5), 415–431 (2009)
23. Wainer, J., Barthelmess, P., Kumar, A.: W-RBAC a workflow security model incorporating controlled overriding of constraints. Int. J. Coop. Inf. Syst. **12**(04), 455–485 (2003)
24. Wainer, J., Kumar, A.: A fine-grained, controllable, user-to-user delegation method in RBAC. In: Proceedings of the Tenth ACM Symposium on Access Control Models and Technologies, pp. 59–66. ACM (2005)

25. Wüllenweber, K., Beimborn, D., Weitzel, T., König, W.: The impact of process standardization on business process outsourcing success. Inf. Syst. Front. **10**(2), 211–224 (2008)
26. Zhang, L., Ahn, G.J., Chu, B.T.: A rule-based framework for role-based delegation and revocation. ACM Trans. Inf. Syst. Secur. (TISSEC) **6**(3), 404–441 (2003)

LASARUS: Lightweight Attack Surface Reduction for Legacy Industrial Control Systems

Anhtuan Le[✉], Utz Roedig, and Awais Rashid

Security Lancaster Institute, Lancaster University, Lancaster, UK
a.le@lancaster.ac.uk

Abstract. Many operational Industrial Control Systems (ICSs) were designed and deployed years ago with little or no consideration of security issues arising from an interconnected world. It is well-known that attackers can read and write sensor and actuator data from Programmable Logic Controllers (PLCs) as legacy ICS offer little means of protection. Replacing such legacy ICS is expensive, requires extensive planning and a major programme of updates often spanning several years. Yet augmenting deployed ICS with established security mechanisms is rarely possible. Legacy PLCs cannot support computationally expensive (i.e., cryptographic) operations while maintaining real-time control. Intrusion Detection Systems (IDSs) have been employed to improve security of legacy ICS. However, attackers can avoid detection by learning acceptable system behaviour from observed data. In this paper, we present LASARUS, a lightweight approach that can be implemented on legacy PLCs to reduce their attack surface, making it harder for an attacker to learn system behaviour and craft useful attacks. Our approach involves applying obfuscation to PLC data whenever it is stored or accessed which leads to a continuous change of the target surface. Obfuscation keys can be refreshed depending on the threat situation, striking a balance between system performance and protection level. Using real-world and simulated ICS data sets, we demonstrate that LASARUS is able to prevent a set of well-known attacks like random or replay injection, by reducing their passing rate significantly—up to a 100 times.

1 Introduction

Industrial Control Systems (ICSs) are used to monitor and control systems such as power plants, power grids, water treatment plants, oil refineries and gas distribution networks. Many ICS are legacy systems and offer little means of protection. Specifically, attackers are able to read and write sensor and actuator data of Programmable Logic Controllers (PLCs) in much the same way as the operator of the plant does (see, e.g., [1,2]). Thus, an attacker is able to inject false command instructions to control the physical process (managed by the PLCs), while at the same time injecting false response packets to mislead remote monitoring stations and operators. Such Man-In-The-Middle (MitM) attacks can enable attackers to: steal physical resources (oil, gas, water); alter production processes or bypass safety procedures, all the while leaving remote operators

© Springer International Publishing AG 2017
E. Bodden et al. (Eds.): ESSoS 2017, LNCS 10379, pp. 36–52, 2017.
DOI: 10.1007/978-3-319-62105-0_3

blind to such actions [3]. Attackers may also hide their activities from operators for a long time by falsifying data carefully, based on long-term observation of normal behaviour before starting an attack. The security vulnerabilities of ICS have been demonstrated by a number of high profile attacks such as Maroochy water services (2000), Stuxnet (2007), Turkish pipeline (2008), and the German steel mill (2014) [4].

Many ICS services need to be operated in real time, which restricts the performance latency within a strong bound. For example, according to IEC 61850 (reference architecture for electric power systems), the latency bound for fault isolation and protection services is 3 ms [4]. On the other hand, applying access control and cryptographic solutions can create significant delay, for instance, the latency of applying a 1024 bit DSA algorithm in an average system is 14.9 ms while that of applying the 2048 bit RSA is 61.04 ms [4]. The delay created by cryptographic solutions may exceed largely from the required bounds, which will disable certain ICS real-time operations. Therefore, augmenting legacy ICS with well known access control and cryptographic protocols to address the aforementioned issues is rarely possible as the required major system upgrades are not feasible to satisfy such performance requirements. In many cases, ICS are in operation for more than 20 years and it is not possible to augment these systems as necessary. Replacement of the entire control infrastructure is also often not possible as it is too costly and would require system shutdown for lengthy periods. Finally, in many cases, real-time control requirements make it impossible to use time consuming cryptographic procedures.

A number of Intrusion Detection Systems (IDSs) have been proposed, e.g., [1,5,6]. However, capable attackers can study system behaviour over long periods and manipulate the system state such that it still falls within acceptable bounds not detected by the IDS [7]. In a worst-case scenario, the attacker may have all past system data and the same detection algorithm available and can craft attacks that are undetectable.

As current legacy ICS give an attacker too much information, in this paper we focus on reducing their attack surface in order to make it harder for an adversary to carry out a successful attack. Our proposed approach, LASARUS, is designed to operate under real-world constraints in ICS environments, namely:

- Deployment of sophisticated access control and cryptographic solutions is not possible due to architectural and resource constraints.
- The approach must be implementable using available functionality in legacy PLCs.
- The approach must be lightweight so as not to compromise the real-time properties of an ICS.

LASARUS involves the use of an obfuscation key K_d to obfuscate data deposited in the data block of a PLC, with the obfuscation pattern changing on a per session basis. The obfuscation key K_d is shared between all components that have to access the data block (i.e. shared between operator and PLC). The obfuscation key is updated periodically whereby the frequency of key updates is determined by system needs. The obfuscation function is a simple XOR operation, making it possible to be implemented by existing legacy PLC programming frameworks while fast and lightweight enough to limit the latency and processing overhead so as not to compromise real-time PLC operations.

The novel contributions of this paper are as follows:

– We propose a lightweight approach to reduce the attack surface of legacy ICS that can be implemented on legacy PLCs.
– We demonstrate the effectiveness of the approach by evaluating it against three types of attacks: (i) injecting random values; (ii) replaying eavesdropped values; (iii) injecting estimated values. We show that adding LASARUS to a legacy ICS can help to reduce the probability of these attacks to bypass an IDS (even one using a simple algorithm) significantly, up to a 100 times.
– We provide an analysis of security and usability trade-offs of LASARUS, supporting system configuration decisions so that the additional security features introduced by LASARUS do not compromise operation.

The structure of the paper is as follows. Section 2 presents the background on ICS and related work on ICS security. Section 3 describes the Man-In-The-Middle (MitM) attacks that are the focus of our approach. Section 4 introduces the proposed approach while Sect. 5 shows the evaluation and presents a discussion of the insights. Finally, Sect. 6 concludes the paper.

2   Background and Related Work

2.1   Industrial Control Systems

ICSs are used to control physical processes in a range of critical infrastructure such as, power plants, water works, oil refineries and gas distribution. Programmable Logic Controllers (PLCs) are used at the heart of any ICS to implement control logic, interacting with sensors and actuators. PLCs store data computed by the control process, sent to actuators and obtained from sensors locally, often referred to as "data block"[1]. Data in the data block is used to control the PLC behaviour and, thus, the physical process. The data block is also accessed externally by other ICS equipment, including management systems and other PLCs. For example, an operator console will fetch data from the PLC's data block to visualise system state. A historian, a database to store long-term process data, will fetch data periodically from the data block. In a Supervisory Control and Data Acquisition (SCADA) system other PLCs may obtain data from the data block to facilitate complex distributed control tasks.

Although ICSs are used to control many critical infrastructures, their security is rarely considered properly. A reason can be found in their historic development. In the past, ICS were air-gapped systems using specialist system parts,

---

[1] This term is used for Siemens PLC equipment but a similar data construct is used by other vendors too.

including software and hardware, with which only few people were familiar. Thus, attacks were unlikely as physical presence of highly skilled personnel was required. Today this situation has changed. To improve operational efficiency, ICS are now connected to enterprise systems and, in many cases, also to the Internet [8]. Also, the systems are easier to use and to program, and knowledge to interact with these computer systems is much more widespread. Attacks are, therefore, now more likely and ICS security must step up.

2.2 Security of ICS

Apart from real world reported ICS attacks, recent research has also highlighted various potential threats to ICS. For instance, Stouffer et al. [9] present a wide range of probable adversaries – from inexperienced attackers utilising pre-written scripts through to complex and organised Advanced Persistent Threats (APT), which are crafted carefully aiming at system manipulation over long period of time. Morris and Gao [10] describe 17 attacks on ICS, grouping them into four main types, namely: reconnaissance attacks, response and measurement injection attacks, command injection attacks, and denial of service attacks. MitM attacks in ICSs are also discussed widely in the literature, and shown to be feasible in testbed environments, for instance, see [11,12]

Although security mechanisms are well developed for other IT systems, these cannot be simply transferred to the ICS domain [2,13]. A number of intrusion detection systems (IDS), specific to ICS, have been proposed. For instance, Sainz et al. [6] apply modal interval analysis to derive suitable envelopes, including upper and lower bounds for values according to time, in order to check the veracity of the data. Hadziosmanovic et al. [5] model logged data using an autoregressive model to predict the next value to detect potential tampering. Almalawi et al. [1] introduce a detection approach, which first clusters the process parameters to identify the normal and critical states of the system. They then apply data mining techniques to extract the proximity-based detection rules from such states. Given that the MitM attacker may have access to the logged data as much as the operator does, the attacker can also predict the next value with similar accuracy. Therefore, such attacks may not be readily detected by IDSs.

As discussed earlier, augmenting deployed ICS with well known access control and cryptographic protocols is not feasible due to the cost of updating the infrastructure or constraints arising from real-time properties. Therefore, any security solution needs to be lightweight and must require little change to be compatible with existing parts of the system. Existing research on Moving Target Denfense (MTD) has considered the problem of reducing the attack surface of systems. Davidson and Andel [14] are among the first to point out the feasibility and effectiveness of applying MTD to ICS security. However, to the best of our knowledge, there has been no attempt to design such a system so far. LASARUS can thus be seen as a concrete instantiation of such an MTD approach.

3   Problem Definition

3.1   Threat Model

Figure 1 shows a simplified MitM attack in ICS. As shown, the physical system communicates with the PLC through its actuators and sensors. The PLC controls the physical side based on parameters received from the system operator. The state of the physical system is reported to and recorded by the PLC. State information is also transmitted periodically to the operator who observes the system and may tune parameters in response. In practice the control side may be connected to multiple PLC and multiple physical systems at the same time. However, for simplification we consider here a single PLC and operator.

The MitM attacker is able to interact with the PLC in a fashion similar to that of the operator. He can request recorded physical system state logged by the PLC and can inject operation parameters into the PLC. He may also simply modify data passed between operator and PLC without direct manipulation of the PLC's data block. Such attacks can be implemented using a variety of techniques. For example, by uploading malicious control logic to gain control of devices that the PLC manages [15]; compromising Address Resolution in the network to manipulate communication between operator and PLC [9]; or eavesdropping on the communication followed by analysing and altering its contents [16].

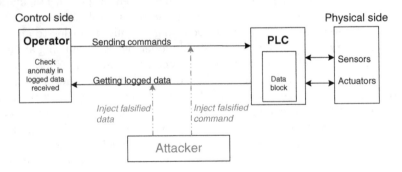

Fig. 1. ICS Man-In-The-Middle (MitM) attack model.

3.2   Example ICS

We consider an ICS used to control a water tank as typical example to illustrate MitM attacks. We also use this example application later for our evaluation. The physical system in this particular example is a water system, which consists of: a tank, a pump to fill the tank and a sensor to record water level. The PLC controls the pump according to the following parameters set by the operator: HH, H, LL, L [17]. HH and LL are two alarm values. If the water level rises higher than HH or falls lower than LL, the operator will raise an alarm. H and

L are the two values to control the pump. If the water level is higher than H, the pump will need to be turned off. If it falls lower than L, the pump will need to be turned on. These operation parameters submitted to the PLC are stored in the data block. The filling level is read periodically and these readings are stored as well in the PLC's data block. Filling levels are requested periodically by the operator from the data block to monitor the process.

The system can be attacked by injecting false values into the data block. For example, Morris et al. [18] have shown that simple replay attacks (storing a previous value as the next value in the data block) are only detected in 12% of cases. Improved attacks by Morris et al. [10] simulate the value trend and estimate the next value, making the detection accuracy even worse. If the attacker can collect a significantly large sample of data and apply robust techniques to learn the pattern, the chances to bypass the detection system are likely to be even higher. In the worst case, when the attacker knows and applies the algorithm that the system uses to check the data, he can always inject a legal value into the system and the attack will go undetected. The operator will loose control of the system while thinking that everything is in order.

Obviously, anomaly detection can be improved but the attacker can adjust accordingly. As operational parameters and sensor readings are available to the operator and attacker via the data block, the problem remains.

4 Lightweight Attack Surface Reduction with LASARUS

As the problem arises from the large attack surface easily accessible to the attacker, we propose an approach whereby data maintained in a PLC's data block is obfuscated, with the obfuscation pattern changing on a per session basis. An obfuscation key K_d is used to obfuscate data deposited in the data block. Likewise, data obtained from the data block must be de-obfuscated using K_d. The obfuscation key K_d is shared between all components that have to access the data block (i.e. shared between operator and PLC). The obfuscation key is updated periodically whereby the frequency of key updates is determined by system needs (we discuss this aspect in detail in our evaluation for a specific application case). The obfuscation function is a simple XOR operation. We chose this simple approach as obfuscation can then be implemented by existing legacy PLC programming frameworks and processing overhead is limited as required for real-time PLC operations.

We aim at manipulating the data block in a PLC such that an attacker has a limited view on system behaviour. The attacker should not be able to learn acceptable value ranges in order to craft sophisticated attacks by injecting seemingly acceptable values. In order to do so, we assume that there is a shared secret key K between the PLC and other system components (such as the operator). This key can be stored at a specific memory address in the PLC which cannot be written to or read by any other party. We assume that this key is valid over a long time. The issue of key distribution is beyond the scope of this paper. However, other research has tackled this question, e.g., [19].

As shown in Fig. 2, the shared secret K is used to calculate a session key K_d for each session d. K_d is used within each session to obfuscate data in the PLC's data block. A session is active for an agreed duration T_s and, after this time elapses, a new session key will be used. Note that we can generate this new key right after the last logging cycle of the session instead of waiting until session ends. As the logging frequency is considerably longer (e.g., 10 s) compared to the time needed to generate a key (e.g., under a millisecond using hash), generating a new session key right after the last logging cycle will eliminate the impact of any delay it may cause. Session keys are generated based on a time stamp T_d and the shared secret K. Therefore, session keys do not need to be distributed; they are computed by all involved ICS components based on the same time base. It is feasible to follow this approach in an ICS context as components require tight time synchronisation to facilitate real-time control operations. An attacker can disrupt time synchronisation; however, this will generally lead to system faults which are immediately obvious. Also, manipulating time synchronisation will lead to de-synchronisation of obfuscation keys which will lead to parts of the ICS not being able to access data which is also immediately detectable. The timestamp for session d is calculated as $T_s \cdot (d-1)$. The session key K_d for session d is calculated as: $K_d = hash(K \oplus T_d)$.

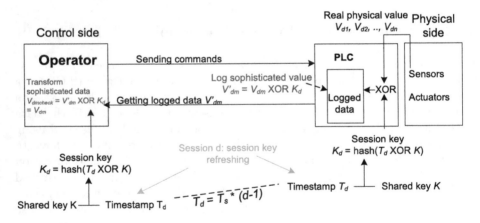

Fig. 2. Obfuscating the logged values using the session key to prevent MitM attacks.

The obfuscation pattern changes in every session, though the real physical values may remain the same. A Man-In-The-Middle who does not know the shared key and time reference will not be able to generate useful values for an attack.

Assume that for session d, the physical values are $V_{d1}, V_{d2}, V_{d3}, ..., V_{dn}$. The PLC will store the obfuscated representation of these values, $V'_{d1}, V'_{d2}, V'_{d3}, ..., V'_{dn}$, in which:

$$V'_{dm} = V_{dm} \oplus K_d, \ m = 1, 2, ..., n$$

When the control side receives data from session d, it will use the session key K_d to obtain the original values:

$$V_{dmcheck} = V'_{dm} \oplus K_d = V_{dm} \oplus K_d \oplus K_d = V_{dm}, \ m = 1, 2, ..., n$$

These original values may be used to detect if any anomaly is present in the physical system. For an attacker, it will be challenging to predict which obfuscated values to inject such that an anomaly detection system (even a very simple one) does not trigger an alarm.

5   Evaluation

We evaluate the effectiveness of LASARUS on three types of attacks: (i) injecting random values; (ii) replaying eavesdropped values; (iii) injecting estimated values. These three attack scenarios are the best options for a MiTM attacker to bypass the defense system as shown in other work [10,17].

5.1   Evaluation Scenario and Datasets

We use the water storage tank dataset from [18]. The dataset was recorded from a water tank ICS testbed under normal and attack conditions. It contains attributes such as pump states, the automatic thresholds for turning the pump on/off or raising alarm, the physical water level, the response time of the PLC, and so on. We use only the water level attribute as test value in our experiment which is sampled every 11.5 s. We pre-processed the data to exclude values recorded under attack, only using data from normal operation conditions. We use 10044 water level values collected over a duration of approximately 32 h for our experiments. We refer to this real-world dataset as *Set-Real*.

We assume that the attackers have the ability to learn patterns from the eavesdropped data, so we are also interested in seeing whether the obfuscated data contains patterns that can be manipulated. Therefore, we generate three artificial datasets with clear patterns: *Set-Linear:* the water level is a function of the time and pump velocity; *Set-Repeated:* a range of the Set-Real is chosen and repeated continuously; *Set-Constant:* all values are constant, e.g., when the system is inactive and the logged water values are not changed.

5.2   Experiment Setup

Session Duration. Obfuscation keys K_d change after a time period (the session duration T_s). In our experiments we use the following configurations for T_s: $T_s = 10$ s; $T_s = 250$ s and $T_s = 500$ s. The PLC will use the session key to obfuscate the sampling water level and record to a data block. The operator will use the session key to transform values back to the real physical water level.

Intrusion Detection. We assume that the control side (the operator) employs a means to detect intrusions. We assume the following two detection rules:

- Rule-Simple (R-S): This rule checks whether the water level is within a believable range. We assume the range to be between 20% and 80% of tank capacity. This rule is named simple because it does not involve any particular data learning algorithm.
- Rule-Advanced (R-A): This rule checks whether the water level falls into a legitimate envelope, which is not 10% higher or 10% lower than the true value. We assume here a prediction algorithm is in place which can estimate true values. This rule is called advanced because it emulates a more sophisticated intrusion detection mechanism.

These rules are used to demonstrate how LASARUS supports an existing IDS.

Random Attack. We assume two attack conditions which differ regarding the attacker's knowledge of data obfuscation being in place or not:

- Normal Range Random (NRR) attack: The attacker does not know that obfuscation is used. Random value generation assumes values should fall in the normal data range of water values.
- Obfuscated Range Random (ORR) attack: The attacker knows that obfuscation is used. The attacker generates values falling in the range of the valid obfuscated data range.

Replay Attack. The attacker can choose to replay data differently to bypass the system. For Set-Real, the attacker is able to capture a value (obfuscated or not) and use this value for replay. For Set-Linear, Set-Repeated, Set-Constant, the attacker can replay a set of values in the pattern that he learnt.

5.3   Results and Discussions

Dataset Observation. Figure 3 illustrates the first 250 values of the dataset S-Real. Figure 3a shows the real water level, while Fig. 3b–d shows the obfuscated values with session duration $T_s = 10$ s, 250 s, and 500 s respectively. As can be seen, when values are similar, their obfuscated counterparts will also be similar if transformed with the same key. When the keys are updated for every value ($T_s = 10$ s), the transformed values fluctuated strongly as shown in Fig. 3b, which makes it hard for an attacker to predict future values. On the other hand, all the obfuscated datasets have a large standard deviation at about 1200 (compared with 8.48 of the original dataset), with the values spread over a large range from about -2100 to 2100, which indicates such datasets are not stable. The initial observations of the dataset shows it would be much more difficult for the attackers to inject a legal value into the obfuscated datasets compared with injecting into the original dataset.

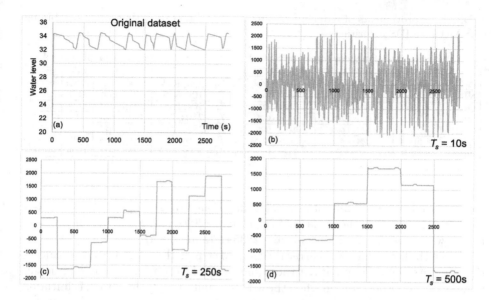

Fig. 3. The first 250 values of the water level dataset S-Real and the obfuscated datasets with $T_s = 10$ s, 250 s, and 500 s.

Random Attack. We now investigate the effectiveness of the two types of random attacks previously described. For each type of the random attack (NRR, ORR), we generate random values in the [Min Max] range for every entry in the dataset and check if these are detected by the two detection rules (R-S, R-A).

Table 1a shows the passing rates of the two types of random attacks. We first apply the random attacks on the original dataset without obfuscation in place. The results show that R-S cannot detect either of the random attacks because all the injected values fall in the legitimate data range [20, 80]. R-A improves the detection ability significantly, which lets the passing rates fall to values between 10.91% and 12.33%. LASARUS, however, reduces the passing rate even more, which is less than 2% if using R-S, and less than 0.25% if using R-A to detect the attacker. With the same detection technique, the obfuscated solutions are about 100 times more effective when compared with the non-obfuscated solution.

The length of the session key does not affect the passing rate. This is because after being obfuscated, the range and the standard deviation of the dataset values are similar, which create similar results when dealing with the random attacks.

Replay Attack. Next we investigate the effectiveness of replay attacks. First, we select a random time at which to initiate the attack. From that time till the end of the dataset, we replace the water level value with the selected replay value. We then check the modified dataset using the two detection rules to measure how long it takes to detect the attacker. We run 1000 attacks for each experiment.

Table 1b shows the time to detect the replay attacker for each setting. For the original dataset (no obfuscation), R-S cannot detect the replay attacker because

Table 1. Improvements of reducing passing rates and detection time when combining
LASARUS to IDS algorithms.

(a) Passing rate of random attacks on S-Real

	Rule-Simple	Rule-Advance
Original dataset	100%	10.91-12.33%
NRR; $T_s = 10$s	1.4% - 1.59%	0.12 - 0.19%
ORR; $T_s = 10$s	1.24% - 1.62%	0.09% - 0.23%
NRR; $T_s = 250$s	1.07% - 1.26%	0.12% - 0.2%
ORR; $T_s = 250$s	1.24% - 1.66%	0.09% - 0.2%
NRR; $T_s = 500$s	1.19% - 1.44%	0.12% - 0.25%
ORR; $T_s = 500$s	1.24% - 1.5%	0.12% - 0.2%

(b) Time needs to detect a replay attacker

	Min	Max	Avg.	SDev.
Original; R-A	10.84	28354	6209.4	6884.1
$T_s = 10$s; R-S	10.58	23.72	12.12	2.59
$T_s = 10$s; R-A	10.58	22.73	11.52	0.45
$T_s = 250$s; R-S	10.87	463.1	132.01	74.53
$T_s = 250$s; R-A	10.87	255.3	118.3	74.45
$T_s = 500$s; R-S	10.8	958.8	259.3	148.97
$T_s = 500$s; R-A	11.16	505.7	236.01	146.98

any replayed value will fall into the legitimate value range of [20, 80]. Using R-A
the system can catch the replay attacker after 6209 s (approx. 2 h), on average.
In the worst-case scenario, it will take 28354 s (almost 8 h).

Table 1b shows that the shorter the time to change the session key, the quicker
the defense system can point out the anomaly on the dataset. The time to detect
a replay attacker depends on when the attack is initiated. If the attack is initiated
at the beginning of a session, it is likely to be undetected until a new key is
replaced. On the other hand, when the attack is initiated at the end of a session,
it will be spotted quickly when a new key is used.

Table 1b also shows the maximum time that is required to detect a replay
attacker. If using R-S, the maximum time is approx. twice the session length.
This is because the XOR function applied on the value will likely jump out of
the legal range [20, 80] after two key changes. While using R-A, the maximum
time to detect a replay attacker is only approx. the length of the session. This
is due to the checking range of R-A being much narrower compared with R-S,
which helps to detect the attacker right after changing the session key.

Attacks on Data with Patterns. Once the attackers find the pattern, the best
chance they have to bypass the system is to do the replay attack which inject
data following the found pattern. Figure 4 illustrates the differences between the
original and obfuscated datasets of the three most common patterns.

Figure 4a compares the pattern of a linear rising water level in Set-Linear
with its obfuscated versions. The figure clearly shows that a linear original value
will not lead to similar pattern on the transformed value. The flat lines present
in the obfuscated figures are due to the similarity of the original values.

Figure 4b presents the repeated pattern in Set-Repeated and its obfuscations.
When the session length is smaller than the length of the pattern, the obfuscated
datasets are not repeated like the original pattern. This is because different keys
were applied in the same dataset. However, when the session is longer than
the pattern duration, the repeated real values XORing with the same session
key create repeated obfuscated values. Nevertheless, unlike in the original Set-
Repeated, the pattern in the obfuscated set does not repeat over more than one
session due to the session key change.

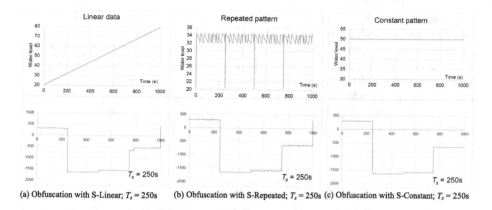

(a) Obfuscation with S-Linear; $T_s = 250s$ (b) Obfuscation with S-Repeated; $T_s = 250s$ (c) Obfuscation with S-Constant; $T_s = 250s$

Fig. 4. Patterns of the three data sets.

Figure 4c shows the comparisons between the original patterned dataset Set-Constant and the obfuscated values when the original data is constant. As can be seen, a transformed constant value will also be constant given the same obfuscation key. When the session key is not changed, a replay attack will be successful for any detection algorithm. However, at the moment when the session key is changed (or the starting of a new session), the attackers will likely fail as they cannot predict the next value.

The experiments show that replay attacks on patterned dataset will not be successful in multiple sessions. In Fig. 5, we illustrate the passing possibility of such attack within one session. The linear pattern of Set-Linear does not help the attacker to increase the chance to bypass the system. On the other hand, repeated pattern of Set-Repeated can create repeated patterns of obfuscated dataset, which helps the replay attack to be successful after the first cycle of the pattern. The worst case for the detection system happens with Set-Constant, where the attacker only fails in the first sampling time of the session. However,

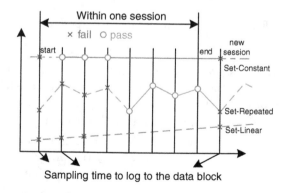

Fig. 5. Comparison of passing rate in one session for the three pattern sets.

protecting the constant dataset from the replay attack is also a challenge for any other defending mechanisms. If the system operator knows that their dataset contains patterns, s/he can adjust the session duration to interrupt the pattern in the obfuscated set. For example, if the data is a repeated pattern (not constant), setting the session duration smaller than the pattern's length eliminates the chance of replay attacks. If the system operator cannot do so, s/he will face the risk of not detecting the attackers at some points in the session. However, the attacker will always fail at the beginning of a new session.

5.4   Possible Attacks on Obfuscation Keys

The previous sections show that common injection attacks on the obfuscated dataset are not effective. However, attackers may aim to expose the session and, ultimately, secret keys instead. Once the key is revealed, an attacker can transform between obfuscated and normal values to inject accurate data values. We are aware of two fundamental approaches (see Fig. 6) to obtain session keys with we detail here. The first method does not rely on any information about the data values; it is agnostic to the data obfuscated with the session key. The second method, which converges much faster, uses known information about obfuscated values. For example, in an ICS context the range of valid values may be known which limits the search space to find the session key.

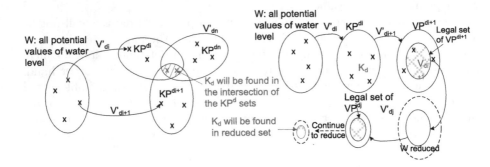

Fig. 6. Examples of methods to expose K_d

Session Key Extraction Without Data Insight. Assume that in session d, an attacker has knowledge of the set of all potential real water values W. He also obtains a sequence of obfuscated values $V'_{di}, V'_{di+1}, ..., V'_{dn}$. The first method to expose the session key is to compute a set KP^{dj} for each $V'_{dj}, j = i, i+1, .., n$, in which $\mathrm{KP}^{dj} = \{\mathrm{KP}^{dj}_k | \mathrm{KP}^{dj}_k = V'_{dj} \oplus W_k, \forall k \in W\}$. As W contains all possible values, $\exists W_m \in W : W_m = V_{dj}$ as a result $\mathrm{KP}^{dj}_m = W_m \oplus V'_{dj} = V_{dj} \oplus V_{dj} \oplus K_d = K_d$. The attacker knows that K_d is contained in every KP^{dj} set. An attacker can derive K_d from the intersection of all these sets (see Fig. 6a). The number of candidate session keys in the intersection reduces with the number of collected obfuscated values. The intersection will contain a single element (the session key) when enough obfuscated values are observed by the attacker.

Session Key Extraction with Data Insight. The second method relies on knowledge of the physical process behind the data. For example, it might be known that a value will be in a particular range (e.g., the filling level of a tank). More detailed information, such as process behaviour over time, might also be available. This knowledge can be used to further reduce the search space for the session key leading to faster exposure of the obfuscation key. The search space of potential keys is reduced recursively (see Fig. 6b), using the following steps.

Step 1. Using the first obfuscated value V'_{di}, compute KP^{di}. Now the attacker has $KP = KP^{di}$, which contains all potential K_d.

Step 2. Compute V^{di+1} from KP and V'_{di+1}, in which $V^{di+1} = \{V_k^{di+1} | V_k^{di+1} = V'_{di+1} \oplus KP_k, \forall k \in KP\}$. KP contains all the potential K_d and $\exists m \in KP : KP_m = K_d$. We have $V_m^{di+1} = V'_{di+1} \oplus KP_m = V_{di+1} \oplus K_d \oplus K_d = V_{di+1}$. So attackers know that V^{di+1} contains V_{di+1}.

Step 3. V_{di+1} represents the real value. Now constraints using process knowledge (e.g., legitimate value ranges) can be applied. The attacker can use these constrains to eliminating all the unsatisfied values in the V^{di+1} set. The size of KP will also be reduced by tracing back from the reduced V^{di+1}.

Step 4. Step 2 is repeated with the reduced KP and the obfuscated V'_{di+2}.

Discussion. Once the session key is exposed, an attacker can perform a dictionary attack to retrieve the secret key. To do so, T_d must also be exposed. The attacker can XOR all the dictionary values with T_d and hash these. The hashed results are then compared with K_d and a match will reveal the secret key.

Thus, attacks with the aim to expose session keys are reasonable, but note that such attacks cannot bypass the system longer than one session duration. This is because in the session interchange time, the attackers do not have time for collecting enough data to expose the next session key, while they still need to inject the falsified values. If they do not inject anything, the real states of the physical system will be revealed to the system operators, who will spot the abnormal changes and detect the attacks. If they inject without knowing the session key, the chance of success is very low. Therefore, the session interchange time is likely the time that the attackers will be detected. Besides, exposed session keys should not lead to an exposed secret key if it is complex enough. Secret keys may also be renewed from time to time.

5.5   System Configuration Options

We have shown that the shorter the T_s, the smaller the attack surface and the impact of attacks on patterned data or session keys. However, such reductions commonly come with cost. We next consider the trade-off between security and usability to ensure that the security does not compromise operation.

Cost Consideration. The overheads created by LASARUS, C, are the combination of the obfuscating cost, C_o, and the key refreshing cost, C_k. We will consider such overhead in a time T. The period to log the physical value is T_l; the cost for running each XOR operator is x; the period to refresh the session key is T_s; the cost for generating a session key is y. The system will process approximately T/T_l obfuscating operating, so we will have:

$$C_o = \frac{T}{T_l} \cdot x$$

The key will be refreshed T/T_s over time T, so we have:

$$C_k = \frac{T}{T_s} \cdot y$$

Overall, the total overhead will be:

$$C = C_o + C_k = \frac{T}{T_l} \cdot x + \frac{T}{T_s} \cdot y \tag{1}$$

Note that costs x and y are computable and constant for a specific PLC. Besides, T_l is set according to specific ICS applications so we will not consider varying T_l for security purposes. As a result, from Eq. (1), only T and T_s will have an effect on C.

We illustrate the relations between the factors in Fig. 7a, which shows that the shorter the T_s, the higher the overhead. If we know the specific values of x, y, T and T_l, and given the cut out point of cost, which means the maximum cost we can afford, we can derive the value of T_s. Such values are the intersections between the cost lines and the constant vertical lines, which represent T_s. The overall time T to run the system also affects the cost. The longer it runs, the more overhead it will create. That suggests the operator to stop LASARUS when the resource is limited, or to run it only when there is a risk.

System Configuration Consideration. The main factor that can be configured to control the trade-off is T_s. We illustrate the way that an operator can configure T_s in Fig. 7b. The red line indicates the harm that the attacker can create over time while the blue line shows the overhead that LASARUS adds. Assume that the operators have a maximum of cost that they can afford, represented by the cost cut out line. On the other hand, they need to protect their system from damage by the undetected attacker, represented by the harm cut out line. In order to satisfy these cost-harm trade-offs, T_s should be larger than $T_{sMinCost}$ to save cost, and smaller than $T_{sMaxHarm}$ to prevent harm.

Note that cost and harm are not necessary correlated in the system, so $T_{sMinCost}$ may not always be smaller than $T_{sMaxHarm}$. Figure 7b illustrates the case when $T_{sMinCost} < T_{sMaxHarm}$. In this case, when T_s falls into the $[T_{sMinCost}, T_{sMaxHarm}]$ range, the conditions of cost and harm are always satisfied. As a result, operator can always configure T_s to have a value between these two points.

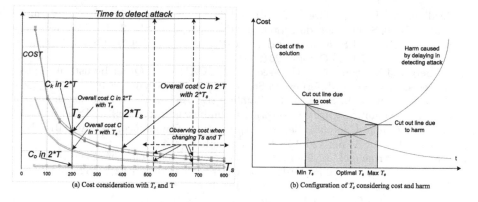

Fig. 7. Cost consideration with T_s and T (Color figure online)

The intersection point of the cost (blue line) and harm (red line) is the optimal value of T_s to balance the cost and security need.

There may be cases where $T_{sMinCost} > T_{sMaxHarm}$, whereby any implementation of T_s will exceed either cost or harm. When that happens, the operator can consider other configurations such as lowering T to save cost, or using stronger detection mechanisms, to detect the attackers faster and lower the harm.

6   Conclusion

We have designed and experimented with LASARUS, a system to continuously obfuscate data stored or accessed from a PLC in order to reduce the attack surface of legacy ICS. We show that LASARUS represents a significant challenge for attackers, decreasing the passing rate of attacks by up to 100 times with even simple detection systems. We also show that our obfuscated solution hides the patterns in the original data effectively, which stops the attackers from learning and predicting the next values successfully. We have also analysed the trade-off between security and cost by adjusting the length of the session, which adds more flexibility for the system operator. In future work, we plan to implement and evaluate LASARUS on a real-world ICS testbed available to us [20].

Acknowledgements. Supported by EPSRC/Chist-Era grant: EP/N021657/1.

References

1. Almalawi, A., Fahad, A., Tari, Z., Alamri, A., AlGhamdi, R., Zomaya, A.Y.: An efficient data-driven clustering technique to detect attacks in SCADA systems. IEEE Trans. Inf. Forensics Secur. **11**(5), 893–906 (2016)
2. Antrobus, R., Frey, S., Green, B., Rashid, A.: SimaticScan: towards a specialised vulnerability scanner for industrial control systems. In: Proceedings of the 4th International Symposium on ICS and SCADA Cyber Security Research (ICS-CSR 2016) (2016)

3. Jardine, W., Frey, S., Green, B., Rashid, A.: Selective non-invasive active monitoring for ICS intrusion detection. In: Proceedings of the 2nd ACM Workshop on Cyber-Physical Systems Security and Privacy, CPS-SPC@CCS 2016, Vienna, Austria, pp. 23–34, 28 October 2016
4. Colbert, E.J.M., Kott, A.: Cyber-security of SCADA and Other Industrial Control Systems. Advances in Information Security. Springer, Cham (2016)
5. Hadziosmanovic, D., Sommer, R., Zambon, E., Hartel, P.H.: Through the eye of the PLC: semantic security monitoring for industrial processes. In: Proceedings of the 30th Annual Computer Security Applications Conference, ACSAC 2014, New Orleans, LA, USA, pp. 126–135, 8–12 December 2014
6. Sainz, M., Armengol, J., Vehi, J.: Fault detection and isolation of the three-tank system using the modal interval analysis. J. Process Control **12**(2), 325–338 (2002)
7. Evans, D., Nguyen-Tuong, A., Knight, J.: Effectiveness of moving target defenses. In: Jajodia, S., Ghosh, A.K., Swarup, V., Wang, C., Wang, X.S. (eds.) Moving Target Defense, pp. 29–48. Springer, New York (2011)
8. Infracritical: Project SHINE findings report (2014). http://www.slideshare.net/BobRadvanovsky/project-shine-findings-report-dated-1oct2014. Accessed 12 Apr 2016
9. Stouffer, K., Falco, J., Scarfone, K.: Guide to industrial control systems (ICS) security. NIST Special Publication 800(82), p. 16 (2011)
10. Morris, T., Gao, W.: Industrial control system cyber attacks. In: Proceedings of the 1st International Symposium on ICS and SCADA Cyber Security Research, pp. 22–29. BCS (2013)
11. Maynard, P., McLaughlin, K., Haberler, B.: Towards understanding Man-In-The-Middle attacks on IEC 60870-5-104 SCADA networks. In: Proceedings of the 2nd International Symposium on ICS and SCADA Cyber Security Research, pp. 30–42. BCS (2014)
12. Yang, Y., Jiang, H.T., McLaughlin, K., Gao, L., Yuan, Y.B., Huang, W., Sezer, S.: Cybersecurity test-bed for IEC 61850 based smart substations. In: 2015 IEEE Power and Energy Society General Meeting, pp. 1–5. IEEE (2015)
13. Mahan, R.E., Fluckiger, J.D., Clements, S.L., Tews, C.W., Burnette, J.R., Goranson, C.A., Kirkham, H.: Secure data transfer guidance for industrial control and SCADA systems. Pacific Northwest National Lab (PNNL) Report (2011). http://www.pnnl.gov/main/publications/external/technical_reports/PNNL-20776.pdf. Accessed 4 Jan 2016
14. Davidson, C., Andel, T.: Feasibility of applying moving target defensive techniques in a SCADA system. In: 11th International Conference on Cyber Warfare and Security, ICCWS 2016, p. 363. Academic Conferences and Publishing Limited (2016)
15. McLaughlin, S., McDaniel, P.: Specification-based payload generation for programmable logic controllers. In: Proceedings of the 2012 ACM Conference on Computer and Communications Security, pp. 439–449. ACM (2012)
16. Krutz, R.L.: Securing SCADA Systems. Wiley, Hoboken (2005)
17. Gao, W., Morris, T., Reaves, B., Richey, D.: On SCADA control system command and response injection and intrusion detection. In: eCrime Researchers Summit (eCrime), pp. 1–9. IEEE (2010)
18. Morris, T.H., Thornton, Z., Turnipseed, I.: Industrial control system simulation and data logging for intrusion detection system research (2015)
19. Rezai, A., Keshavarzi, P., Moravej, Z.: Key management issue in SCADA networks: a review. Eng. Sci. Technol. Int. J. **20**, 354–363 (2017)
20. Green, B., Frey, S.A.F., Rashid, A., Hutchison, D.: Testbed diversity as a fundamental principle for effective ICS security research. In: SERECIN (2016)

Exploring the Relationship Between Architecture Coupling and Software Vulnerabilities

Robert Lagerström[1,2(✉)], Carliss Baldwin[2], Alan MacCormack[2],
Dan Sturtevant[3], and Lee Doolan[3]

[1] KTH Royal Institute of Technology, Stockholm, Sweden
robertl@kth.se
[2] Harvard Business School, Boston, USA
[3] Silverthread Inc., Boston, USA

Abstract. Employing software metrics, such as size and complexity, for predicting defects has been given a lot of attention over the years and proven very useful. However, the few studies looking at software architecture and vulnerabilities are limited in scope and findings. We explore the relationship between software vulnerabilities and component metrics (like code churn and cyclomatic complexity), as well as architecture coupling metrics (direct, indirect, and cyclic coupling). Our case is based on the Google Chromium project, an open source project that has not been studied for this topic yet. Our findings show a strong relationship between vulnerabilities and both component level metrics and architecture coupling metrics. 68% of the files associated with a vulnerability are cyclically coupled, compared to 43% of the non-vulnerable files. Our best regression model is a combination of low commenting, high code churn, high direct fan-out within the main cyclic group, and high direct fan-in outside of the main cyclic group.

Keywords: Security vulnerabilities · Software architecture · Metrics

1 Introduction

Cyber security incidents and software vulnerabilities cause big problems with increasing societal impact. Both individual home users and large corporations face similar problems with exploited software vulnerabilities leading to loss in confidentiality, integrity, and availability, and at the end of the day - time and money. Many seem to agree that software architecture complexity is a key issue when it comes to software vulnerabilities. Quoting a well-cited blog post by Bruce Schneier[1] "The worst enemy of security is complexity". The basic argument is that poorly designed and maintained software systems tend to embed highly complex code and architectures, which in turn increase the likely occurrence of vulnerabilities waiting to be exploited. However, few studies have explored the relationship of complexity to vulnerabilities and the findings to this point are inconclusive [1, 2] and far from generalizable.

---

[1] www.schneier.com/essays/archives/1999/11/a_plea_for_simplicit.html.

© Springer International Publishing AG 2017
E. Bodden et al. (Eds.): ESSoS 2017, LNCS 10379, pp. 53–69, 2017.
DOI: 10.1007/978-3-319-62105-0_4

Some existing studies of software vulnerabilities include direct coupling as a predictive variable, e.g. [3–5]. However, to our knowledge, other coupling measures such as indirect coupling and cyclic coupling have not been tested in relation to vulnerabilities. These measures have been shown to affect other software performance outcomes such as defects e.g. [6], productivity e.g. [7], and maintenance cost e.g. [8]. Our theory is that this is also the case for software vulnerabilities.

In this paper, we measure (and visualize) the Google Chrome software architecture and explore the correlation between software vulnerabilities and component-level metrics and different architecture coupling measures. Our component metrics include: code churn, source lines of code, cyclomatic complexity, and comment ratio. Our coupling measures fall into three categories: direct coupling (fan-in & fan-out), indirect coupling (fan-in & fan-out), and cyclic coupling. Studying 16,268 C-files of the March 2016 Chrome release and linking them to 290 files that were changed in order to fix 185 vulnerabilities, we found that both component metrics and the different coupling measures are significantly correlated with vulnerabilities. However, due to limitations of the sample, when testing a set of regression models, we could not untangle the impact of the different coupling measures.

Our main contribution in this paper is to add new findings to the work on software metrics and vulnerabilities, bringing the field closer to generalizable and conclusive results. To this end, we focus on the Chromium project, which has not been studied from the perspective of vulnerabilities. Our correlations are both strong and significant. They indicate that architectural coupling measures might be used in addition to component-level metrics to improve vulnerability prediction models, although this needs additional exploration.

The rest of this paper is organized as follows: Sect. 2 presents related work in three areas; software metrics and defects, software metrics and vulnerabilities, and impact of architectural coupling on different performance measures. In Sect. 3 we describe our measures of complexity and coupling. The Chromium project is described in Sect. 4, followed by our analysis of Chrome and software vulnerabilities in Sect. 5. Our study and potential future work are discussed in Sect. 6. Section 7 concludes the paper.

2   Related Work

For purposes of exposition, we have divided related work in three categories: studies relating software metrics and defects; studies relating software metrics and vulnerabilities; and studies relating architecture coupling measures to different performance outcomes.

2.1   Software Metrics and Defects

Numerous studies have looked at the relationship between software metrics and defects. We discuss those that use measures most closely related to the ones we test. For the interested reader [9, 10] present comprehensive literature studies on this topic.

In [11] Kitchenham et al. found that the number of files used by a given file, a coupling measure we label "direct fan out," is associated with defects, although source lines of code, a code measure, was a stronger indicator. A similar study by Basili et al. [12] found the opposite: that coupling measures were better able to predict faults traditional code metrics, such as lines of code. In [13], Nagappan and Ball showed that code churn, a relative measure of change in a file, is an early indicator of defect density. Schröter et al. looked at usage dependencies, a form of coupling between components and showed that these are good predictors of defects [14]. Zimmermann and Nagappan studied network measures of coupling, such as density and centrality, for defect prediction and found that these perform better than other complexity metrics [15]. Steff and Russo then showed that dependency changes are strong defect indicators [16].

From these and other studies, it appears that both coupling measures and component-level metrics have proven successful in defect prediction. Since vulnerabilities are a special class of defects, our working hypothesis is that the coupling measures and code metrics should also predict vulnerabilities.

2.2 Software Metrics and Vulnerabilities

While much attention has been paid to defects, less work has been done to examine the relationship between coupling measures and code metrics and vulnerabilities. However, elevated concerns about cyber security have brought more attention to this topic.

Neuhaus et al. studied the Mozilla project and found correlation between vulnerabilities and include statements [17]. In [18], the same authors used Red Hat to investigate the correlation between package dependencies and vulnerabilities. Zimmermann et al. also found weak correlation between a set of software metrics and vulnerabilities [19]. Nguyen and Tran used dependency graphs to look at vulnerabilities in the Mozilla Firefox Javascript Engine [20]. Shin et al. investigated the same codebase, but focused on complexity metrics [3]. Moshtari et al. [5] replicated and extended this work by including a more complete set of vulnerabilities and looking at more software applications, including Eclipse, Apache Tomcat, Firefox, Linux Kernel, and OpenSCADA. They concluded that their software (complexity) metrics are good predictors of vulnerabilities. Chowdhury and Zulkernine [21] investigated the relation between complexity, coupling, cohesion, and vulnerabilities in Mozilla Firefox. They were able to predict a majority of the files associated with vulnerabilities with tolerable false positive rates. Hovsepyan et al. [22] looked at design churn as a predictor of vulnerabilities in ten Android applications and found a statistically significant relationship between design churn and vulnerabilities in some but not all applications.

Morrison et al. [2] did not find any significant relation between complexity and vulnerabilities in their study of Microsoft products. They suggested that a set of security-specific metrics might be needed in vulnerability prediction models. Shin and Williams 1 similarly found the relationship between software complexity and vulnerabilities to be weak, and also recommended that new complexity metrics be developed for understanding security related defects.

The studies on software vulnerabilities and various metrics provide a mixed picture of the relationship. Most find some correlation or predictability, but some don't and the overall findings are weak. Most agree that there is a need to continue exploring this topic. We note that studies to date have not looked at architectural measures in conjunction with code-level complexity metrics. In most cases, coupling is omitted as a predictive variable: when included it is limited to direct coupling.

2.3 Coupling Metrics for Outcome Prediction

In [23] MacCormack et al. used indirect coupling and cyclic coupling to measure modularity and show that modular organizations produce modular software products, verifying the so-called mirroring hypothesis. Sturtevant [7] and Akaikine [8] also studied indirect and cyclic coupling in two separate cases. They found significant differences in defect density, defect resolution time, and developer productivity as a function of coupling measures.

Baldwin et al. present empirical work using 1,286 software releases from 17 different software applications showing that most of the software systems contain one large cyclic group of interdependent files (high cyclic coupling/high levels of indirect coupling), calling it the Core [24]. Heiser et al. [25] studied cyclic coupling and indirect coupling (using the suggested method in [24]) for organizational transformation planning in a development organization. In [26], they used the same methodology to develop a strategy to prioritize software feature production.

MacCormack and Sturtevant looked at the impact of coupling (indirect and cyclic) on software defect related activity [6]. Lagerström et al. used cyclic and indirect coupling in a biopharmaceutical case to visualize and measure modularity in an enterprise architecture [27]. In subsequent work, the same authors showed that it was more costly to change software applications with many cyclic dependencies than those with few or no cyclic dependencies [28, 29].

In summary, software metrics have been successful in studies predicting the location of general defects. Work on vulnerabilities, however, is not as extensive or as conclusive, although there have been promising findings. Moreover, coupling measures have not been widely used in vulnerability studies, although they known to be correlated with other performance measures including defects. In this paper, we aim to explore software metrics including architecture coupling measures in relation to software vulnerabilities by studying the Google Chrome codebase.

3   Measuring Component and Architecture Coupling Metrics

As noted in the previous section software metrics have been used as predictors of behavior in many studies. We focus on the most common and widely used component metrics, as well as a set of architectural coupling measures.

3.1   Software Component Metrics

The most common and also the simplest software metrics is measuring source lines of code (*SLOC*), basically counting the number of lines in a software file not including comments. This is a measure of size and has been shown to predict defects, cost and complexity e.g. [30, 31].

In 1976 McCabe proposed the cyclomatic complexity (*MCCABE*) measure [32]. It is now one of the most common complexity metrics used in software studies [9]. Basically, the McCabe metric counts the number alternative execution paths that can be followed as a program executes. Alternative paths through a procedure result from conditional branching statements (if statement, switch/case statement, while loops, et cetera). McCabe scores may be calculated for procedures (called functions in C or C++) or class methods. We calculate cyclomatic complexity for all functions and methods within a C-file, and then use the maximum figure observed within that file. In prior work, McCabe scores have been predictive of higher defect rates and lower productivity.

The comment ratio (*COMMR*) is a measure of how well commented the source code is. It is a comments-to-code ratio rather than a pure count of number of comment lines. This measure is also frequently used when analyzing software, e.g. [33]. However, there is no theoretical prediction as to correlation of comments to complexity or defects (i.e. complex or defective code may generate many comments or few comments).

Code churn (*CHURN*) measures the activity within each file in terms of number of lines of code being added, modified, or deleted. This metric is also frequently used in software studies, especially for defect prediction e.g. [13]. Recently it has proved predictive in some vulnerability studies e.g. [3].

3.2 Architecture Coupling Measures

Files in a software can be coupled in different ways: directly, indirectly, or cyclically.

Figure 1(1) represents the base case, in which the files are not coupled to any other files. In Fig. 1(2), file A is directly coupled with files B and C, i.e. B and C depend on A, but A does not depend on B and C. Thus A has a direct fan-in (*DFI*) of two and a direct fan-out (*DFO*) of zero. Modular systems theory predicts that files with higher levels of direct coupling are more defect prone, given the difficulty assessing the potential impact of changing the coupled files on the dependent files [34]. Hence we predict that coupled files would be more likely to contain vulnerabilities than a similar file with no coupling (e.g., as indicated in Fig. 1(1)). Support for such a relationship is found in empirical studies of software, in which the components are source files or classes, and dependencies denote use relationships between them [3].

Figure 1(3) depicts a more complex set of relationships between software files. File A is directly coupled to B and is indirectly coupled to files C and D (through B). That is, A has an indirect fan-in (*IndFI*) of three and an indirect fan-out (*IndFO*) of zero. In this architecture, changes may propagate between files that are not directly connected, via a "chain" of dependencies. While indirect coupling relationships are likely to be weaker than direct coupling relationships, the former are not as visible to a software developer, hence may be overlooked and more likely to produce unintended system behaviors. Measures of indirect coupling have been shown to predict both the

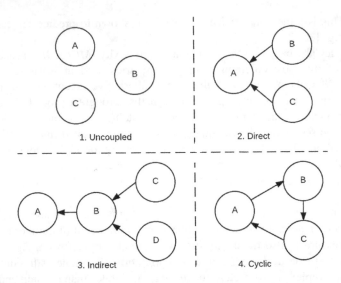

Fig. 1. Different coupling relationships between software files.

number of defects and the ease (or difficulty) with which a software system can be adapted 635.

Figure 1(4) illustrates a third pattern of coupling between files, called cyclic coupling (*CYCLIC*) 3637. In this architecture, A is coupled with C, C is coupled with B, and B is coupled with A. These files form a cyclic group – a group of files that are mutually interdependent. In contrast to Fig. 1(3), there is no ordering of these files, such that one can be changed (or developed) before the others. Rather, files in cyclic groups must often be changed concurrently, to ensure that they continue to work together effectively. When cyclic groups are large, this presents a significant challenge, increasing the likelihood of defects [35], and possibly vulnerabilities. We measure cyclic coupling as whether a file belongs to the largest cyclic group in the architecture or not, as explained in [24].

The patterns described above represent related, but conceptually distinct, patterns of coupling that exist between files. We note however, that measures of these different types are likely to be correlated. Specifically, files with high levels of direct coupling are, all else being equal, more likely to have high levels of indirect coupling. And files with high levels of indirect coupling are, all else being equal, more likely to be members of cyclic groups. It will be important to be sensitive to these issues in our empirical tests.

Table 1 presents the different types of metrics we use. It differentiates between component level metrics (source lines of code, cyclomatic complexity, commenting ratio, and code churn) and the architectural coupling measures, (direct coupling, indirect coupling, and cyclic coupling).

Table 1. Component-level and architecture coupling metrics used in this study.

Component-level metrics	Architecture coupling metrics
Source lines of code (*SLOC*)	Direct coupling (*DFI & DFO*)
Cyclomatic complexity (*MCCABE*)	Indirect coupling (*IndFI & IndFO*)
Commenting ratio (*COMMR*)	Cyclic coupling (*CYCLIC*)
Code churn (*CHURN*)	

4 The Chromium Project

The Google Chromium project[2] is an open source web-browser project from which the Chrome browser gets its source code. It is mainly written in C++ and is available for multiple platforms such as Linux, OS X 10.9 and later, Windows 7 and later, and iOS. The earliest version was released late 2008, while the first stable non-beta version (5.0.306.0) was released in early 2010. Our main focus in this study is the March 31st 2016 version called 50.0.2661.57.

4.1 Chrome Metrics and Coupling

We have measured the Chrome software architecture in terms of traditional software metrics; source lines of code (*SLOC*), cyclomatic complexity (*MCCABE*), commenting ratio (*COMMR*), and the amount of activity (*CHURN*) spent in each file to fix "regular" defects (not vulnerabilities). We also calculated the different coupling measures; direct (*DFI & DFO*), indirect (*IndFI & IndFO*), and cyclic (*CYCLIC*). All metrics and the architecture visualization (Fig. 2) were derived using a commercial analysis tool from Silverthread[3] and each metric is explained in Sect. 3. All variables are measured as positive integers, except *COMMR* which is a positive rational number and *CYCLIC* which is a binary (1/0) number.

The binary cyclic coupling metric indicates whether a file belongs to the largest cluster of cyclically dependent files (1) or not (0). The largest cyclic group is labeled the Core in Fig. 2: it contains 44% of the files in the codebase. The next largest cyclic group is much smaller containing only 118 files. How this cluster is derived is explained in detail in [24]. In Table 2 all metrics are presented with their real numbers. Due to the nature of our data all variables (except the binary *CYCLIC* variable) are converted to their natural logarithms (LN) in calculating correlations (Table 4) and in our regression models (Table 5).

Our dependent variable (*VULN*, 1/0) has a value of one if the file in question was changed to fix a defect classified as a vulnerability, and zero otherwise.

In an attempt to untangle the coupling measures relation to vulnerabilities we have also used direct coupling within the main cyclic group (*DFIxC & DFOxC*) and outside of this group (*DFIxNoC & DFOxNoC*).

---

[2] https://www.chromium.org.

[3] https://silverthreadinc.com.

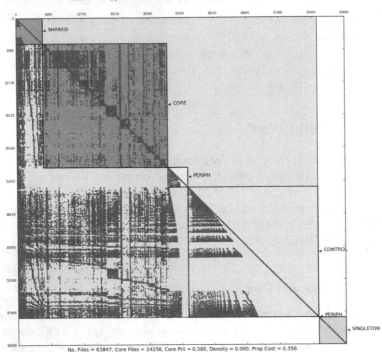

Fig. 2. A visualization of the Google Chrome 2016 software architecture showing all direct dependencies and sorted by different coupling categories. This figure shows the full set of files associated with Chrome, thus a larger number of files than what is used in our analysis. The Silverthread analysis tool produced the figure, see [6] for more information. The coupling categories shown in the figure are based on the number of indirect fan-in and fan-outs, where; the "Shared" group contains files that have high fan-in and low fan-out, "Core" is the largest cyclic group with both high fan-in and fan-out, "Peripheral" files have low indirect coupling, the "Control" group has low fan-in and high fan-out, and the "Singletons" have no coupling at all.

Table 2. Descriptive statistics for 2016 Google Chrome metrics.

2016/n = 16,268	Max	Min	Mean	Median	St. dev
VULN	1	0	0.02	0	0.13
SLOC	69,702	0	196.18	79	854.61
MCCABE	868	0	9.13	5	20.13
COMMR	39	0	0.33	0.17	0.88
CHURN	634,536	1	883.40	249	5,734
DFI	9,381	1	6.09	2	76.97
DFO	355	1	15.69	12	16.05
IndFI	49,570	1	22,996	23	24,705
IndFO	29,949	1	27,227	29,314	7,554
CYCLIC	1	0	0.44	0	0.50

4.2   Chrome Vulnerabilities

We collected the Google Chrome related vulnerabilities using the bug Tracker system[4] used by the developers in the Chromium project. In Tracker, bugs classified as vulnerabilities are registered with both their external CVE[5] ID and the internally used bug ID. (CVE, which stands for Common Vulnerabilities and Exposures, is a published list of security vulnerabilities that provides unique IDs for publicly known security issues. Some CVEs are associated with multiple internally defined bugs.)

We then used the internal bug IDs to track the files in the Chrome architecture that were changed in order to fix each vulnerability-classified bug. We did this by extracting the commits that specified fixing a vulnerability bug that was tagged with the internal bug ID.

As noted in [36] many CVEs are associated with external projects, thus not identifiable using the Chrome commits. Nguyen and Massacci claim that two thirds of the Chrome vulnerabilities are unverifiable due to this issue, which seems to be in line with our findings. We found 1,063 unique CVEs (on April 14th, 2016) associated with 1,070 bugs in the Chrome bug Tracker. Going through the commits gave us 407 bugs associated with 390 CVEs, which were fixed by patching 965 C- & header-files.

The architecture displayed in Fig. 2 contains the complete Google Chrome architecture as of March 31st, 2016, including both C-files and header files. These in turn were associated with 288 CVEs corresponding to 294 internal vulnerability bugs fixed by modifying 621 files. At this point, we excluded the header-files since these come hand in hand with the C-files and are thus associated with the same bugs and CVEs. In doing so we found only nine non-redundant CVEs and vulnerability bugs, and decreased the total number of files for analysis by 32,418 files.

The 2016 Chrome architecture contains a directory called "third_party/WebKit" which is a recently (2015) merged set of files from another vendor (Apple). From an architectural coupling perspective this directory, and its recent bulk merge, creates a

Table 3. CVE and Chrome file data leading to our analysis set of files.

	CVEs	Bugs	Vuln. files	Total files
Total contained in tracker	1,063	1,070	Not known	Not appl.
C- & h-files fixed by Google commits	390	407	965	Not appl.
Found for March 2016 architecture	288	294	621	63,847
Subtract:				
h-files	9	9	223	32,418
third_party/WebKit	94	95	108	3,015
Missing data	0	0	0	12,146
Final:				
Analysis sample	185	190	290	16,268

---

[4] http://bugs.chromium.org/p/chromium/issues/.

[5] https://cve.mitre.org/

situation where most of the directory is not a part of the overall architectural structure. It has its own special structure that is not representative of the rest of the system. To avoid mixing systems with different histories and structure, we excluded this directory as well. Ninety-four CVEs were associated with this directory. Finally, one of our key variables, code churn (CHURN), had missing data for many of the C-files. Dropping these files did not reduce the CVE count, but did reduce the number of files by 12,146 to 16,268.

In summary, our final dataset contains 185 unique CVEs associated with 190 vulnerability bugs fixed in patches of 290 C-files, and the total C-file set to compare with is 16,268. The numbers for this data cleanse are detailed in Table 3.

5   Chrome Metrics and Vulnerable Files

In this section we explore the relationship between software component metrics and different architecture coupling metrics in vulnerability-associated files of the Google Chrome architecture from 2016.

5.1   Findings

Table 4 presents a correlation matrix for the variables we study. As indicated, we have taken the natural logarithm of each variable except the binary variable *CYCLIC*. From the table, we can see that *CHURN* is highly correlated with source lines of code (*SLOC*), cyclomatic complexity (*MCCABE*), and direct fan-out (*DFO*). That is, files that are associated with many changes in general (excluding vulnerability bug changes) also have more source lines of code, higher cyclomatic complexity, and a higher number of direct fan-out dependencies. Further, we see that all of our software metrics, including the different types of coupling, are significantly correlated with vulnerability bug files (*VULN*). Namely, files that have been changed a lot, that have a low comment ratio, many source lines of code, high cyclomatic complexity, and high coupling are all associated with vulnerability bugs.

Unfortunately, due to the high correlation between variables we can't include them all in the same regression model. For the metrics code churn, source lines of code, cyclomatic complexity, and direct fan-out we basically need to choose one to include in the regression. Code churn has been proven before to be a good predictor (see e.g. [3]) and it also has the highest correlation with our *VULN* variable. Therefore, we chose to include *CHURN* in our regression models and not the others.

Model 1 in our regression contains three traditional software metrics used in defect and vulnerability prediction; code churn, comment ratio, and direct fan-in. This is a good starting model since these all have been used successfully before. As can be seen in Table 5 all three variables significantly contribute to our model. Since we want to explore coupling further, Model 2 tests whether indirect fan-in (*IndFI*) and indirect fan-out (*IndFO*) add any explanatory power over *DFI*. Model 3 looks at cyclic coupling (*CYCLIC*) instead of *IndFI* and *IndFO*. So far, we can see that the indirect coupling metrics perform better together with code churn and commenting ratio

Table 4. Correlation table for vulnerability bugs and complexity metrics in the 2016 Google Chrome software architecture.

	VULN	SLOC	MCCABE	COMMR	CHURN	DFI	DFO	IndFI	IndFO	CYCLIC	DFIxC	DFOxC	DFIxNoC	DFOxNoC
VULN	1													
SLOC	.135*	1												
MCCABE	.110*	.804*	1											
COMMR	-.021*	-.299*	-.199*	1										
CHURN	.180*	.801*	.675*	-.103*	1									
DFI	.084*	.203*	.128*	-.062*	.195*	1								
DFO	.140*	.707*	.622*	-.248*	.656*	.136*	1							
IndFI	.063*	.144*	.114*	-.022*	.134*	.603*	.149*	1						
IndFO	.026*	.384*	.400*	-.226*	.277*	.043*	.577*	.048*	1					
CYCLIC	.066*	.202*	.188*	-.085*	.183*	.508*	.245*	.929*	.243*	1				
DFIxC	.088*	.218*	.177*	-.073*	.219*	.816*	.203*	.718*	.188*	.774*	1			
DFOxC	.115*	.338*	.296*	-.109*	.333*	.480*	.437*	.859*	.225*	.925*	.725*	1		
DFIxNoC	-0.014	-.042*	-.094*	.023*	-.059*	.222*	-.125*	-.248*	-.248*	-.494*	-.382*	-.457*	1	
DFOxNoC	-.022*	.155*	.138*	-.065*	.123*	-.415*	.263*	-.813*	.181*	-.813*	-.629*	-.753*	.399**	1

* Correlation is significant at the 0.01 level, bold numbers indicate high correlation problematic for regression model

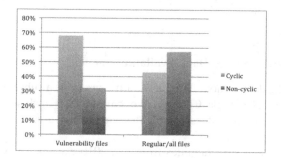

Fig. 3. Vulnerability associated files in the Cyclic and Non-cyclic groups.

compared to direct and cyclic coupling. This is not surprising since it is a more coarse grained metric that includes more information than both cyclic and direct coupling.

In Model 4 and 5 we test if direct fan-in and fan-out within the main cyclic group and outside this group adds any explanatory power. Again, due to the correlation among the measures, we have to divide our direct coupling measures from each other. DFI within the cyclic files (*DFIxCyc*) is tested in Model 4 and *DFO* within the cyclic files (*DFOxCyc*) in Model 5. Our best model seems to be the one including code churn, comment ratio, direct fan-out within the cyclic group (*DFOxCyc*) together with direct fan-in within the non-cyclic group (*DFIxNoCyc*), that is Model 5. Meaning that files that are cyclically coupled together in a large co-dependent network with a high degree of direct fan-out coupling and files that are not in this large cyclic group but have a high degree of direct fan-in coupling (the group in Fig. 2 called Shared), and with many changes in the past and a low commenting ratio – are more likely to contain vulnerabilities.

These results are in line with related work and this is where we are at with vulnerability prediction today.

Table 5. Binary logistic regression for vulnerability bug files in 2016 Chrome architecture.

VULN	Model 1	Model 2	Model 3	Model 4	Model 5
COMMR	−1.003**	−.880*	−.878*	−.993**	−.714*
CHURN	.861***	.874***	.876***	.859***	.805***
DFI	.215***				
IndFI		.063***			
IndFO		.004			
CYCLIC			.568***		
DFIxC				.216***	
DFOxC					.286***
DFIxNoC				.137	.381**
Constant	−9.683***	−9.999***	−9.869***	−9.647***	−9.710***
Chi-square	531.038***	538.206***	534.718***	531.613***	553.748***
Cox&Snell R^2	0.032	0.033	0.032	0.032	0.033
Nagelkerke R^2	0.197	0.199	0.198	0.197	0.205

n = 16,268, * $p < 0.05$, ** $p < 0.01$, and ***$p < 0.001$

5.2   Use of Different Sets of Data Available

As mentioned in the data section our dataset only represents a subset of the files in the 2016 March release of Google Chrome. We have run all analyses on the different subsets (cf. Table 3) as a robustness check, there are some variance but the main story looks similar.

One could argue that vulnerabilities from e.g. 2010 can't be analyzed based on an architecture from 2016. As a robustness check we have also looked at the 2010 architecture (the first stable release of Chrome). We also divided our vulnerability data in two equally large sets and looking at the older half of vulnerabilities for the 2010 architecture, and the younger half of vulnerabilities for the 2016 architecture.

The correlations and regressions with the 2010 and 2016 architecture and all vulnerability bugs, as well as the division of bugs between 2010 and 2016 look fairly similar. We did lose some power when dividing the bug dataset between the architectures, this had us chose the architecture associated with most vulnerabilities, that is the 2016 architecture and all vulnerability related bugs.

If we compare Table 2 (2016 Chrome stats.) and Table 6 (2010 Chrome stats.) we can see that some of the software metrics have changed, e.g. the comment ratio and direct fan-in and fan-out. Although the maximum values have significant increases, the differences when considering the means or medians are not that large. For cyclomatic complexity and code churn the means actually went down between 2010 and 2016. The main differences can be seen in the coupling measures for indirect fan-in and fan-out, where the means increased from 3,000–4,000 to 23,000–27,000. This is related to the considerable increase in size of the main cyclic group of dependent files, the "Core" in 2010 contained 4,049 files and in 2016 it had grown to 24,258 files.

Regarding the visualization of the architecture seen in Fig. 4 one can conclude that the 2010 and 2016 architectures look very similar in terms of coupling. For both architectures we have a large "Core" (that is, a large cyclic group where everyone depends on one another). In 2010 the Core was 33% of the architecture and in 2016 38%, thus even though this group of files grew considerably in number, it grew in proportion to the rest of the codebase. Both architectures also have large Control groups (files with high indirect fan-out and low indirect fan-in), and small groups of Shared files (files with high indirect fan-in and low indirect fan-out), Peripheral files (low indirect coupling), and Singletons (no coupling). This architectural similarity we interpret as an indication that our coupling measures are comparable with vulnerabilities for either architecture as long as the file associated with the vulnerability bug is present in the architecture.

6 Discussion and Future Work

Our work is the first study to use the Google Chromium project to explore the relationship between software metrics and vulnerabilities. As such it adds evidence to the total body of knowledge on this topic, which is still fairly unexplored (especially in comparison with the relationship between software metrics and generic defects).

The main weakness in our study we believe is that, because of their high level of collinearity, the different coupling measures have essentially equal predictive power in our regressions. The component-level metrics—source lines of code, code churn, cyclomatic complexity—are also highly correlated with each other and with direct fan-out. For this reason, we are unable (in this codebase) to tease apart the separate contribution of conceptually distinct, but empirically indistinguishable, types of complexity on vulnerability. Hopefully, we (or others) can explore these questions further using other software architectures in order to better understand the linkages between complexity, coupling and vulnerabilities.

We are not alone in having difficulty determining the relationship between software metrics and vulnerabilities. As reported in the section on related work, other studies also report weak power or non-statistically significant variables e.g. [1, 2]. Prediction models report either too many false positives or low precision. Thus this seems to be a generally difficult area to research.

Statistical problems, like collinearity, make it difficult to identify the causal mechanisms linking complexity and coupling with vulnerabilities. However, most studies are able to report valid correlations. Thus a growing body of collective evidence shows that variables like size, complexity, code churn, and coupling are associated with and thus likely to increase the incidence of vulnerabilities. The correlations reported in Table 4 and the regressions in Table 5 indicate a significant relation between vulnerable files, traditional software metrics and coupling measures, hence add to this mounting body of evidence. However, future work is needed.

Many studies present vulnerability prediction models with a large set of variables. However, very few describe the details of the variables included. What variables do actually contribute to the prediction model and which do not? This is especially interesting for architecture coupling and component complexity, since some of the

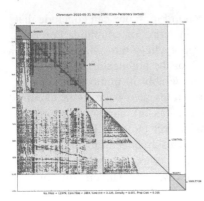

Fig. 4. Google Chrome 2010 software architecture showing a large cyclic cluster (here called the core) and other similar features as the 2016 version.

Table 6. Descriptive statistics for complexity metrics in Google Chrome 2010.

2010 / n = 6,333	Max	Min	Mean	Median	St.dev
VULN	1	0	0.02	0	0.15
SLOC	72,847	0	300.72	121	1,554.97
MCCABE	700	0	10.75	5	25.15
COMMR	163	0	0.44	0.23	2.24
CHURN	213,099	10	2,096.52	846	6,248.25
DFI	2,281	1	6.03	2	36.19
DFO	189	1	14.23	11	13.33
IndFI	8,649	1	3,204.69	9	4,146.90
IndFO	5,125	1	4,349.66	4,916	1,589.18
CYCLIC	1	0	0.36	0	0.48

papers we have studied report these as good predictors e.g. [3] while other say it shows weak or no relation to vulnerabilities e.g. [1, 2]. In general it would have been interesting to get this information from all studies, in e.g. the form of a correlation table or detailed prediction models.

As indicated, our findings on the relationship between of software metrics and vulnerabilities are mixed. Thus, future work is very much needed. First, we believe doing more studies in general on this topic is necessary. So far, there are few studies and thus few software systems have been investigated. For generalizability, more work is needed, including not only open source projects but also commercial software. Secondly, we have only found one study that compares general defects and vulnerabilities using the same data set. Camilo et al. [37] also studied the Google Chromium project and found "that bugs and vulnerabilities are empirically dissimilar groups, warranting the need for more research targeting vulnerabilities." More studies of this kind are necessary. Specifically we would like to be able to say what the main differences between a vulnerability bug and regular bug are in terms of complexity, size, code churn, commenting, and coupling. This could help us build more accurate prediction models.

7   Conclusions

Managing software vulnerabilities has become one of the top issues in today's society. Previous research on software defects, and to some extent vulnerabilities, showed that component level metrics (e.g. complexity and code churn) and architecture measures (e.g. coupling) can be good predictors of where problems are likely to occur. In this study we studied the Google Chromium project and found that all our metrics, both component and architecture level, are highly correlated with files that have been patched in order to fix vulnerability classified bugs. We also set out to test whether different software architecture coupling measures were correlated with a higher incidence of vulnerabilities. In our tests we found it difficult to conclusively distinguish between our different measures of coupling, but the indication is that indirect coupling performs better than direct coupling, and the best model is a combination of cyclic coupling and direct coupling. We strongly believe that the indications in our study together with other related research show that software metrics of different kinds can be very helpful in locating vulnerabilities, but that more work is needed.

References

1. Shin, Y., Williams, L.: Is complexity really the enemy of software security?. In: Proceedings of the 4th ACM Workshop on Quality of Protection, pp. 47–50 (2008)
2. Morrison, P., Herzig, K., Murphy, B., Williams, L.: Challenges with applying vulnerability prediction models. In: Proceedings of the 2015 Symposium and Bootcamp on the Science of Security, p. 4 (2015)
3. Shin, Y., Meneely, A., Williams, L., Osborne, J.A.: Evaluating complexity, code churn, and developer activity metrics as indicators of software vulnerabilities. IEEE Trans. Software Eng. 37(6), 772–787 (2011)
4. Walden, J., Stuckman, J., Scandariato, R.: Predicting vulnerable components: software metrics vs text mining. In: IEEE 25th International Symposium on Software Reliability Engineering, pp. 23–33 (2014)
5. Moshtari, S., Sami, A., Azimi, M.: Using complexity metrics to improve software security. Comput. Fraud Secur. 5, 8–17 (2013)
6. MacCormack, A., Sturtevant, D.: Technical debt and system architecture: the impact of coupling on defect-related activity. J. Syst. Software 120, 170–182 (2016)
7. Sturtevant, D.J.: System design and the cost of architectural complexity. Doctoral dissertation, Massachusetts Institute of Technology (MIT) (2013)
8. Akaikine, A.: The impact of software design structure on product maintenance costs and measurement of economic benefits of product design. Master thesis, Massachusetts Institute of Technology (MIT) (2010)
9. Catal, C., Diri, B.: A systematic review of software fault prediction studies. Expert Syst. Appl. 36(4), 7346–7354 (2009)
10. Hall, T., Beecham, S., Bowes, D., Gray, D., Counsell, S.: A systematic literature review on fault prediction performance in software engineering. IEEE Trans. Software Eng. 38, 1276–1304 (2012)
11. Kitchenham, B., Pickard, L., Linkman, S.: An evaluation of some design metrics. Software Eng. J. 5(1), 50–58 (1990)
12. Basili, V.R., Briand, L.C., Melo, W.L.: A validation of object-oriented design metrics as quality indicators. IEEE Trans. Software Eng. 22, 751–761 (1990)
13. Nagappan, N., Ball, T.: Use of relative code churn measures to predict system defect density. In: Proceedings of the 27th International Conference on Software Engineering (ICSE), pp. 284–292 (2005)
14. Schröter, A., Zimmermann, T., Zeller, A.: Predicting component failures at design time. In: Proceedings of the ACM/IEEE International Symposium on Empirical Software Engineering, pp. 18–27 (2006)

15. Zimmermann, T., Nagappan, N.: Predicting defects using network analysis on dependency graphs. In: Proceedings of the 30th International Conference on Software Engineering (ICSE), pp. 531–540 (2008)
16. Steff, M., Russo, B.: Measuring architectural change for defect estimation and localization. In: Proceedings of the International Symposium on Empirical Software Engineering and Measurement, pp. 225–234 (2011)
17. Neuhaus, S., Zimmermann, T., Holler, C., Zeller, A.: Predicting vulnerable software components. In: ACM Conference on Computer and Communications Security (CCS), pp. 529–540 (2007)
18. Neuhaus, S., Zimmermann, T.: The beauty and the beast: vulnerabilities in red hat's packages. In: Proceedings of the Annual Technical Conference on USENIX, p. 30 (2009)
19. Zimmermann, T., Nagappan, N., Williams, L.: Searching for a needle in a haystack: predicting security vulnerabilities for windows vista. In: Proceedings of the International Conference on Software Testing, Verification & Validation, pp. 421–428 (2010)
20. Nguyen, V.H., Tran, L.M.: Predicting vulnerable software components with dependency graphs. In: Proceedings of the 6th International Workshop on Security Measurements and Metrics, pp. 3:1–3:8 (2010)
21. Chowdhury, I., Zulkernine, M.: Using complexity, coupling, and cohesion metrics as early indicators of vulnerabilities. J. Syst. Archit. **57**(3), 294–313 (2011)
22. Hovsepyan, A., Scandariato, R., Steff, M., Joosen, W.: Design churn as predictor of vulnerabilities? Int. J. Secure Software Eng. **5**(3), 16–31 (2014)
23. MacCormack, A., Baldwin, C., Rusnak, J.: Exploring the duality between product and organizational architectures: a test of the "mirroring" hypothesis. Res. Policy **41**(8), 1309–1324 (2012)
24. Baldwin, C.A., MacCormack, A., Rusnak, J.: Hidden structure: using network methods to map system architecture. Res. Policy **43**(8), 1381–1397 (2014)
25. Heiser, F., Lagerström, R., Addibpour, M.: Revealing hidden structures in organizational transformation – a case study. In: Persson, A., Stirna, J. (eds.) CAiSE 2015. LNBIP, vol. 215, pp. 327–338. Springer, Cham (2015). doi:10.1007/978-3-319-19243-7_31
26. Lagerström, R., Addibpour, M., Heiser, F.: Product feature prioritization using the hidden structure method: a practical case at Ericsson. In: Proceedings of the Portland International Center for Management of Engineering and Technology (PICMET) Conference. IEEE, September 2016
27. Lagerström, R., Baldwin, C., MacCormack, A., Dreyfus, D.: Visualizing and measuring enterprise architecture: an exploratory biopharma case. In: Grabis, J., Kirikova, M., Zdravkovic, J., Stirna, J. (eds.) PoEM 2013. LNBIP, vol. 165, pp. 9–23. Springer, Heidelberg (2013). doi:10.1007/978-3-642-41641-5_2
28. Lagerström, R., Baldwin, C., MacCormack, A., Dreyfus, D.: Visualizing and measuring software portfolio architecture: a flexibility analysis. In: Proceedings of the 16th International DSM Conference (2014)
29. MacCormack, A., Lagerström, R., Dreyfus, D., Baldwin, C.: Building the agile enterprise: IT architecture, modularity and the cost of IT change. Harvard Business School Working Paper, No. 15-060, (2015) (revised August 2016)
30. Albrecht, A.J., Gaffney, J.E.: Software function, source lines of code, and development effort prediction: a software science validation. IEEE Trans. Software Eng. **6**, 639–648 (1983)
31. Kan, S.H.: Metrics and Models in Software Quality Engineering. Addison-Wesley Longman Publishing Co., Inc., Boston (2002)
32. McCabe, T.J.: A complexity measure. IEEE Trans. Software Eng. **4**, 308–320 (1976)
33. Aggarwal, K.K., Singh, Y., Chandra, P., Puri, M.: Sensitivity analysis of fuzzy and neural network models. ACM SIGSOFT Software Eng. Notes **30**(4), 1–4 (2005)

34. Simon, H.A.: The architecture of complexity. Proc. Am. Philos. Soc. **106**, 467–482 (1962)
35. Sosa, M., Mihm, J., Browning, T.: Linking cyclicality and product quality. Manufact. Serv. Oper. Manage. **15**(3), 473–491 (2013)
36. Nguyen, V.H., Massacci, F.: The (un) reliability of NVD vulnerable versions data: an empirical experiment on google chrome vulnerabilities. In: Proceedings of the 8th ACM SIGSAC Symposium on Information, Computer and Communications Security, pp. 493–498. ACM (2013)
37. Camilo, F., Meneely, A., Nagappan, M.: Do bugs foreshadow vulnerabilities? A study of the chromium project. In: Proceedings of the 12th IEEE/ACM Working Conference on Mining Software Repositories (MSR), pp. 269–279. IEEE (2015)

Natural Language Insights from Code Reviews that Missed a Vulnerability

A Large Scale Study of Chromium

Nuthan Munaiah[1]([⊠]), Benjamin S. Meyers[1], Cecilia O. Alm[2],
Andrew Meneely[1], Pradeep K. Murukannaiah[1], Emily Prud'hommeaux[2],
Josephine Wolff[2], and Yang Yu[3]

[1] B. Thomas Golisano College of Computing and Information Sciences,
Rochester Institute of Technology, Rochester, NY 14623, USA
{nm6061,bsm9339,axmvse,pkmvse}@rit.edu
[2] College of Liberal Arts, Rochester Institute of Technology,
Rochester, NY 14623, USA
{coagla,emilypx,jcwgpt}@rit.edu
[3] Saunders College of Business, Rochester Institute of Technology,
Rochester, NY 14623, USA
yyu@saunders.rit.edu

Abstract. Engineering secure software is challenging. Software development organizations leverage a host of processes and tools to enable developers to prevent vulnerabilities in software. Code reviewing is one such approach which has been instrumental in improving the overall quality of a software system. In a typical code review, developers critique a proposed change to uncover potential vulnerabilities. Despite best efforts by developers, some vulnerabilities inevitably slip through the reviews. In this study, we characterized linguistic features—inquisitiveness, sentiment and syntactic complexity—of conversations between developers in a code review, to identify factors that could explain developers missing a vulnerability. We used natural language processing to collect these linguistic features from 3,994,976 messages in 788,437 code reviews from the Chromium project. We collected 1,462 Chromium vulnerabilities to empirically analyze the linguistic features. We found that code reviews with lower inquisitiveness, higher sentiment, and lower complexity were more likely to miss a vulnerability. We used a Naïve Bayes classifier to assess if the words (or lemmas) in the code reviews could differentiate reviews that are likely to miss vulnerabilities. The classifier used a subset of all lemmas (over 2 million) as features and their corresponding TF-IDF scores as values. The average precision, recall, and F-measure of the classifier were 14%, 73%, and 23%, respectively. We believe that our linguistic characterization will help developers identify problematic code reviews before they result in a vulnerability being missed.

1 Introduction

Vulnerabilities in software systems expose its users to the risk of cyber attacks. The onus of engineering secure software lies with the developers who must assess

© Springer International Publishing AG 2017
E. Bodden et al. (Eds.): ESSoS 2017, LNCS 10379, pp. 70–86, 2017.
DOI: 10.1007/978-3-319-62105-0_5

the potential for an attack with each new line of code they write. Over the years, software development teams have transitioned toward a proactive approach to secure software engineering. Modern day software engineering processes now include a host of security-focused activities from threat modeling during design to code reviews, static analysis, and unit/integration/fuzz testing during development. The code review process, in particular, has been effective in uncovering a wide variety of flaws in software systems, [27] to vulnerabilities [7,9,29]. Code reviews have now become such an essential part of software development lifecycle that large software development organizations like Google [13] and Microsoft [25] mandate code review of every change made to the source code of certain projects.

Developers make mistakes. Code reviews provide an opportunity for these mistakes to be caught early, preventing them from becoming an exploitable vulnerability. Done in an systematic way, code reviews have the potential to uncover almost all defects in a software system [14].

Code reviews contain a wealth of information from which one can gain valuable insights about a software system and its developers. Conversations between developers participating in a code review often represent instances of constructive criticism and a collaborative effort to improve the overall quality of the software system. However, in some cases, the same conversations could contain clues to indicate potential reasons for a mistake, such as a vulnerability, to have been missed in the review. As with software development, code reviews involve humans—the developers. Developers participating in code reviews could exhibit a wide variety of socio-technical behaviors; some developers may be verbose, inquisitive, overly opinionated, and security-focused, while others may be succinct, cryptic, and uncontroversial. The natural language analysis of code review conversations can help identify these intrinsic (linguistic) characteristics and understand how they may contribute to the likelihood of a code review missing a vulnerability. Furthermore, we can use automated natural language processing techniques to identify these characteristics on a massive scale aiding developers by highlighting problematic code reviews sooner.

Our goal in this study is *to characterize the linguistic features that contribute to the likelihood that a code review has missed a vulnerability.* We empirically analyzed 3,994,976 messages across 788,437 code reviews from the Chromium project. We addressed the following research questions:

RQ1 Feedback Quality Do linguistic measures of inquisitiveness, sentiment, and syntactic complexity in code reviews contribute to the likelihood that a code review has missed a vulnerability?

RQ2 Lexical Classifier Can the words used differentiate code reviews that have missed a vulnerability?

The remainder of this paper is organized as follows: we begin with brief summary of prior literature closely related to ours in Sect. 2. In Sect. 3, we describe the approach used to obtain the data from a variety of sources, collect various metrics from the data, and statistically analyze the metrics. We present our results in Sect. 4, highlight some of the limitations in Sect. 5, and conclude the paper with a brief summary in Sect. 6.

2   Related Work

Code reviews are used widely in the software engineering field with the goal of improving the overall quality of software systems. Despite the popularity and evidence justifying the benefit of code reviews [5,27], some research suggests that code reviews are not always carried out properly, diminishing their utility in the software development cycle [14,15]. The focus of prior research on code reviews has been to understand attributes of code reviews that express their usefulness [8] and identify aspects of the code review process that enable timely conclusion of reviews [4]. While some studies from prior literature [5,16,29] have questioned the effectiveness of code reviews in finding vulnerable code, these studies do not provide an insight into the factors that may have led to the code reviews missing vulnerabilities.

Bosu and Carver [7], who found evidence to support the notion that code reviews are effective at uncovering vulnerabilities, used text mining techniques to compile a list of keywords related to various types of vulnerabilities. Using a similar approach, Pletea *et al.* [35] performed sentiment analysis of comments on GitHub pull requests and found that security-oriented comments were typically more negative. Guzman *et al.* [22] performed similar analysis but with correlating sentiment in commit messages with social and environmental factors. While these studies present interesting findings, they still do not explain why code reviews often overlook vulnerabilities. To address this question, we not only use sentiment analysis and lexical information, but also explore more complex natural language processing approaches for analyzing code reviews at the structural and word frequency distribution level. To the best of our knowledge, our work is one of the first to attempt analyses of this nature, especially in the context of a large-scale data set of 788,437 code reviews from the Chromium project.

3   Methodology

In the subsections that follow, we describe the methodology used in the empirical analysis. At a high-level, our methodology may be organized into three steps: (1) data collection, (2) metric collection, and (3) statistical analysis.

3.1   Data Collection

Data Sources. The data set used in the empirical analysis is a collection of code reviews with their associated messages and metadata (bug and vulnerability identifiers), which was obtained from a variety of managed sources. The code reviews, specifically, the messages posted by reviewers, were the central pieces of information in our data set. The Chromium project uses Rietveld[1] to facilitate the code review process. We used Rietveld's RESTful API to retrieve all code reviews (2008–2016) for the Chromium project as JSON formatted documents.

---

[1] https://codereview.chromium.org/.

A typical code review in the Chromium project is created when a developer wishes to have changes to the source code integrated with the Chromium repository. The group of files changed is called a patchset. A code review may have one or more patchsets depending on the changes the developer had to implement to address the comments in the code review. In retrieving the code reviews, we also retrieved any associated patchsets. The patchsets were used to identify the files that were reviewed and those that were committed as part of the code review.

The goal in our study is to characterize the linguistic features of code reviews and their relationship with the likelihood of missing a vulnerability. A code review is said to have missed a vulnerability if at least one of the files reviewed was later fixed for a vulnerability. Therefore, the key piece of information needed in the analysis is a mapping between code reviews and vulnerabilities. In the Chromium project, the association between code reviews and vulnerabilities is achieved through an issue tracking system. The Chromium project tracks bugs using Monorail.[2] The report of bugs that resulted in the resolution of a vulnerability have the Common Vulnerabilities and Exposure (CVE) identifier of the vulnerability as a label. We used the bulk export feature supported by Monorail's web interface to download, in CSV format, a list of all bugs in the Chromium project. All code reviews that have bugs associated with them are expected to have the bug identifier(s) mentioned (using the template: BUG=<bug_id>,<bug_id>) in the description of the reviews. We parsed the code review description to identify the bug(s) that were associated with a code review.

We compared the vulnerabilities obtained from Monorail to those obtained from the National Vulnerability Database (NVD[3]) to ensure completeness. We found a small set of vulnerabilities that were resolved by the Chromium project team but no record of a mapping between the vulnerability and a bug existed in Monorail. We manually identified the mapping between the vulnerability and bug using posts from the Chrome Releases Blog[4] and the references list from the vulnerability report on NVD.

Data Annotations. The code reviews in our data set were annotated with labels to enable us to group reviews into categories that were relevant to our empirical analysis. In the subsections that follow, we introduce these labels and describe the approach we used to assign those labels to code reviews.

(1) Code Reviews that Fixed Vulnerabilities - We used the label *fixed vulnerability* to identify code reviews that facilitated the review of a fix for a vulnerability. In our data set, we annotated all code reviews that were associated with a bug that resolved a vulnerability with the *fixed vulnerability* label. The fixed vulnerability code reviews were crucial in identifying the files that were reviewed (and possibly committed) in resolving a vulnerability. Intuitively, the fixed vulnerability code reviews represent the conversations that

---

[2] https://bugs.chromium.org/p/chromium.
[3] https://nvd.nist.gov/.
[4] https://chromereleases.googleblog.com/.

the developers should have had in the past to potentially discover and resolve vulnerabilities.

(2) Code Reviews that Missed Vulnerabilities - We used the label *missed vulnerability* to identify code reviews that *potentially* missed a vulnerability. We identify missed vulnerability code reviews by searching for code reviews that reviewed a file that was later fixed for a vulnerability. In our study, We followed a two step process to identify missed vulnerability code reviews:

Step 1 For each fixed vulnerability code review, identify all files committed.

Step 2 For each committed file, identify all code reviews, created before the review in question, that included the file.

Intuitively, the missed vulnerability code reviews represent the *missed opportunities* in which vulnerabilities could have been discovered. We base our intuition on prior research by Meneely *et al.* [30], who found that vulnerabilities tend to exist in software for over two years before being discovered. While no single code review can be blamed for missing a vulnerability, we believe that, in aggregate, the missed vulnerability code reviews constitute an opportunity in which the vulnerability could have been discovered.

(3) Neutral Code Reviews - We used the label *neutral* to identify code reviews that neither reviewed the fix for a vulnerability nor missed a vulnerability. The neutral code reviews serve as the control group in our analysis. The choice of using the generic label "neutral" is intentional; one cannot definitively say that a code review did not miss a vulnerability since there may be latent vulnerabilities in the source code that are yet to be discovered [30]. Intuitively, the set of neutral reviews could potentially include those reviews in which reviewers may have overlooked a vulnerability.

Summary. The data set used in the empirical analysis consists of 788,437 code reviews containing a total of 3,994,976 messages posted by 8,119 distinct participants. On average, each review had 2 participants, reviewed 9 files, had 6 messages, and lasted 67 days. The data set also includes 436,191 bugs and 1,462 vulnerabilities. Among the code reviews, 877 were labeled as *fixed vulnerability*, 92,030 were labeled as *missed vulnerability* and 695,530 were labeled as *neutral*.

3.2   Metric Collection

In the subsections that follow, we describe the metrics used to address the research questions and the approaches used to extract these metrics. All metrics are defined at the message level; however, we aggregate them at the review level for empirical analysis. We used the Natural Language Toolkit (NLTK) [6], the Stanford CoreNLP [26], and the Speech Processing & Linguistic Analysis Tool (SPLAT) [32] in collecting these metrics from the code review messages.

Inquisitiveness. Uncovering security flaws in a software system involves a speculative thought process. A reviewer must consider the possibility that even the most unlikely scenario could have an impact on the piece of code being reviewed.

The *inquisitiveness* metric is an attempt to quantify this speculative type of conversation in code reviews.

The inquisitiveness metric is estimated by counting the number of questions in a code review message. We have used a naïve approach to estimate the value of this metric by the frequency of the symbol "?" in the message text. The assumption here is that the number of questions in a message is correlated with the number of occurrences of "?". We validated this assumption by manually counting the number of questions in a sample of 399 code review messages obtained by random stratified sampling of messages with zero, one, and more than one occurrences of the symbol "?". In the manual analysis, we not only looked for the "?" symbol but also read the content of the messages to consider sentences phrased as a question but not terminated by "?". For instance, here is an excerpt from a message that contains a question (terminated by "?") and a sentence that is phrased as a question but without being terminated by "?": "I'm not sure ... immutable. Is it OK ... is called? If it's OK, why we don't ... of MIDIHost.". We used Spearman's rank correlation co-efficient (ρ) to quantify the correlation between the manually estimated number of questions and the number of occurrences of the symbol "?". We found a strong, statistically significant (p-value $\ll 0.01$), positive correlation with $\rho = 0.93$.

In our approach to calculating the inquisitiveness metric, we used NLTK to tokenize the data (i.e. break up sentences into words, separating out punctuation marks) and to compute the frequency of "?". In the manual analysis of the 399 code review messages, we found that the inquisitiveness metric tends to over-estimate the actual number of questions in cases when a single question is terminated with multiple question marks or when a URL is incorrectly terminated at the "?" by the NLTK tokenizer. The inquisitiveness metrics also misses questions if they are not terminated by "?". We, however, found only a few instances of these cases in our manual analysis.

We chose to use the seemingly simplistic approach rather than more sophisticated ones such as regular expressions or syntactic parse trees because, unlike traditional natural language, code review messages tend to be informal and, sometimes, fragmented. Furthermore, the notion of a question in code review messages tends to go beyond the message itself, requiring additional context such as the line of source code that the sentence in a message is associated with.

The number of questions is likely to be positively correlated with the size of the message. We accounted for this likelihood by expressing the metric as inquisitiveness per sentence in the message. We used Stanford CoreNLP to split a message into sentences to count the number of sentences.

Sentiment. Conversations about the security of a software system tend to have a non-neutral sentiment [35]. The *sentiment* group of metrics is an attempt to capture the sentiment associated with code review messages. Each of the sentiment metrics is calculated as the proportion of sentences in a code review message exhibiting that sentiment. We used proportion of sentences, rather than the actual number of sentences, to control for message size.

We used the sentiment analysis model [39] from the Stanford CoreNLP to identify the sentiment expressed in sentences. The model uses information about words and their relationships to classify sentences into one of five sentiment classes: very positive, positive, neutral, negative, and very negative. In our study, we merge very negative and negative into a single negative class and very positive and positive into a single positive class. Furthermore, we do not consider the neutral sentiment in the analysis of the sentiment metrics. In effect, we only consider the positivity (proportion of positive sentiment sentences) and negativity (proportion of the negative sentiment sentences) in the analysis.

Term-Frequency Inverse-Document-Frequency (TF-IDF). Widely used in the field of information retrieval [38], TF-IDF is a measure of the relative importance of a term (word) within a document with the term's frequency (TF) in that document normalized by its frequency in the corpus to which that document belongs (inverse document frequency, IDF). In our data, a single code review is a document and the corpus is the collection of all code reviews.

There are many ways to calculate TF-IDF. We have used the approach implemented by the TextCollection[5] class of NLTK to compute the TF-IDF metric. In this approach, the TF-IDF of a term (t) in a document (d) is computed as $tf\text{-}idf_{(t,d)} = tf_{(t,d)} \times df_t$, where $tf_{(t,d)}$, the term frequency, is the ratio of the frequency of the term t (in document d) to the total number of terms in d and df_t, the document frequency, is the natural logarithm of the ratio of the number of documents in the corpus to the number of documents containing the term t.

As with the inquisitiveness metric, we used NLTK to tokenize code review messages, but we perform a key preprocessing of the tokens before computing the TF-IDF: map token to base form, or lemma. We compute the TF-IDF of lemmas instead of tokens to account for morphological variation (i.e., suffixes we add to words to express different grammatical functions); the words *compiles, compiling* and *compiled*, for instance, are all forms of the lemma *compile*.

Syntactic Complexity. Software engineers participating in a code review are required to process a considerable amount of information in reviewing a piece of code. The structural complexity of the language used in code review messages could lead a developer to misunderstand a comment and consequently introduce a spurious change. The *syntactic complexity* group of metrics is aimed at quantifying the complexity that may be in code review messages.

A variety of metrics have been proposed to quantify the syntactic complexity of natural language sentences. While some of these metrics focus simply on sentence or utterance length [34] or on part of speech information, others use information about the structure of sentences that can be extracted from syntactic parses or trees. In particular, there are several parse-based measures of complexity relying on the assumption that deviations from a given language's typical branching structure (in the case of English, right branching) are indicative of higher complexity [18, 42]. In our study, we use three measures of syntactic

---

[5] http://www.nltk.org/api/nltk.html#nltk.text.TextCollection.

complexity to quantify the complexity of code review messages: (1) Yngve score (2) Frazier score, and (3) propositional density. We describe the three metrics in greater detail below. The implementation of these metrics, which are adaptations of the algorithms described in Roark *et al.* [37] and Brown *et al.* [10], have been borrowed from the previously mentioned open-source tool SPLAT [32].

– Yngve Score: The Yngve score [42] is a measure of syntactic complexity that is based on cognitive load [28,40], specifically on the limited capabilities of the working memory [2,3,33]. The Yngve score is computed using the tree representation of a sentence obtained by syntactically parsing the sentence. The tree is scanned using a pushdown stack in a top-down, right-to-left order. For every level of the tree, branches are labeled starting with 0 for the rightmost branch and incrementing by 1 as the parse progresses toward the left branch. Each word is then assigned a word score by summing up the labels for each branch in the path from the root node to the word (leaf node) as seen in Fig. 1.

  We used the Stanford CoreNLP in conjunction with NLTK to obtain syntactic parse trees for code review messages. In this study, we use the mean Yngve score over all words in a sentence. The Yngve score is then averaged for each sentence in a message and for each message in a code review. See Table 1 for sample Yngve scores.

– Frazier Score: The Frazier score is similar to the Yngve score with one key distinction: while Yngve score is a measure of the the breadth a syntactic tree, Frazier score measures of the depth of the tree [37]. The Frazier score emphasizes embedded clauses (sub-sentences) based on the notion that the number of embedded clauses is associated with greater complexity [18–21].

  The algorithm to compute the Frazier score of a sentence is similar to that used to compute its Yngve score. Starting with the leftmost leaf node, each branch leading up to the root of an embedded clause (sentence node) is labeled as 1, with the exception of the branch on the uppermost level of the tree that leads directly to the sentence node, which is labeled as 1.5. This process is repeated for every leftmost leaf node. Labeling stops when the path upward from the leaf node reaches a node that is not the leftmost child of its parent, as shown with dotted lines in Fig. 1.

– Propositional Density: The propositional density metric (often referred to as p-density) is a socio-linguistic measure of the number of assertions in a

Table 1. Sample sentences with syntactic complexity scores

Sentence	Yngve	Frazier	p-density
This CL will add a new H264 codec to the SDP negotiation when H264 high profile is supported	2.056	0.722	0.278
There is a 3.9% decrease in initial load time observed	1.500	0.750	0.200
Fixed as spec says	0.750	1.500	0.750
Lgtm then	0.500	1.750	0.500

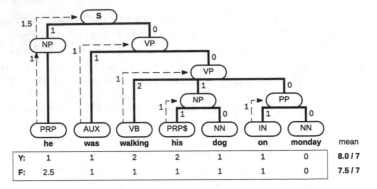

Fig. 1. Parse tree with Yngve (Y) and Frazier (F) scores on the solid and dotted lines, respectively. Word scores are boxed, with the mean score for the sentence to the right.

sentence. For example, Chomsky's famous sentence "colorless green ideas sleep furiously [12]" makes two assertions: (1) colorless green ideas sleep, and (2) they do it furiously. Part-of-speech tags and word order are used to determine likely propositions, and a series of rules is applied to determine how many propositions are expressed in a sentence [10]. After propositions have been identified, p-density is simply the ratio of the number of expressed propositions in a sentence to the number of words in that sentence.

Although sentence length can serve as a proxy for syntactic complexity, we chose to use more sophisticated metrics because these metrics take the structure of the sentence into consideration. We did, however, assess the correlation between our complexity metrics, aggregated at the message level, and message length, expressed as number of words. We found a statistically significant (p-value $\ll$ 0.01) positive correlation (Spearman's $\rho = 0.69$) between Yngve score and message length. We normalized the Yngve score metric using message length to account for this correlation. The other two syntactic complexity metrics, Frazier score and propositional density, were not significantly correlated with message length in our data.

3.3   Analysis

In the subsections that follow, we describe the various statistical methods used in the empirical analysis of the metrics proposed in our study. All statistical tests were executed with R version 3.2.3 [36].

Correlation. We used Spearman's rank correlation coefficient (ρ) to assess the pairwise correlation between the various metrics that were introduced earlier. We considered two metrics to be strongly correlated if $|\rho| >= 0.70$ [24].

Association. We used the non-parametric Mann-Whitney-Wilcoxon (MWW) test for association between the various metrics and the code reviews that missed a vulnerability. We assume statistical significance at $\alpha = 0.05$. We compare mean of the populations to assess if the value of a metric tends to be higher or lower between two populations (neutral and missed vulnerability code reviews).

Classification. To assess if the words used in code reviews can be a differentiator between neutral and missed vulnerability code reviews, we built a Naïve Bayes classifier with lemmas of the words from code reviews as features and their corresponding TF-IDF as values. A typical code review could have hundreds of distinct lemmas; to constrain the number of features in the model, we used the criteria described below to filter the lemmas before attempting to build the classifier.

(1) We only considered alphanumeric lemmas that were fewer than 13 characters in length. We chose 13 characters to be a reasonable limit for lemma length because over 99% of the all words in the Brown [17], Gutenberg [23], and Reuters [1] natural language data sets are fewer than 13 characters in length.
(2) We only considered the top ten lemmas, ordered by the TF-IDF values, in each code review. In other words, we only considered the ten most important lemmas in code reviews.

In addition to constraining the number of features, we also had to constrain the number of observations (code reviews) in the data set used to build the classifier. We used random sampling to select 5% of neutral and 5% of missed vulnerability code reviews. We repeated the random sampling to generate ten (possibly) different data sets to be used to build the classifier. We used the information gain [41] metric to assess the relevance of features in differentiating the code reviews and removed all features with a zero information gain. We then used the relevant features to train and test a Naïve Bayes classifier using 10×10-fold cross validation. We used SMOTE [11] to mitigate the impact of the imbalance in the number of neutral and missed vulnerability code reviews on the performance of the classifier. We used precision, recall and F-measure metrics to assess the performance of the classifier.

4   Results

In the subsections that follow, we address our research questions through the empirical analysis of our metrics.

4.1   RQ1 Feedback Quality

Question: Do linguistic measures of inquisitiveness, sentiment, and syntactic complexity in code reviews contribute to the likelihood that a code review has missed a vulnerability?

We began the analysis by evaluating the correlation between the metrics themselves to understand if any of the metrics were redundant due to high correlation. The correlation analysis did not reveal any strong correlations between the metrics and the highest value of $|\rho|$ was 0.45, between inquisitiveness and Yngve score metrics. We then used the MWW test to assess the strength of association between the metric and the likelihood of a code review missing a vulnerability. The results are shown in Table 2, with all associations statistically significant at least p-value < 0.01. Shown in Fig. 3 in the Appendix are the comparative box plots of the inquisitiveness, sentiment, and complexity metrics.

Table 2. Mann-Whitney-Wilcoxon (MWW) test outcome for association between the linguistic measures and the likelihood of a code review missing a vulnerability

Metric	p-value	Mean$_{neutral}$	Mean$_{missed}$
Inquisitiveness	3.28e−12	0.1785	0.1711
Negativity	< 2.2e−16	0.3707	0.4091
Positivity	< 2.2e−16	0.0625	0.0783
Yngve score	< 2.2e−16	0.0498	0.0442
Frazier score	0.0031	0.8568	0.8548
Propositional density	1.77e−124	0.2634	0.2708

These results reveal some interesting insights into the nature of code reviews that have missed vulnerabilities. First, the lower inquisitiveness values in code reviews that missed a vulnerability suggest that the participants in these reviews may not have been as actively trying to unearth flaws. The approach to uncovering security vulnerabilities requires review participants to question the behavior of the code being reviewed in scenarios that are unlikely but still plausible.

> Code reviews with lower inquisitiveness i.e. fewer questions per sentence tend to miss vulnerabilities.

Secondly, participants in code reviews that missed vulnerabilities expressed a higher degree of both positive and negative sentiment. The higher negativity in code reviews that missed a vulnerability confirms the results observed by Pletea et al. [35] in security-specific discussions in GitHub pull requests. However, the higher positivity in code reviews that missed a vulnerability is interesting because it seems that the conversation may have started on a negative sentiment but culminated on a positive sentiment, or vice versa. We may have to chronologically analyze messages to better understand the evolution of sentiment.

> Code reviews with higher sentiment, regardless of the polarity of that sentiment, tend to miss vulnerabilities.

Lastly, the complexity metrics, specifically Yngve and Frazier scores, show that code reviews that missed a vulnerability tend to be less complex. While the result may seem counterintuitive, the lack of complexity could be an indicator that the code review conversation may be lacking substance. The propositional density metric, on the other hand, is higher for code reviews that missed a vulnerability indicating that those code reviews tend to have more assertions.

> Code reviews with lower complexity in terms of Yngve and Frazier and higher complexity in terms of propositional density tend to miss vulnerabilities.

4.2 RQ2 Lexical Classifier

Question: Can the words used differentiate code reviews that have missed a vulnerability?

In RQ1, we found that the inquisitiveness, sentiment, and syntactic complexity in code reviews are associated with the likelihood of a code review missing a vulnerability. In this research question, however, we wanted to understand if the words used in the code reviews itself was different between reviews that were neutral and those that missed a vulnerability.

We computed the TF-IDF of the lemmas of the words used in a code review, and using these features, built a classifier to identify code reviews as neutral or missed vulnerability. Each random sample of data used to build the classifier contained 39,377 code reviews and an average of 25,652 features. Shown in Table 3 is the total number of features and the number of those features deemed relevant (i.e. non-zero information gain) in each of the ten random samples.

Table 3. Number of relevant features in each of the ten randomly sampled sets of code reviews

Sample set	1	2	3	4	5	6	7	8	9	10
# Features	25,636	25,535	25,456	25,550	25,761	25,805	25,592	25,709	25,651	25,827
# Relevant	1,092	889	959	885	910	1,012	986	910	1,091	898

We incrementally selected increasing number of relevant features to build and evaluate the performance of a Naïve Bayes classifier. Figure 2 shows the distributions of precision, recall, and F-measure obtained from each of the ten random samples for varying number of relevant features selected. As seen in the figure, the classifier built with 18 relevant features performs the best in terms of F-measure. The average precision, recall, and F-measure of the best performing classifier was 14%, 73%, and 23%, respectively. We note that, in classifying code reviews that are likely to miss a vulnerability, a higher recall is desired even at the cost of lower precision [31] since the cost of revisiting a few misclassified reviews is relatively small when compared to the cost of a missed vulnerability.

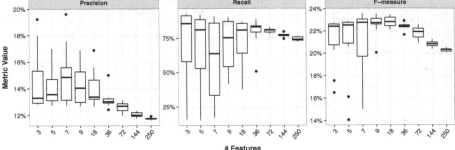

Fig. 2. Distribution of classifier performance metrics—precision, recall, and F-measure—obtained from ten random samples of code reviews for varying number of relevant features used in training the classifier

The ability of our classifier to differentiate between neutral and missed vulnerability code reviews indicates that the distribution of words used in these two types of code reviews is indeed different. In a code review framework, such a classifier could be used to identify code reviews that are potentially missing vulnerabilities. The development team could then revisit these flagged code reviews to ensure that the necessary steps are taken to uncover any latent vulnerabilities.

> Yes. The accuracy of our classifier indicates that the words used in code review can be a differentiator between neutral and missed vulnerability code reviews.

5 Limitations

The scale of our data set posed certain computational limitations, specifically in the process of building a lexical classifier. We used the lemma of words in the code review as features in the lexical classifier, however, our data set contains 2,089,579 unique lemmas obtained through lemmatization of 2,197,114 unique words. An attempt to build a classifier using the entire data set $788,437 \times 2,089,579$ seemed intractable. We overcame this limitation by filtering lemmas by length and non-alphanumeric characters, by randomly sampling a small percentage of code reviews, and by selecting the top 10 lemmas by their relative importance. We mitigated the arbitrariness in the sampling process by repeating it ten times and averaging the results.

The sentiment analysis model that we used was trained with movie reviews and may have misclassified sentences since code reviews tend to have variable names or other artifacts that could skew the analysis. A mitigation could be to train the sentiment analysis model with a sufficiently large sample of manually classified code review messages.

The default parser used to parse the syntax of sentences in Stanford CoreNLP is based on Probabilistic Context-Free Grammar (PCFG). In our initial of analysis, the parser would timeout when parsing long code review messages. In the subsequent analyses, we have used a faster but marginally less accurate Shift-Reduce Constituency Parser (SR). We do not believe that the use of the SR parser may have had an impact on any downstream operations performed on the syntactic parse trees.

6   Summary

In this study, we used natural language processing to characterize linguistic features—inquisitiveness, sentiment and syntactic complexity—in conversations between developers participating in a code review. We collected these features from 3,994,976 messages spread across 788,437 code reviews from the Chromium project. We collected 1,462 vulnerabilities and identified code reviews that had the opportunity to prevent the vulnerability in the past. We then used association analysis to evaluate if the linguistic features proposed were associated with the likelihood of code reviews missing a vulnerability. We found that code reviews with lower inquisitiveness, higher sentiment, and lower complexity were more likely to miss a vulnerability. In addition to the linguistic features, we computed the relative importance measure—TF-IDF—of 2,089,579 unique lemmas obtained from words in code reviews messages. We used a subset of the lemmas as features to build a Naïve Bayes classifier capable of differentiating between code reviews that are neutral and those that had missed a vulnerability. The average precision, recall, and F-measure of the classifier were 14%, 73%, and 23%, respectively.

We believe that our characterization of the linguistic features and the classifier will help developers identify potentially problematic code reviews before a vulnerability is missed.

A   Comparing Distribution of Inquisitiveness, Sentiment and Complexity Metrics

The comparison of the distribution of inquisitiveness, sentiment and complexity metrics for neutral and missed vulnerability code reviews is shown in Fig. 3.

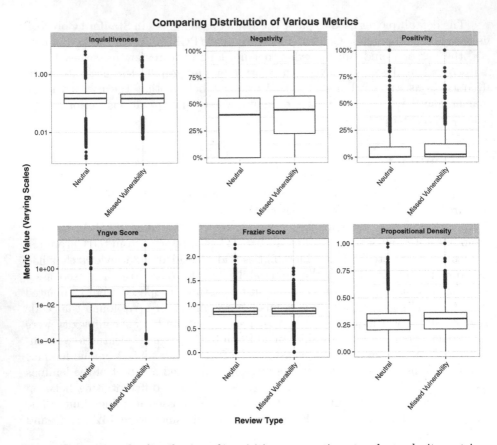

Fig. 3. Comparing the distribution of inquisitiveness, sentiment and complexity metrics for neutral and missed vulnerability code reviews

References

1. Reuters-21578, Distribution 1.0. http://kdd.ics.uci.edu/databases/reuters21578/reuters21578.html
2. Baddeley, A.: Recent developments in working memory. Curr. Opin. Neurobiol. **8**(2), 234–238 (1998)
3. Baddeley, A.: Working memory and language: an overview. J. Commun. Disord. **36**(3), 189–208 (2003)
4. Baysal, O., Kononenko, O., Holmes, R., Godfrey, M.W.: The influence of non-technical factors on code review. In: 2013 20th Working Conference on Reverse Engineering (WCRE), pp. 122–131, October 2013
5. Beller, M., Bacchelli, A., Zaidman, A., Juergens, E.: Modern code reviews in open-source projects: which problems do they fix? In: Proceedings of the 11th Working Conference on Mining Software Repositories, MSR 2014, New York, NY, USA, pp. 202–211. ACM, New York (2014)
6. Bird, S., Klein, E., Loper, E.: Natural Language Processing with Python: Analyzing Text with the Natural Language Toolkit. O'Reilly Media Inc, Sebastopol (2009)

7. Bosu, A., Carver, J.C.: Peer code review to prevent security vulnerabilities: an empirical evaluation. In: 2013 IEEE Seventh International Conference on Software Security and Reliability Companion, pp. 229–230, June 2013

8. Bosu, A., Greiler, M., Bird, C.: Characteristics of useful code reviews: an empirical study at microsoft. In: 2015 IEEE/ACM 12th Working Conference on Mining Software Repositories, pp. 146–156, May 2015

9. Bosu, A., Carver, J.C., Hafiz, M., Hilley, P., Janni, D.: Identifying the characteristics of vulnerable code changes: an empirical study. In: Proceedings of the 22nd ACM SIGSOFT International Symposium on Foundations of Software Engineering, FSE 2014, New York, NY, pp. 257–268. ACM, New York (2014)

10. Brown, C., Snodgrass, T., Kemper, S.J., Herman, R., Covington, M.A.: Automatic measurement of propositional idea density from part-of-speech tagging. Behav. Res. Methods **40**(2), 540–545 (2008)

11. Chawla, N.V., Bowyer, K.W., Hall, L.O., Kegelmeyer, W.P.: SMOTE: synthetic minority over-sampling technique. J. Artif. Intell. Res. **16**, 321–357 (2002)

12. Chomsky, N.: Syntactic Structures. Mouton, The Hague (1957)

13. Chromium: Chromium OS developer's guide (2017). https://www.chromium.org/chromium-os/developer-guide

14. Ciolkowski, M., Laitenberger, O., Biffl, S.: Software reviews: the state of the practice. IEEE Software **20**(6), 46–51 (2003)

15. Czerwonka, J., Greiler, M., Tilford, J.: Code reviews do not find bugs: how the current code review best practice slows us down. In: Proceedings of the 37th International Conference on Software Engineering, ICSE 2015, vol. 2, pp. 27–28. IEEE Press, Piscataway (2015). http://dl.acm.org/citation.cfm?id=2819009.2819015

16. Edmundson, A., Holtkamp, B., Rivera, E., Finifter, M., Mettler, A., Wagner, D.: An empirical study on the effectiveness of security code review. In: Jürjens, J., Livshits, B., Scandariato, R. (eds.) ESSoS 2013. LNCS, vol. 7781, pp. 197–212. Springer, Heidelberg (2013). doi:10.1007/978-3-642-36563-8_14

17. Francis, W.N., Kucera, H.: A standard corpus of present-day edited American English, for use with digital computers. Coll. Engl. **26**(4), 267 (1965)

18. Frazier, L.: Syntactic complexity. In: Dowty, D.R., Karttunen, L., Zwicky, A.M. (eds.) Natural Language Parsing, pp. 129–189. Cambridge University Press (CUP), Cambridge (1985)

19. Frazier, L.: Sentence Processing: A Tutorial Review (1987)

20. Frazier, L.: syntactic processing: evidence from Dutch. Nat. Lang. Linguist. Theor. **5**(4), 519–559 (1987)

21. Frazier, L., Taft, L., Roeper, T., Clifton, C., Ehrlich, K.: Parallel structure: a source of facilitation in sentence comprehension. Mem. Cogn. **12**(5), 421–430 (1984)

22. Guzman, E., Azócar, D., Li, Y.: Sentiment analysis of commit comments in GitHub: an empirical study. In: Proceedings of the 11th Working Conference on Mining Software Repositories, MSR 2014, NY, pp. 352–355. ACM, New York (2014)

23. Hart, M.S., Austen, J., Blake, W., Burgess, T.W., Bryant, S.C., Carroll, L., Chesterton, G.K., Edgeworth, M., Melville, H., Milton, J., Shakespeare, W., Whitman, W., Bible, K.J.: Project Gutenberg Selections. Freely available as a Corpus in the Natural Language ToolKit. http://www.nltk.org/nltk_data/#25

24. Hinkle, D.E., Wiersma, W., Jurs, S.G.: Applied Statistics for the Behavioral Sciences. Houghton Mifflin, Boston (2002)

25. Lipner, S.: The trustworthy computing security development lifecycle. In: 20th Annual Computer Security Applications Conference, pp. 2–13, December 2004

26. Manning, C.D., Surdeanu, M., Bauer, J., Finkel, J., Bethard, S.J., McClosky, D.: The Stanford CoreNLP natural language processing toolkit. In: Association for Computational Linguistics (ACL) System Demonstrations, pp. 55–60 (2014)

27. Mäntylä, M.V., Lassenius, C.: What types of defects are really discovered in code reviews? IEEE Trans. Software Eng. **35**(3), 430–448 (2009)

28. Mayer, R.E., Moreno, R.: Nine ways to reduce cognitive load in multimedia learning. Educ. Psychol. **38**(1), 43–52 (2003)

29. McGraw, G.: Software security. IEEE Secur. Priv. **2**(2), 80–83 (2004)

30. Meneely, A., Srinivasan, H., Musa, A., Tejeda, A.R., Mokary, M., Spates, B.: When a patch goes bad: exploring the properties of vulnerability-contributing commits. In: 2013 ACM/IEEE International Symposium on Empirical Software Engineering and Measurement, pp. 65–74, October 2013

31. Menzies, T., Menzies, A., Distefano, J., Greenwald, J.: Problems with precision: a response to "comments on 'data mining static code attributes to learn defect predictors'". IEEE Trans. Softw. Eng. **33**(9), 637–640 (2007). doi:10.1109/TSE.2007.70721. ISSN: 0098-5589

32. Meyers, B.S.: Speech processing & linguistic analysis tool (SPLAT). https://github.com/meyersbs/SPLAT

33. Miller, G.: Human memory and the storage of information. IRE Trans. Inf. Theor. **2**(3), 129–137 (1956)

34. Miller, J.F., Chapman, R.S.: The relation between age and mean length of utterance in morphemes. J. Speech Lang. Hear. Res. **24**(2), 154–161 (1981)

35. Pletea, D., Vasilescu, B., Serebrenik, A.: Security and emotion: sentiment analysis of security discussions on GitHub. In: Proceedings of the 11th Working Conference on Mining Software Repositories, MSR 2014, NY, pp. 348–351. ACM, New York (2014)

36. R Core Team: R: A Language and Environment for Statistical Computing. R Foundation for Statistical Computing, Vienna, Austria (2015). https://www.R-project.org/

37. Roark, B., Mitchell, M., Hosom, J., Hollingshead, K., Kaye, J.: Spoken language derived measures for detecting mild cognitive impairment. Trans. Audio Speech Lang. Proc. **19**(7), 2081–2090 (2011)

38. Salton, G., Buckley, C.: Term-weighting approaches in automatic text retrieval. Inf. Process. Manage. **24**(5), 513–523 (1988)

39. Socher, R., Perelygin, A., Wu, J.Y., Chuang, J., Manning, C.D., Ng, A.Y., Potts, C.: Recursive deep models for semantic compositionality over a sentiment treebank. In: Proceedings of the 2013 Conference on Empirical Methods in Natural Language Processing. Association for Computational Linguistics, October 2013

40. Sweller, J., Chandler, P.: Evidence for cognitive load theory. Cogn. Instr. **8**(4), 351–362 (1991)

41. Yang, Y., Pedersen, J.O.: A comparative study on feature selection in text categorization. In: ICML, vol. 97, pp. 412–420 (1997)

42. Yngve, V.H.: A Model and an Hypothesis for Language Structure, vol. 104, pp. 444–466. American Philosophical Society (1960)

Idea: Optimized Automatic Sanitizer Placement

Gebrehiwet Biyane Welearegai$^{(\boxtimes)}$ and Christian Hammer

University of Potsdam, Potsdam, Germany
welearegai@uni-potsdam.de, hammer@cs.uni-potsdam.de

Abstract. Sanitization is a primary defense mechanism against injection attacks, such as cross-site scripting (XSS) and SQL injection. Most existing research on sanitization focuses on vulnerability detection and sanitization correctness, leaving the burden of sanitizer placement with the developers. However, manual sanitizer placement is complex in realistic applications. Moreover, the automatic placement strategies presented in the literature do not optimize the number of sanitizer positions, which results in *inconsistent multiple-sanitization* errors and duplicated code in our experience.

As a remedy this paper presents an optimized automatic sanitizer placement to reduce the number of positions where sanitization is required. To that end, we analyze the dataflow of a program via static analysis. We optimize the number of sanitizer positions by preferring nodes common to multiple paths as sanitizer positions. Our evaluation displays equal sanitization coverage as previous approaches with a reduced number of sanitizers, and reduces the number of sanitization errors to 0.

Keywords: Vulnerability · Sanitization · Automatic sanitizer placement

1 Introduction

Web applications are often vulnerable to script injection attacks, such as *cross-site scripting (XSS)* and *SQL injection*. XSS vulnerabilities allow an attacker to inject client-side scripting code into the output of an application which is then sent to another users web browser [1]. The scripting code can be crafted to send sensitive data, such as user login credentials, credit card numbers, to a third party when executed in the browser. Likewise, SQL injection vulnerabilities allow an attacker to execute malicious SQL statements that violate the application's desired data integrity or confidentiality policies [2]. The predominant first-line approach to prevent such attacks is *sanitization*, the practice of encoding or filtering untrusted inputs of an application. Existing research on sanitization mainly deals with vulnerability detection [3,4]. These approaches assume that an application is secure if sanitization is applied on all paths from sources to sinks. However, this does not always hold as the sanitization process itself might be buggy or incomplete. This triggered a line of research on sanitizer correctness

© Springer International Publishing AG 2017
E. Bodden et al. (Eds.): ESSoS 2017, LNCS 10379, pp. 87–96, 2017.
DOI: 10.1007/978-3-319-62105-0_6

```
1   main() {
2     exchange = getSource();
3     func1(exchange);
4     func2(exchange);
5   }
6   func1(exchange) {
7     exchange.getIN();
8   }
9   func2(exchange) {
10    exchange.getIN();
11  }
```

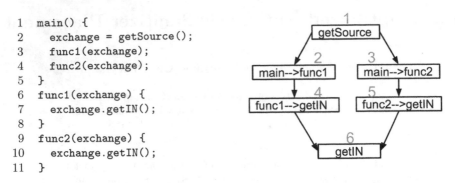

Fig. 1. Path decomposition due to flow-insensitivity (code and its data flow graph)

[4,5]. Yet, having correct sanitizers is not enough to completely mitigate scripting attacks; the sanitizers must also be placed correctly.

Sanitizer placement depends on how input data is being used [6], where it originates from [7] and the context in which it is rendered [6,8]. Hence, manual sanitizer placement is difficult and error prone [4,5]. On top of missing sanitization, common errors are *inconsistent sanitization* (mismatch of sanitizer and context) and *inconsistent multiple sanitization* (sanitizers may not be idempotent) [9]. This motivated research on automatic sanitizer placement [6,8,9].

Automatic sanitizer placement techniques assume that the individual sanitizers are correct, and that the mapping of sanitizers to their contexts [8,9] or source and sink policy [6] is given. The goal of the automatic placement strategy is to place sanitizers on every program path between an untrusted input and a possibly scriptable output of an application while preventing errors due to inconsistent sanitization and inconsistent multiple sanitization. Currently, the automatic placement techniques strive for this goal but do not try to optimize the number of sanitizer calls in the code. In the worst case each path in the code may have its own call to an appropriate sanitizer. However, due to the flow-insensitive points-to-analysis characteristics, a single runtime path can be decomposed into several paths that may lead to inconsistent multiple sanitization. Assuming the policy of Fig. 1 does not allow to put a sanitizer at node n_6, nodes n_4 and n_5 are selected as sanitizer positions according to existing research. However, at runtime these two nodes are being executed subsequently, i.e. the value in exchange is being sanitized twice. Our experiments (cf. Sect. 4) display an error rate of 20% for the non-optimized algorithm, i.e., 20% of all sanitizers might suffer from erroneous inconsistent multiple sanitization. An alternative approach that does not suffer from the shortcomings of flow-insensitivity analysis would be to dynamically taint untrusted input data at runtime and to propagate these taints during computation, but this may incur significant runtime overheads.

In this paper, we propose an optimized automatic sanitizer placement technique by statically analyzing the flow of tainted data. This analysis takes a dataflow graph and the sanitization policy, that specifies the mapping of sanitizers with respect to source and sink combinations, as input. The goal is, then, to automatically find sanitizer positions satisfying sanitization correctness, i.e., every value that flows from a source to a sink must have the given type of sanitizer applied exactly once. Our placement technique uses *static node-based* analysis, and nodes that are common to several paths requiring the same sanitizer type are proposed as the best candidate for optimized sanitizer positions. For the data flow graph in Fig. 1, our optimized approach selects node n_1 as sanitization position, thus eliminating multiple sanitization and code duplication. Our evaluation (in Sect. 4) shows that the reduction of sanitizers due to this optimization reduces or eliminates the sanitization errors of previous approaches.

2   Sanitizer Placement Overview

This section presents background on dataflow graphs and sanitization policies which are the input to the sanitization placement problem, followed by a clarification of the placement problem.

2.1   Dataflow Graph and Sanitization Policy

A dataflow graph is a static representation of a program where nodes represent statements/predicates and edges indicate data dependencies. When the program performs a computation, values may only flow according to the data dependence edges. To guarantee a secure flow of data, we require a sanitization policy that defines an appropriate sanitizer for values that flow from a given source to a given sink. The policy is usually given in the form of a table where sources and sinks are displayed in rows and columns and sanitizers are given as the entries [6]. Throughout this paper, we use the dataflow graph and its sanitization policy in Fig. 2 as an example. Source types $(\bigcirc, \triangle)$ are shown in the rows and sink types $(\blacksquare, \blacklozenge, \bullet, \blacktriangle)$ are shown in the columns. $\oslash$ represents data sources and sinks that are irrelevant for security. We use metavariables P, I and O to range over policies, sources and sinks, respectively. Particularly, we write $P(I, O)$ for the entry in policy P for the source I and sink O. For instance, for the policy P in Fig. 2, data originating from source type $\bigcirc$ going to sink type $\blacksquare$ should have sanitizer S_1 applied to it. If data that flow from source type I to sink type O does not require sanitization, we represent its policy as $P(I, O) = \bot$.

2.2   Sanitizer Placement Problem

The challenge of sanitizer placement is to identify an appropriate sanitizer and its position in the source code in order to prevent untrusted data flowing from a source to a sink with dangerous scripts to be injected in the sink context. This problem arises as the result of the source, sink and context-sensitivity property of sanitization placement [6–8]. In large applications, with a multitude of nodes and paths, manual sanitizer placement is hard to get right. Consequently, an automatic decision procedure is required whose goal is to ensure correct sanitization of data in an application given its dataflow graph and sanitization policy, i.e., according to the correctness definition [6] (Definition 1).

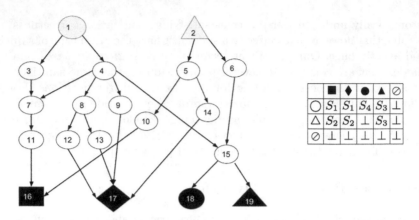

Fig. 2. Dataflow graph example (sources on top, sinks at bottom) and sanitization policy

Definition 1. Given a dataflow graph $G = \langle N, E \rangle$, sanitization for the graph is valid for a policy P, if for all source nodes s and all sink nodes t:

- if $P(s,t) = S$, then every value that flows from source node s to sink node t has sanitizer S applied exactly once, and no other sanitizer is applied.
- if $P(s,t) = \bot$, then every value that flows from source node s to sink node t has no sanitizer applied.

The reason why sanitizers must be applied only once on a single path is that they are not necessarily idempotent [3]. Specifically, applying a sanitizer several times on a path may lead to inconsistent multiple sanitization errors [9]. However, untrusted input may be coming from a source in multiple contexts, which implies different sanitizers might be required within a single path leading to a sink. For this type of situation, multiple (potentially nested) sanitizers are modeled as a single (composite) sanitizer [6].

3 Our Approach

To solve the sanitizer placement problem, we propose two types of static node-based strategies: a *less-optimized* and a *fully-optimized* solution. The less-optimized solution optimizes the number of sanitizer positions only when there is a common node for all paths from a source to a sink. Other than that, it follows the same approach as Livshits et al. [6]. The fully-optimized solution, however, always reduces the number of sanitizer positions by selecting nodes common to many paths requiring the same sanitizer as a sanitization positions. This optimization removes code duplication and the occurrence of inconsistent multiple-sanitization error that could appear as the result of flow-insensitive static analysis. Due to space limitation, we present detailed explanations only for the fully-optimized solution. However, the result of both approaches is evaluated in Sect. 4.

Table 1. S_i-possible and S_i-exclusive nodes for Fig. 2

Sanitizers	Possible	Exclusive
S_1	1, 3, 4, 7, 8, 9, 11, 12, 13, 16, 17	3, 7, 8, 9, 11, 12, 13
S_2	2, 5, 10, 14, 16, 17	5, 10, 14
S_3	1, 2, 4, 6, 15, 19	19
S_4	1, 4, 15, 18	$\emptyset$
$\perp$	2, 6, 15, 18	$\emptyset$

3.1 Fully Optimized Approach

For i, j ranging from 1 to k where k is the number of sanitizer types, a node n is called S_i-*possible* if it is found on a path from source s to sink t that requires sanitizer S_i, i.e., $P(s, t) = S_i$. This implies that at least some of the data traversing from source s to sink t through node n needs to be sanitized with sanitizer S_i. Likewise, a node n is called S_i-*exclusive* if it is S_i-possible and not S_j-possible for all $i \neq j$ [6].

Definition 2. Node $n \in N$ is S_i-possible if there is a source node s and a sink node t such that n is on a path from s to t and $P(s, t) = S_i$.

Definition 3. Node $n \in N$ is S_i-exclusive if it is S_i-possible and for all source nodes s and sink nodes t, if n is on a path from s to t, then $P(s, t) = S_i$.

For the dataflow graph example (Fig. 2), the possible and exclusive nodes for sanitizers S_1, S_2, S_3, S_4 and $\perp$ are given in Table 1. According to the correctness definition (Definition 1), sanitizer nodes must be selected from the S_i-exclusive sets. However, sanitizer S_4 has no exclusive nodes, hence values flowing from source type ○ to sink type ● cannot be sanitized statically. This is due to the inability of static analysis to identify the source and/or destination of input data at nodes that are not exclusive to a sanitizer type. Additionally the correctness definition prohibits placing the same sanitizer more than once on a single path. Hence, our solution selects the node that provides most optimal placement if there is more than one exclusive node on a single path.

In addition to the S_i-possible and S_i-exclusive sets, we need the following definitions to elaborate our approach.

Definition 4. The S_i-*node-frequency* for a node $n \in N$ is the number of paths through n that satisfy $P(s, t) = S_i$, for a source node s and a sink node t.

Definition 5. Node $n \in N$ is S_i-*exclusive-p_j-previous* if it is S_i-exclusive and it is found on any of the paths traversed before path p_j during the depth first path search of path analysis.

Definition 6. Node $n \in N$ on a path p_j is S_i-*exclusive-p_j-exclusive* if it is S_i-exclusive and not S_i-exclusive-p_j-previous.

Definition 7. Node $n \in N$ is called the S_i-*position* if it is selected to be sanitization node for sanitizer S_i.

Definition 8. S_i-*backtracking-map* collects the mapping of S_i-position nodes, at every path iteration, to paths requiring sanitizer S_i.

For each path p_j our fully-optimized placement algorithm traverses the S_i-exclusive-p_j-exclusive nodes and selects the last node on that path with maximum[1] S_i-node-frequency as the temporary[1] S_i-position. However, more than one sanitizer could be included on a single path with this strategy alone, which violates the correctness definition (Definition 1). To resolve this problem, we consider three conditions based on the number of previously identified sanitizer position nodes S_i on the current path p_j.

First, if there is no S_i-position on p_j, we apply the strategy described above and add p_j into the S_i-backtracking-map.

Second, there is exactly one S_i-position on p_j. Thus the current path p_j already has a S_i-position node, hence we do nothing. However, that S_i-position node might be removed later due to backtracking in which case p_j would lack a sanitizer. For this reason, p_j is entered into a map of skipped paths which will be re-added to the iteration if its corresponding S_i-position node is removed.

Third, when there is more than one S_i-position node on p_j, we backtrack to find the paths that provided these nodes and assign a different sanitization node for all except one path. To select that one, we consider the intersection of the current path with all paths that have provided the S_i-position nodes causing multiple sanitization errors. Then, taking two intersection sets at a time starting from the sink, we compare the number of incoming edges to the top node in the bottom intersection set with the number of outgoing edges from the bottom node in the top intersection set. After that, the path whose S_i-position node in the intersection set had the lower number is removed and another intersection set is compared with the one that had the higher number. When all intersection sets are considered, only the path that results in the maximum number remains and serves as the source of S_i-position for the current path, as well. The reason behind this is that if the S_i-position node is removed with the path, we have to apply S_i at all its previous/next nodes depending on its relative position in the two intersection sets. Thus, it is preferable to remove the ones that have lower in-/out-degrees. Lastly, these removed paths as well as the skipped paths that contain these removed S_i-positions are again included to the path iteration to select another S_i-position node.

To exemplify our fully-optimized solution, we use the S_i-*exclusive* graph shown in Fig. 3. The path numbers in the graph indicate the iteration order during the analysis to find a single S_i-position node on every path. For p_1 n_3 is selected as sanitization node according to the first condition since it has node frequency 3. Path p_2 already contains n_3 (second condition). Next, node n_8 is selected as S_i-position for p_3 (first condition).

---

[1] The S_i-position for path p_j can be changed later due to backtracking.

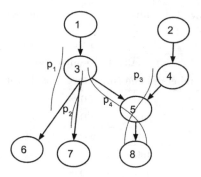

Fig. 3. S_i-exclusive graph example for fully-optimized solution explanation

The fourth iteration results in backtracking, as p_4 contains two sanitization nodes: n_3 and n_8. From the intersection of p_4 with p_3, we get the top node n_5 and from the intersection of p_4 with p_1 we get the bottom node n_3. Comparing the out-degree of n_3 (3 edges) with in-degree of n_5 (2 edges), n_3 is chosen to remain sanitizer node. Finally n_4 is selected as new sanitization node for path p_3 (subpath excluding n_5 and n_8) using condition one. Placing S_i at nodes n_3 and n_4 is sufficient to sanitize all values that flow along these paths.

In the end, the S_i-position nodes using our fully-optimized solution for the dataflow graph and the policy in Fig. 2 are: S_1 at nodes n_{11}, n_8, n_9, S_2 at node n_5 and S_3 at node n_{19}. S_4 and $\perp$ have no exclusive node, hence sanitization is not statically possible. Using our less-optimized solution, n_{12} and n_{13} would be selected for S_1 instead of n_8, similar to previous approaches [6].

4   Evaluation

We evaluate our approaches using WALA [10] on an application whose call graph consists of 15,214 nodes, 119,026 edges, 14,070 methods, and 724,806 bytes. Sanitization coverage, sanitization errors, the number of sanitizer positions and time taken by the analyses are used as evaluation parameters. The sanitization coverage indicates the ratio of untrusted inputs passed through the correct sanitizers. The sanitization errors are multiple sanitization errors due to WALA's flow-insensitive pointer analysis that decomposes one path to multiple paths. Table 2 reports the result of the fully-optimized and less-optimized approaches on a Mac-Book Pro with a 2.9 GHz Intel Core i7 processor and 16 GB RAM. N in the first column indicates a call-string based context-sensitivity parameter. The ratio of sanitization errors is relative to the required correct sanitizer positions.

Maximum sanitization coverage was achieved for $N = 2$ for both approaches, and we took that for comparison as missing sanitization may have devastating effects. The missing 10% are caused by paths lacking sanitizer-exclusive nodes. However, for these paths runtime tracking of input data can be applied instead of static sanitizer placement [6]. For example, in Fig. 2 one might want to add

Table 2. Results of placement approaches

	Fully-optimized				Less-optimized			
	Sanitization			Analysis	Sanitization			Analysis
N	Coverage	Errors	Numbers	Time (m)	Coverage	Errors	Numbers	Time (m)
1	50 %	0%	5	2:31	50 %	20%	8	2:40
2	90 %	0%	9	2:09	90 %	40 %	14	2:01
3	80 %	0%	8	2:44	90 %	40 %	14	2:42
4	80 %	0%	9	4:46	90 %	40 %	14	5:19
5	90 %	0%	9	9:30	90 %	40 %	14	9:02

code that registers whether data was flowing to node 15 from node 4 or from node 6. Then in node 18 one would be able to decide whether sanitizer S_4 needs to be applied (flow from 4) or not (flow from 6).

As expected, the number of sanitizer positions is reduced for the fully-optimized approach since it always attempts to find common nodes for paths that require the same sanitizer type. Unlike the less-optimized approach, which is only slightly more precise than previous work [6], the fully-optimized approach does not result in sanitization errors. The analysis time is almost identical for each context-sensitivity value N. But the less-optimized solution can provide its maximum coverage at a lower value of N, hence analysis time could be lower.

Note that the less-optimized solution follows exactly the same approach as *Livshits et al.* [6] in its non-optimized variant. Hence, the evaluation of the fully-optimized solution with respect to the less-optimized solution also elaborates on how our fully-optimized solution resolves the multiple sanitization error and code duplication problems of existing research. The correctness (sanitization coverage) of both our solutions is in sync with *Livshits et al.* [6], since we use the same node-based static analysis approach, i.e., every piece of data which flows through a path that has at least one exclusive node is sanitized. This has been confirmed using several test cases although we use only one application for a final evaluation. The optimality of the fully-optimized approach is also confirmed in a similar way, i.e., it finds the least sufficient number of sanitizer positions.

To the best of our knowledge, previous research does not consider optimization of sanitizer placement and this paper is the first to report that such an optimization has benefits beyond code clone elimination, namely a reduction in the sanitization error rate.

5   Related Work

The automatic sanitizer placement of Livshits et al. [6] is closely related to our approach. They propose two solutions: a static node-based solution, and an edge-based solution based on static analysis and runtime taint tracking. The former is similar to ours but does not attempt to optimize the number of sanitizer positions. Another research that shares our goal is presented by Samuel et al. [8]. They provide static type inference-based approach to automatically apply sanitizers. It is unclear whether type inference based analysis is scalable as they focus on a small program (less than 4000 lines of code) in Google Closure. Saxena et al. [9] propose *SCRIPTGARD* that can detect and repair incorrect placement of sanitizers in ASP.NET applications. *SCRIPTGARD* assumes that developers have manually applied context-sensitive sanitization correctly. A dynamic analysis detects and auto-corrects context-inconsistency errors in sanitization. In contrast, our approach can correctly apply sanitizers in an application completely lacking developer-supplied annotations. Additionally, we leverage static analysis in order to eliminate runtime overhead of dynamic analysis.

6 Conclusion

This paper presents an automatic sanitizer placement mechanism that optimizes the number of sanitizer positions. Due to the reduced number of sanitizer positions we did not experience any inconsistent multiple sanitization errors. Hence, the fully-optimized algorithm is a valuable solution for real world applications. However, in some cases runtime information is required to identify the valid sanitizer type. Thus, a hybrid analysis that leverages runtime tracking in such situations is proposed to guarantee full sanitization coverage.

Acknowledgements. This work was supported by the German Federal Ministry of Education and Research (BMBF) through the project SimoBA (16KIS0440).

References

1. Vogt, P., Nentwich, F., Jovanovic, N., Kirda, E., Kruegel, C., Vigna, G.: Cross-site scripting prevention with dynamic data tainting and static analysis. In: Proceedings of Network and Distributed System Security, p. 12 (2007)
2. Halfond, W., Viegas, J., Orso, A.: A classification of SQL-injection attacks and countermeasures. In: IEEE International Symposium on Secure Software Engineering (ISSSE), pp. 13–15. IEEE (2006)
3. Xie, Y., Aiken, A.: Static detection of security vulnerabilities in scripting languages. In: 15th USENIX Security Symposium, pp. 179–192 (2006)
4. Balzarotti, D., Cova, M., Felmetsger, V., Jovanovic, N., Kirda, E., Kruegel, C., Vigna, G.: Saner: composing static and dynamic analysis to validate sanitization in web applications. In: Symposium on Security and Privacy, pp. 387–401 (2008)
5. Hooimeijer, P., Livshits, B., Molnar, D., Saxena, P., Veanes, M.: Fast and precise sanitizer analysis with BEK. In: 20th USENIX Conference on Security, p. 1. USENIX Association (2011)
6. Livshits, B., Chong, S.: Towards fully automatic placement of security sanitizers and declassiefiers. In: ACM SIGPLAN Notices, pp. 385–398. ACM (2013)
7. Weinberger, J., Saxena, P., Akhawe, D., Finifter, M., Shin, R., Song, D.: A systematic analysis of XSS sanitization in web application frameworks. In: Atluri, V., Diaz, C. (eds.) ESORICS 2011. LNCS, vol. 6879, pp. 150–171. Springer, Heidelberg (2011). doi:10.1007/978-3-642-23822-2_9

8. Samuel, M., Saxena, P., Song, D.: Context-sensitive auto-sanitization in web templating languages using type qualifiers. In: CCS, pp. 587–600. ACM (2011)
9. Saxena, P., Molnar, D., Livshits, B.: SCRIPTGARD: automatic context-sensitive sanitization for large-scale legacy web applications. In: CCS, pp. 601–614 (2011)
10. T.J. Watson Libraries for Analysis (WALA). http://wala.sourceforge.net

FPRandom: Randomizing Core Browser Objects to Break Advanced Device Fingerprinting Techniques

Pierre Laperdrix[1]([✉]), Benoit Baudry[2],
and Vikas Mishra[3]

[1] INSA de Rennes & INRIA, Rennes, France
`pierre.laperdrix@insa-rennes.fr`
[2] INRIA, Rennes, France
`benoit.baudry@inria.fr`
[3] Birla Institute of Technology and Science, Sancoale, Goa, India
`vikasmishra95@gmail.com`

Abstract. The rich programming interfaces (APIs) provided by web browsers can be diverted to collect a browser fingerprint. A small number of queries on these interfaces are sufficient to build a fingerprint that is statistically unique and very stable over time. Consequently, the fingerprint can be used to track users. Our work aims at mitigating the risk of browser fingerprinting for users privacy by 'breaking' the stability of a fingerprint over time. We add randomness in the computation of selected browser functions, in order to have them deliver slightly different answers for each browsing session. Randomization is possible thanks to the following properties of browsers implementations: (i) some functions have a nondeterministic specification, but a deterministic implementation; (ii) multimedia functions can be slightly altered without deteriorating user's perception. We present FPRandom, a modified version of Firefox that adds randomness to mitigate the most recent fingerprinting algorithms, namely canvas fingerprinting, AudioContext fingerprinting and the unmasking of browsers through the order of JavaScript properties. We evaluate the effectiveness of FPRandom by testing it against known fingerprinting tests. We also conduct a user study and evaluate the performance overhead of randomization to determine the impact on the user experience.

1 Introduction

Browser fingerprinting has reached a state of maturity where it is now used by many companies alongside cookies to identify and track devices for a wide range of purposes from targeted advertising to fraud prevention. Several studies have shown the growth of this technique along the years with both the discovery of new attributes and its spread on the web [1,2,18]. Englehardt et al. notably

---

The stamp on the top of this paper refers to an approval process conducted by the ESSoS artifact evaluation committee chaired by Karim Ali and Omer Tripp.

© Springer International Publishing AG 2017
E. Bodden et al. (Eds.): ESSoS 2017, LNCS 10379, pp. 97–114, 2017.
DOI: 10.1007/978-3-319-62105-0_7

showed in 2016 that "the number of sites on which font fingerprinting is used and the number of third parties using canvas fingerprinting have both increased by considerably in the past few years" [8]. Third-parties are starting to turn to the most recent browser APIs to collect as much device-specific information as possible. Olejnik et al. demonstrated that recent APIs like the Battey API [20] or the Ambient Light Sensor API [21] can leak device-specific information. Englehardt et al. discovered that some online scripts use the AudioContext API to get data on the audio capabilities of a device [8]. However, in the fast evolving landscape of Web standards, only a very low number of works have explored approaches to mitigate or thwart tracking through fingerprinting. The main challenge in designing a good defense is to preserve the user experience while sending information that will render device identification impossible. Since most of the different attributes that constitute a fingerprint are essential for browsing the web, changing a single one incorrectly can result in the complete loss of functionalities and the user is then unable to get access to the desired service. In this paper, we explore the use of browsers' flexibility to prevent tracking through advanced fingerprinting techniques along with an implementation in a Firefox browser called FPRandom.

Key insight. Several API functions used to build a browser fingerprint are unnecessarily deterministic and provide device-specific information as a side effect. Browsers present untapped flexibility that can be exploited to obtain a constantly changing fingerprint. We especially investigate the two following areas:

- Browsers' JavaScript engines make deterministic implementation choices, even for some functions which are meant to be non-deterministic according to the ECMAScript. We show that by removing some of these deterministic coding choices, we can prevent the leakage of device-specific information.
- Randomness can be used to diversify how HTML multimedia elements are rendered in the browser. Leveraging human's perception of colors and sound, we introduce controlled noise into the rendering process of canvas and audio elements. Consequently, fingerprinting scripts constantly collect new values, but we preserve the user experience.

By introducing randomness into key browser subroutines, we break the stability of a fingerprint without artificially replacing values with pre-existing ones. This hampers user tracking since a server cannot rely on the stability of the fingerprint.

Implementation and evaluation. The landscape of browser fingerprinting has greatly evolved in the past few years with the push of HTML5 by developers to make the web more secure and more complete. The lists of plugins and fonts used to be two key attributes to identify devices, but they are now slowly becoming remnants of the past. Yet, more recent techniques such as canvas fingerprinting [1], AudioContext fingerprinting [8] and the unmasking of the browser through JavaScript properties' order [18] offer strong foundations for effective fingerprinting. Our work focuses on these three techniques. For each technique, we look at the official JavaScript specification with a special attention for the inner-workings of the targeted HTML elements. Then we design behavioural modifications that can impact the fingerprinting process without altering the user experience. We developed a working prototype based on Firefox called FPRandom and we evaluate both its performance and its resilience against known fingerprinting scripts. The performed benchmarks show that the overhead introduced by our solution is negligible and that all scripts using the targeted attributes are affected.

The paper is organized as follows. Section 2 gives an overview of our approach along with details on existing techniques to break the linkability of fingerprints. Section 3 details the FPRandom browser with the different fingerprinting techniques we target. Section 4 provides an evaluation of the browser's performance and its ability to deceive known fingerprinting scripts. Section 5 discusses the related work while Sect. 6 concludes this paper.

2   Breaking Linkability of Fingerprints

Fingerprint uniqueness and stability are the two key properties that make browser fingerprint tracking a reality. In this work, we aim at breaking the stability of fingerprints so that collected fingerprints are not *linkable*. Diversity is a strong solution as constantly-changing information can be sent to fingerprinters without impacting the user experience. Below, we present two state of the art solutions that specifically target the linkability of fingerprints before we detail our approach.

2.1   Current Solutions

Blink. In a previous study, we explored with *Blink* the use of dynamic software reconfiguration "to establish a moving target defense against browser fingerprint tracking" [13]. By leveraging virtualization and assembling components from a large pool of operating systems, browsers, plugins and fonts, *Blink* is able to build environments that exhibit very different fingerprints over time. The strong advantage of this solution is that the generated browsing platforms are genuine: they do not present any inconsistencies contrary to the spoofing extensions discussed in Sect. 5. However, its major drawback is the complete machinery involved in the synthesis of these browsing platforms. To exhibit diverse fingerprints, *Blink* relies on a pool of hundreds of components that can occupy a large amount of disk space and the use of virtual machines can be very costly on less powerful computers. Moreover, *Blink* requires the use of several different browsers to increase its success rate at breaking fingerprint linkability. It is a sacrifice that not all users may be willing to make to increase their online privacy.

PriVaricator. Nikiforakis et al. explore with *PriVaricator* how randomization can be used to render browser fingerprints unreliable for tracking [18]. The main insight of their study is that making fingerprints non-deterministic on multiple visits makes them hard to link across browsing sessions. They state that "creatively misrepresenting—or lying—about [collected] values introduces an element of non-determinism" and that "subtly misrepresenting key properties of the browser environment goes a long way towards combating fingerprinters". As a proof of concept, they introduced into Chromium the concept of *randomization policies*, protection strategies that are activated when specific requirements are met. They designed policies against the collection of offset measurements of HTML elements and the enumeration of the list of plugins.

2.2 Our Approach: Exploiting Browsers' Flexibility

In this work, we propose to exploit browsers' untapped flexibility to introduce randomness. Instead of changing software components at runtime like Blink or lying on specific values like PriVaricator, we want to increase non-determinism in browsers to reduce side-effects that cause fingerprintable behaviors.

Flexibility of the implementation of the JavaScript specifications. The official ECMAScript specification, the de facto standard for scripting language on the web, allows some flexibility in actual JavaScript implementations. Different parts of the specification give some leeway by clearly indicating that specific choices are left for the implementation. The ECMA organization strictly codifies the interpretation of the language but the exact details of how it works remain in the hands of browser vendors. For example, as we will see in the next Section, the enumeration order of JavaScript properties are not detailed by the ECMAScript specification but each browser presents its own unique order. Developers have made deterministic choices when they implemented these functions. By taking a step back and removing what can be interpreted as a surspecification of the standard, we are able to thwart fingerprinting vectors that rely on these detectable side-effects.

Flexibility of the renderings of multimedia elements. Vendors are constantly striving to improve their browsers to provide the latest innovations and the best possible experience to their users. Changing some attributes collected in a browser fingerprint like the user agent or the screen resolution can negatively impact how a page is displayed to the detriment of users. However, the rendering of HTML multimedia elements can be made more flexible and less deterministic without degrading the user experience. Especially, we can exploit users' perception of color and sound to introduce imperceptible noise that impacts the stability of specific browser routines. The key challenge here is to apply very small modifications that no user will notice while a fingerprinting script will output constantly changing values at every execution.

3 Implementation

To experiment with randomization, we target three of the most recent fingerprinting techniques: canvas fingerprinting as it is a prime example of a dynamic media element and "in the top 5 of the most discriminating attributes" [14]; the Web Audio API recently observed in fingerprinting scripts by Englehardt et al. [8]; the leakage of system information through JavaScript properties' order found by Nikiforakis et al. in the Cookieless Montster study [18]. All the miti-gation techniques detailed in this section are implemented in a modified version of Firefox called FPRandom. The complete patch for Firefox 54 is available on GitHub[1] along with a fully-compiled prototype for Linux systems.

3.1 Canvas API

Definition. Canvas fingerprinting was firstly introduced by Mowery et al. [16] and observed on the Internet by Acar et al. [1]. Its goal is to use the Canvas API of a browser to draw an image that can help differentiate one device from another. Each device executes the exact same set of instructions and depending on both hardware and software, rendered images present variations. Figure 1 shows the canvas test we run on the AmIUnique website. The test consists in displaying two lines of text with different shapes merged together. Here, depending on the hardware and the installed drivers, the rendering of shapes and colors slightly vary between devices. Then, depending on the software and most especially on the list of installed fonts, the lines of text can present great differences. In our previous study [14], we showed that one of the strength of canvas fingerprinting is its stability and that it is "in the top 5 of the most discriminating attributes". It is notably the "second highest source of entropy for mobile devices".

Modification. The first modification we made to the Firefox source code is to introduce randomness inside the *ParseColor* function of the *CanvasRendering-Context2D* class. Every time a color is set inside a canvas fingerprinting script, the browser changes the actual RGB values of the parsed color by adding or removing a very small number for each color channel. For example, if a script asks to draw an orange rectangle, the browser will paint the canvas element as requested. However, for every browsing session, the browser will use a slightly different orange than the last time. Modifying the *ParseColor* method enables us to support the full range of color declaration (for example, you can chose a color by directly setting its RGB values or you can simply write its name like "gold" or "orange"). The impact on the user experience is almost non-existent as the difference in color is very hard to see with the naked eye. Finally, it should be noted that we differentiate ourselves from tools called "canvas poisoners" that change the RGB values of each pixel of the rendered image independently from one another. Mowery et al. wrote that they are not "a feasible defense" against current scripts because the noise can be lifted by repeating a test a few times and comparing the results. They add that the aggressive introduction of noise "degrades the performance of <canvas> significantly for legitimate appli-cations" [16]. With our approach, the color on a whole surface is consistent as we do not introduce random noise on separate pixels. As discussed in Sect. 3.4, we can apply the exact same modification for every run of a fingerprinting script. If a fingerprinter were to repeat the same canvas test more than once, he will not be able to notice differences whereas canvas poisoners present noticeable varia-tions between runs. The second modification operates in the *SetFont* function of

---

[1] https://github.com/plaperdr/fprandom.

the *CanvasRenderingContext2D* class and changes a font set by a script by one present on the operating system. For the scripts asking for a fallback font, the stability is broken as a font different from the previous session will be presented.

Example. Figure 2 illustrates the impact of FPRandom on the exact same canvas test with all protection features enabled. The blue, orange and green colors are slightly different for each run and the used fonts are chosen among the ones present on the operating system. The more fonts are installed on the user's system, the bigger the diversity of generated canvas renderings will be. By changing at runtime core properties of elements present in a canvas test, we break the stability of this technique while still preserving the user experience.

Fig. 1. Original canvas rendering with standard colors and the default fallback font (Color figure online)

Fig. 2. Canvas renderings with modified colors and fonts (Color figure online)

3.2 AudioContext API

Definition. Discovered by Englehardt et al. while crawling the web looking for trackers [8], AudioContext fingerprinting is a newcomer in the browser fingerprinting domain. The AudioContext API provides an interface to create a pipeline to process audio. By linking audio modules together, you can generate audio signals and apply very specific operations like compression or filtering to generate a very specific output.

In audio, sampling is applied to convert a continuous signal into a discrete one. This way, a computer can easily process audio in distinct blocks called frames. Each frame is composed of samples that represent the value of the audio stream at a specific point in time. Englehardt et al. have shown that, depending on the audio stack of your system (both software and hardware), the exact value of each of these frames slightly vary between devices. An audio fingerprint can then be created similarly to what is done with the Canvas API.

Modification. We performed an analysis of audio fingerprints that we collected on AmIUnique.org and the results can be found in Appendix A. We decided to introduce very small noises directly into the audio processing routines of the browser so that tests using any number of AudioContext modules are all impacted. We operate at the heart of the *AudioBuffers* of the *AudioNodeEngine* as they contain the frames of the processed audio. By modifying key functions, we slightly decrease the volume of processed buffers by a factor ranging between 0.000 and 0.001. This way, a frame can present very small variations where only the smallest decimal digits are affected. With the use of very small factors, it is impossible to detect modified sections from unmodified ones just by listening to the rendered track as the differences between the original and modified track can genuinely be interpreted as side effects or simple noise of the whole audio stack of the device. For fingerprinting scripts, these modifications produce a different hash as the audio routine will be ever so slightly different for each browsing session.

Example. Figure 3 shows three waveforms of the first second of the "Ride of the Valkyries" from Wagner. The audio pipeline we set up for this example performs two operations. It first increases the volume of the track with a *GainNode* and then compresses it through a *DynamicsCompressorNode*. The waveform in Fig. 3a represents the output from an unaltered pipeline and the one in Fig. 3b from a pipeline with our volume modification. The last waveform in Fig. 3c represents the difference between the first two (i.e. the introduced noise). In order to see the impact of FPRandom, the 3rd waveform has been zoomed in at 1000%. The scale is a clear indication that the generated noise is inaudible, proving that the impact on the user experience is non-existent audio wise but it still impacts the created audio fingerprint.

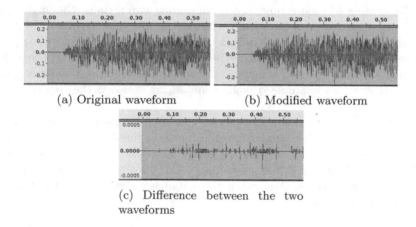

(a) Original waveform   (b) Modified waveform

(c) Difference between the two waveforms

Fig. 3. Visualization of audio rendered through the AudioContext API

3.3   Order of JavaScript Object's Properties

Definition. By analyzing the content of JavaScript objects in the browser, Nikiforakis et al. discovered that "the order of property-enumeration of special browser objects, like the navigator and screen objects, is consistently different between browser families, versions of each browser, and, in some cases, among deployments of the same version on different operating systems" [18]. This way, if someone were to hide the true browser's identity, enumerating the properties of a special object would simply unmask it. As stated by the latest ECMAScript Language Specification ratified in June 2016, "mechanics and order of enumerating the properties is not specified" (see Sect. 13.7.5.15 EnumerateObjectProperties of [7]). This ordering behavior is entirely dependent on the browser's implementation. Chrome and Firefox yield vastly different enumeration orders for native objects like *navigator*. For non-native JavaScript objects, both browsers first return integers in ascending order and then strings in insertion order. This choice is arbitrary and many developers have long debated for the best and most logical behavior as illustrated by this long discussion on the V8 bug tracker [22].

Modification. The browser's unmasking added by the surspecification of the ECMAScript standard can simply be undone by modifying the *jsiter* class of Firefox. A special flag called "JS_MORE_DETERMINISTIC" can be activated at compile time to sort IDs for both native and non-native objects in a deterministic way. By tweaking the behavior of the *SortComparatorIds* structure used with this special flag, we flip its purpose by not making the JavaScript engine more deterministic but by generating a unique enumeration order every time the browser is launched.

With the "JS_MORE_DETERMINISTIC" flag activated, the enumeration of a JavaScript object first returns integers in ascending order and then strings in alphabetical order. By diving even deeper into the source code, we found that the string comparison done by the browser relies on the "Latin-1" or "ISO/CEI 8859-1" encoding of each string. When comparing two strings, the engine goes through one character at a time and performs a simple subtraction of their code points (i.e. their place in the Latin-1 character set, see [27]) to determine which character is in front of the other. When a difference is detected, the engine knows how to order the two strings as the result is either positive or negative. Appendix B gives an example of such comparison between the *appName* and *appVersion* strings.

In order to change the enumeration order for each browsing session, we assign a random order for each combination (i.e. for each possible subtraction result) from the Latin-1 character set. As the first code point starts at position n°32 and the last one is at n°255, we generate in total 223 different booleans to cover all possible combinations. Any attempt to unmask the browser through this technique is then prevented.

3.4   Randomization Strategy

All the modifications described in this section can be executed in different ways when browsing the web. Here, we detail the two randomization strategies present in FPRandom while discussing their own strengths and weaknesses.

Random mode. The first mode that we propose in FPRandom is the "Random" strategy. Every time the modified functions are executed in the browser, they will return random values. The advantage is that it prevents cross-domain tracking as two scripts on two different domains (even from the same provider) would collect different values on both sites. However, the major downside of this solution is that it presents "transparency" problems as discussed by Nikiforakis et al. in the PriVaricator study [17]. If a fingerprinter were to study the presence of randomness, a script could execute the same test several times to detect instability. Depending on the test, a statistical analysis could be performed to reduce or remove the introduced randomness but it requires far more means and a certain insight into the way noise is introduced to get meaningful results. The "Random" mode is the default one in FPRandom as we have no recorded proof of such behaviors from today's major fingerprinting actors.

Per session. The second mode initializes all the randomized variables at startup and they are never modified on subsequent executions. The advantages of this strategy is that it cannot be detected through repeated measurements as the browser will always return the same answers for an identical fingerprinting test. The downside is that it only breaks linkability between browsing sessions as the same fingerprint will be presented to all websites until the browser is rebooted.

4   Evaluation

4.1   Deceiving Fingerprinting Scripts

As pointed out by [17], while it is possible to analyze the JavaScript code that runs inside the browser and detect fingerprinting scripts, it is much more complicated to find fingerprinters that can act as black-box oracles for our work. Some websites give a specific identifier associated with a device's fingerprint but others map collected attributes in a very specific way that is confidential and that is entirely performed on the side of the server. The main challenge in assessing the impact of FPRandom is to find fingerprinting scripts that use the advanced techniques we target and retrieve the right information (either an identifier or the fingerprint data that is sent).

Fingerprintjs2 is the second version of a popular open-source fingerprinting library that collects 25 different attributes and hash them all into a single value [9]. We executed the complete test suite of this library 100 times on both a standard version of Firefox 54 and FPRandom. On Firefox 54, we obtained the same hash for all of the 100 executions. For FPRandom, we collected 100 different ones with the Random mode and a single one in Session mode. These results show how fragile the test suite is for identification. The introduction of noise on a single attribute is sufficient to be considered as a "new" fingerprint.

Maxmind is a company specialized in IP geolocation and online fraud prevention. As part of its fraud detection system, Maxmind has a "device tracking add-on" to identify devices "as they move across networks" [15]. The main add-on script sends the complete device fingerprint at a specific address in a POST request. We manually analyzed the code of the add-on and found that it collects the rendering of a canvas test along with the enumeration order of both the *navigator* and *screen* objects. After 100 runs of the fingerprinting script, FPRandom gives a different canvas hash at each execution whereas a standard Firefox build always send the same result. For the enumeration orders, the behavior of Firefox 54 is the expected one and returns the exact same order for both JavaScript objects. For FPRandom, the browser gives a unique and different enumeration order at each session.

Limitations. Our approach does not deal with static attributes like the user-agent or the timezone but it can mitigate the collection of dynamic attributes from APIs like Canvas or Battery. Scripts that do not rely on the attributes we target can still build their own browser fingerprint and use it for tracking, albeit with a less complete view of the user's system.

4.2 Performance

We use three different JavaScript benchmark suites to assess the performance overhead introduced by FPRandom. The experiments were conducted on a laptop running Fedora 25 with an Intel Core i7-4600U CPU @ 2.10 GHz. The tests were performed using Firefox 54 (Nightly version) with and without our modifications present and enabled.

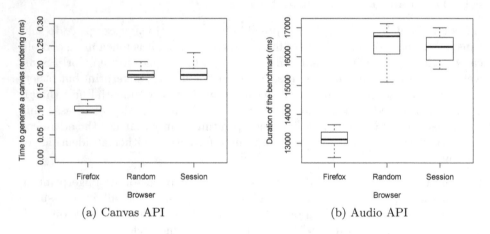

(a) Canvas API   (b) Audio API

Fig. 4. Benchmarking results

Canvas. As there are no benchmarks that specifically target the Canvas API, we developed our own test to asses the overhead introduced by our color and font variations. We repeated the test shown in Fig. 1 1,000 times and measured the time it takes for each image to be fully rendered inside the browser. To get precise measurements, we used the JavaScript Performance API that provides timestamps with an accuracy up to the microsecond [23]. Figure 4a illustrates the difference between a vanilla version of Firefox 54 and FPRandom. While an unmodified version takes 0.12 ms to render the image, our modified browser is about 0.06 ms longer on average in both randomization modes. This difference corresponds to the time it takes to properly choose a new font and introduce variations in the canvas colors. With these reported numbers, we consider the overhead here to be negligible as a rendering time of less than a single millisecond will not impact the user experience.

AudioContext. To assess the impact of FPRandom on the AudioContext API, we use a WebAudio benchmark developed by a Mozilla developer [4]. The benchmark performs a series of 19 different tests from simple gain operations to more complex mixing procedures. Each test instantiates an *OfflineAudioContext* object which is one of the objects we targeted when modifying the Firefox source code. The results in Fig. 4b indicate the time it takes to perform the complete series of 19 tests. It should be noted that we repeated the test suite 30 times. The mean value for FPRandom is about 25% higher than its Firefox counterpart. The "Random" mode is also a little longer than the "Session" one. This increase can be explained by the fact that the modified code is executed a very high number of times in a single test. By comparison, the modification made to the canvas API is only executed once for a test. We instrumented the browser to find a precise number and we found out that a single run of the benchmark enters our modified function more than 8,862,000 times. As a point of reference, the AudioContext test found by Englehardt et al. [8] only enters our function less than 3,000 times. With these numbers, we qualify the benchmark as extremely intensive. The increase in processing time may not be visible for less extreme and more traditional uses of the API. We leave for a future work the exploration of different implementation strategies where only a specific percentage of audio frames would be modified, leading to an increase in performance.

JavaScript enumeration order. As a final performance test for FPRandom, we decided to run a standard JavaScript benchmark to see if the modification made on the enumeration order has an impact on the overall JavaScript engine. We used the recent JetStream benchmark [12] which is developed as part of the WebKit browser engine. Currently, the 1.1 version performs 39 different tests and covers a wide variety of advanced workloads and programming techniques. It integrates tests from well-known benchmarking suites like SunSpider or Octane along with new ones developed specifically for JetStream (more details [11]). The results are present in Table 1 (the bigger the score, the better the performance). As we can see, the scores are almost identical and no real distinction can be made between Firefox and FPRandom. The behavior of the two browsers are similar on both JavaScript throughput and latency and the impact of our order modification is seemingly nonexistent.

Table 1. JetStream benchmark results

	Firefox	FPRandom-random	FPRandom-session
Latency	76.075 ± 1.3250	74.553 ± 1.8074	74.767 ± 1.2530
Throughput	251.97 ± 3.2912	252.32 ± 2.4214	256.02 ± 1.1213
Total	147.45 ± 1.5753	146.23 ± 1.9204	147.61 ± 1.1257

Web crawl. In order to assess more globally the impact of our modifications on day-to-day browsing, we crawled the thousand most popular websites as reported by Alexa [3] on both a vanilla version of Firefox 54 and FPRandom. We used Selenium as the engine for the crawl of both browsers, and we used the Performance API of the browser to measure the time it takes for the DOM of the main page to be completely loaded. Specifically, we used the *domLoading* and *dom-ContentLoadedEventStart* events to make our measurements as they are independent of problems related to network instabilities and congestion. Because of server unavailability and certificate problems encountered during our crawl, we miss loading times for 43 sites. The results can be found in Table 2. In general, load times are extremely close between a vanilla Firefox and FPRandom. Mean times indicate a slightly better performance for Firefox. Yet, in both cases, the standard deviation is very high, meaning that the collected loading times are very dispersed between 0 and 5 s. These numbers demonstrate that the modifications introduced in FPRandom do not have a visible impact on the user experience for day-to-day browsing. Moreover, we can also say that the amount of site breakage is kept to a minimum as only a single script provided us with an error due to our enumeration modification. The modifications on both the Canvas and AudioContext API had no impact on site breakage.

Table 2. Web crawl results

	Times collected	Min (ms)	Max (ms)	Mean (ms)	SD (ms)
Firefox	957	10	64728	1602	3712
FPRandom	958	9	55852	1823	3935

4.3 User Study

An important aspect of FPRandom is that it modifies multimedia elements that can be seen or heard by the user. To make sure that the modified subroutines do not degrade substantially the user experience at the cost of better privacy, we ran a preliminary user study in February 2017. Its goal was to compare multimedia elements as rendered by a normal version of Firefox 54 with modified ones rendered by FPRandom. The study was divided into two phases: the first was focused on the modifications made to canvas elements while the second investigated the impact on the AudioContext API. The link to our survey was communicated through regular channels like social networks and team mailing lists. We received an answer from 20 participants and the results are as follows:

- Half of them noticed a color difference between the original canvas rendering and the 10 modified ones, the other half did not.
- 70% said that some fonts made the strings harder to read and only one person said that it was significantly harder for all of the modified renderings.
- For the AudioContext API, only 25% detected a difference between the original track and the 3 modified ones.

- For people who heard a difference, they all qualified the difference with words like "tiny" or "small".

These results give us confidence in the direction we took with our approach but we plan on conducting a more thorough study to pinpoint more precisely avenues for improvement with more participants. Still, we will investigate how we can exclude some exotic fonts as they can make strings in canvas renderings harder to read for users.

5   Related Work

While we focus in this paper on breaking the linkability of browser fingerprints, other approaches have been designed to tackle fingerprint tracking.

Blocking extensions. Several works report that one strong way to prevent tracking is to block scripts before they are loaded by the browser [1,8,16]. Browser extensions like NoScript [19], Ghostery [10] or Disconnect [6] are illustrations of such solutions. However, these extensions require complete lists of all scripts performing fingerprinting to correctly block them. As the web is constantly evolving and actors in the tracking business are changing, it is very hard to maintain up-to-date lists to protect users' privacy.

Spoofing extensions. Another way to mitigate tracking based on browser fingerprints is to return incorrect information to trackers. Dozens of spoofing extensions already exist for both Chrome and Firefox. With very few steps, a Firefox browser can easily report that it is a Chrome one and vice versa. However, as shown by Nikiforakis et al. [18], these solutions produce inconsistent fingerprints. While the user agent reports one information, a JavaScript property will tell a different story, proving that the browser has deliberately changed its default values. Torres et al. follow in the footsteps of spoofers and created a solution called FP-Block that is an implementation of the concept of separation of web identities [25]. The idea is simple: FP-Block generates a fingerprint (i.e. an identity) for each website that the browser is in contact with. Every time the browser reconnects to the same website, it will reuse the generated identity. As a defense against fingerprinting, the premise is great but unfortunately, the implementation presents the same shortcomings as the extensions stated above. Generated fingerprints are inconsistent and it is easy to find supposedly hidden information as there is an incomplete coverage of methods used for fingerprinting.

Use of multiple browsers. One approach to obtain different browser fingerprints is to use multiple browsers. However, Boda et al. showed the existence of *Cross-browser fingerprinting* [5]. By collecting enough OS-specific data like the list of fonts or plugins, a script can identify a device behind multiple browsers as these information are stable from one browser to the next. A more recent method by Cao et al. can identify with high precision users across different browsers through the use of the WebGL API [28].

Tor browser. The Tor browser is a modified Firefox specifically designed for the Tor network. Its approach towards fingerprinting is to have fingerprints that are as uniform as possible. As stated by the Tor design document [24], its defenses include "value spoofing", "Subsystem Modification or Reimplementation", "Virtualization", "Site Permissions" and "Feature or Functionality Removal". However, this approach poses several problems. First, by design, fingerprints from Tor browser are very specific and thus already known to trackers. Its users can easily be identified as using the Tor browser. Then, the offered protection is extremely brittle since a simple change can change the standard fingerprint to a unique one. To remain effective, customizability and personalization are severely hampered because of this mono-configuration. Finally, by blocking specific browser APIs, the Tor browser restricts users from benefiting from the full array of browser features that could enrich their browsing experience.

6   Conclusion and Future Perspectives

In this work, we aim at breaking the stability of browser fingerprints over time to improve users' privacy. By identifying APIs with restrictive implementation with respect to the JavaScript specification, we introduce randomness to produce slight variations at each execution of a fingerprinting script. We also generate noise inside HTML multimedia elements to alter their rendering without deteriorating user's perception. The approach presented in this work can be generalized to more fingerprinting vectors. For example, there exists other parts in the ECMAScript specification that leave the exact details of the implementation in the hands of developers. The use of Math constants in the browser can be used to unveil information about the device and its browser [26]. If we take a look at Sect. 20.2.2. of the official JavaScript specification [7], it is written that "the choice of algorithms is left to the implementation" and that the behavior of mathematical functions "is not precisely specified". This means that the actual libraries used for these functions could be diversified to prevent the unmasking of the operating system. In the end, the main challenge that remains here is to perform an exhaustive search to identify and anticipate future fingerprinting mechanisms. By locating key functions that could reveal device-specific information, we could preemptively introduce randomness to reinforce users' privacy on the web.

We also developed a working prototype called FPRandom that targets the following attributes of the browser fingerprinting domain: canvas fingerprinting, AudioContext fingerprinting and the unmasking of the browser through the order of special JavaScript objects. By looking at the specification and analyzing the browser's source code, we modified key locations to introduce very small noise that prevents the use of these fingerprinting vectors for identification. Our tests show that our modifications impact known fingerprinting scripts that use the targeted attributes. A careful attention was also given to preserve the user experience as much as possible and our performance benchmarks indicate that the introduced overhead is very small.

A   Analyzing Differences in the AudioContext API

In order to have a better understanding of the diversity of audio fingerprints on the web, we deployed the AudioContext script found by Englehardt et al. on the AmIUnique.org website (used in our Beauty and the Beast study [14]). After discarding more than 1,000 fingerprints from browsers that did not implement the AudioContext API, we collected in total 19,468 audio fingerprints on a period of 100 days between June and September 2016. The results of this study can be found in Table 3. We use the Shannon entropy in bits to better represent the probability distribution of each of the attributes. The higher the entropy is, the more diversity is exhibited between devices.

Table 3. Study of 19,468 audio fingerprints

Name	Entropy (bits)	Size of the biggest set	Number of distinct values	Number of unique values
acSampleRate	1.18	9549	10	3
acState	0.99	10821	2	0
acMaxChannelCount	0.38	18580	11	1
acNumberOfInputs	0.0	19468	1	0
acNumberOfOutputs	0.0	19468	1	0
acChannelCount	0.0	19468	1	0
acChannelCountMode	0.0	19468	1	0
acChannelInterpretation	0.0	19468	1	0
anFftSize	0.0	19468	1	0
anFrequencyBinCount	0.0	19468	1	0
anMinDecibels	0.0	19468	1	0
anMaxDecibels	0.0	19468	1	0
anSmoothingTimeConstant	0.0	19468	1	0
anNumberOfInputs	0.0	19468	1	0
anNumberOfOutputs	0.0	19468	1	0
anChannelCount	0.99	10821	2	0
anChannelCountMode	0.0	19468	1	0
anChannelInterpretation	0.0	19468	1	0
audioDynSum	3.28	5698	53	5
audioDynHash	3.43	5697	72	12

Most of the collected attributes have a single value and do not provide any ground to distinguish one device from another. From the collected audio fingerprints, only 3 attributes have an entropy superior to a single bit:

- *acSampleRate* is the default sample rate of a created track when using the *AudioContext* API. The most common values are 44,1 kHz (49,0% of collected fingerprints) and 48 kHz (48,5%) but some browsers still present some unusual ones (1,7% have 192 kHz and 0,7% 96 kHz).
- *audioDynSum* is the sum of 500 frames generated by a very specific audio processing (compressed audio from an oscillator). The precision of each frame is up to 15 decimal digits. The large majority of values are really close to each other with differences only appearing from the 6th or 7th decimal digit.
- *audioDynHash* is similar to *audioDynSum* as it takes the exact same output but it covers the entirety of the rendered track instead of a few hundreds frames. As it covers a larger space, the entropy is a little higher and this test exhibits more diversity than all other collected attributes.

With these results, we decided to focus only on the differences created by the audio processing performed inside audio nodes. Especially, we want to introduce random noise in the computed frames so that each run of the same test produces different variations. Other values like the default sample rate are still interesting to change but they can easily be modified and they are not the focus of this work.

B   Example of String Comparison When Ordering JavaScript Properties

Figure 5 illustrates the comparison mechanism between the *appVersion* and the *appName* strings. The engine starts with the 'a' letter on both strings. Translating this letter to their corresponding Latin-1 code points yields the decimal numbers '97'. Subtracting 97 from 97 results in 0. As no difference is detected, the engine continues but faces the exact same result for both the second and third characters in each string as they are identical 'p' letters. However, the behavior is different from the fourth character. The first string presents a 'V' and the second an 'N'. Translating to their decimal code points yields '86' and '78'. This time, since the subtraction $86 - 78 = 8$ does not give a zero, it informs the engine that a difference has been detected. As the result is positive, *appName* is placed before *appVersion*. If the result of the subtraction were to be negative, it would have been the opposite order.

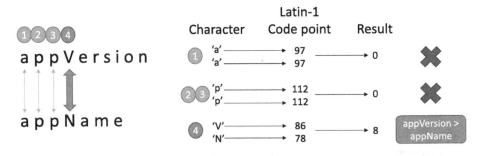

Fig. 5. String comparison between the *appName* and *appVersion* properties

References

1. Acar, G., Eubank, C., Englehardt, S., Juarez, M., Narayanan, A., Diaz, C.: The web never forgets: persistent tracking mechanisms in the wild. In: Proceedings of the 21st ACM Conference on Computer and Communications Security (CCS 2014). ACM (2014)
2. Acar, G., Juarez, M., Nikiforakis, N., Diaz, C., Gürses, S., Piessens, F., Preneel, B.: FPDetective: dusting the web for fingerprinters. In: Proceedings of the Conference on Computer and Communications Security (CCS), pp. 1129–1140. ACM (2013)
3. Alexa: The top 500 sites on the web. http://www.alexa.com/topsites
4. Benchmarks for the WebAudio API. https://github.com/padenot/webaudio-benchmark
5. Boda, K., Földes, Á.M., Gulyás, G.G., Imre, S.: User tracking on the web via cross-browser fingerprinting. In: Laud, P. (ed.) NordSec 2011. LNCS, vol. 7161, pp. 31–46. Springer, Heidelberg (2012). doi:10.1007/978-3-642-29615-4_4
6. Disconnect's official webpage. https://disconnect.me/
7. ECMAScript® 2016 Language Specification. http://www.ecma-international.org/ecma-262/7.0/index.html
8. Englehardt, S., Narayanan, A.: Online tracking: A 1-million-site measurement and analysis. In: Proceedings of the 2016 ACM SIGSAC Conference on Computer and Communications Security, CCS 2016, pp. 1388–1401. ACM, New York (2016)
9. fingerprintjs2, modern and flexible browser fingerprinting library, a successor to the original fingerprintjs. https://github.com/Valve/fingerprintjs2
10. Ghostery's browser extension. https://ghostery.com/our-solutions/ghostery-browser-extension/
11. Introducing the JetStream Benchmark Suite. https://webkit.org/blog/3418/introducing-the-jetstream-benchmark-suite/
12. JetStream benchmark. http://browserbench.org/JetStream/
13. Laperdrix, P., Rudametkin, W., Baudry, B.: Mitigating browser fingerprint tracking: multi-level reconfiguration and diversification. In: 10th International Symposium on Software Engineering for Adaptive and Self-Managing Systems (SEAMS 2015), Firenze, Italy, May 2015
14. Laperdrix, P., Rudametkin, W., Baudry, B.: Beauty and the beast: diverting modern web browsers to build unique browser fingerprints. In: 37th IEEE Symposium on Security and Privacy (S&P 2016) (2016)
15. Maxmind's Device Tracking Add-on for minFraud Services. http://dev.maxmind.com/minfraud/device/
16. Mowery, K., Shacham, H.: Pixel perfect: fingerprinting canvas in HTML5. In: Fredrikson, M. (ed.) Proceedings of W2SP 2012. IEEE Computer Society, May 2012
17. Nikiforakis, N., Joosen, W., Livshits, B.: Privaricator: deceiving fingerprinters with little white lies. In: Proceedings of the 24th International Conference on World Wide Web, pp. 820–830. International World Wide Web Conferences Steering Committee (2015)
18. Nikiforakis, N., Kapravelos, A., Joosen, W., Kruegel, C., Piessens, F., Vigna, G.: Cookieless monster: exploring the ecosystem of web-based device fingerprinting. In: Proceedings of the Symposium on Security and Privacy, pp. 541–555 (2013)
19. NoScript's official webpage. https://noscript.net/
20. Olejnik, L., Acar, G., Castelluccia, C., Daz, C.: The leaking battery: a privacy analysis of the HTML5 battery status API. IACR Cryptology ePrint Archive, 2015:616 (2015)

21. Olejnik, L., Janc, A.: Stealing sensitive browser data with the W3C Ambient Light Sensor API. https://blog.lukaszolejnik.com/stealing-sensitive-browser-data-with-the-w3c-ambient-light-sensor-api/
22. Wrong order in object properties interation - V8 bug tracker. https://bugs.chromium.org/p/v8/issues/detail?id=164
23. High Resolution Time Level 2 (JavaScript Performance API). https://www.w3.org/TR/hr-time/#dom-domhighrestimestamp
24. The Design and Implementation of the Tor Browser - Cross-Origin Fingerprinting Unlinkability. https://www.torproject.org/projects/torbrowser/design/#fingerprinting-linkability
25. Torres, C.F., Jonker, H., Mauw, S.: *FP-Block*: usable web privacy by controlling browser fingerprinting. In: Pernul, G., Ryan, P.Y.A., Weippl, E. (eds.) ESORICS 2015. LNCS, vol. 9327, pp. 3–19. Springer, Cham (2015). doi:10.1007/978-3-319-24177-7_1
26. Tor bug tracker - math routines are OS fingerprintable. https://trac.torproject.org/projects/tor/ticket/13018
27. Codepage layout - ISO/IEC 8859-1. https://en.wikipedia.org/wiki/ISO/IEC_8859-1#Codepage_layout
28. Cao, S.L.Y., Wijmans, E.: (Cross-)browser fingerprinting via OS and hardware level features. In: Proceedings of the 2017 Network and Distributed System Security Symposium, NDSS 2017 (2017)

Control What You Include!
Server-Side Protection Against Third Party Web Tracking

Dolière Francis Somé[✉], Nataliia Bielova, and Tamara Rezk

Université Côte d'Azur, Inria, France
{doliere.some,nataliia.bielova,tamara.rezk}@inria.fr

Abstract. Third party tracking is the practice by which third parties recognize users accross different websites as they browse the web. Recent studies show that more than 90% of Alexa top 500 websites [38] contain third party content that is tracking its users across the web. Website developers often need to include third party content in order to provide basic functionality. However, when a developer includes a third party content, she cannot know whether the third party contains tracking mechanisms. If a website developer wants to protect her users from being tracked, the only solution is to exclude any third-party content, thus trading functionality for privacy. We describe and implement a privacy-preserving web architecture that gives website developers a control over third party tracking: developers are able to include functionally useful third party content, the same time ensuring that the end users are not tracked by the third parties.

Keywords: Program rewriting techniques for security · Security by design

1 Introduction

Third party tracking is the practice by which third parties recognize users accross different websites as they browse the web. In recent years, tracking technologies have been extensively studied and measured [28,29,31,34,36,38] – researchers have found that third parties embedded in websites use numerous technologies, such as third-party cookies, HTML5 local storage, browser cache and device fingerprinting that allow the third party to recognize users across websites [39] and build browsing history profiles. Researchers found that more than 90% of Alexa top 500 websites [38] contain third party web tracking content, while some sites include as much as 34 distinct third party content [33].

But why do website developers include so many third party content (that may track their users)? Though some third party content, such as images and CSS [2] files can be copied to the main (first-party) site, such an approach has a number of disadvantages for other kinds of content. *Advertisement* is the base of the economic model in the web – without advertisements many website providers will not be able to financially support their website maintenance. *Third party*

E. Bodden et al. (Eds.): ESSoS 2017, LNCS 10379, pp. 115–132, 2017.
DOI: 10.1007/978-3-319-62105-0_8

JavaScript libraries offer extra functionality: though copies of such libraries can be stored on the main first party site, this solution will sacrifice maintenance of these libraries when new versions are released. The developer would need to manually check the new versions. *Web mashups*, as for example applications that use hotel searching together with maps, are actually based on reusing third-party content, as well as maps, and would not be able to provide their basic functionality without including the third-party content. Including JavaScript libraries, content for mashups or advertisements means that the web developers cannot provide to the users the guarantee of non-tracking.

Except for ethical decision not to track users, from May 2018 the website owners will have a legal obligation as well. The ePrivacy directive (also know as 'cookie law') will be updated to the regulation, and will make website owners liable for third party tracking that takes place in their websites. This regulation will be applied to all the services that are delivered to the natural persons located in the European Union. This regulation will apply high penalties for any violation. Hence, privacy compliance will be of high interest to all website owners and developers, and today there is no automatic tool that can help to control third party tracking. To keep a promise of non-tracking, the only solution today is to exclude any third-party content[1], thus trading functionality for privacy.

In this paper, we present a new web application architecture that allows web developers to gain control over certain types of third party content. Our solution is based on the automatic rewriting of the web application in such a way that the third party requests are redirected to a trusted web server, with a different domain than the main site. This trusted web server may be either controlled by a trusted party, or by a main site owner – it is enough that the trusted web server has a different domain. A trusted server is needed so that the user's browser will treat all redirected requests as third party requests, like in the original web application. The trusted server automatically eliminates third-party tracking cookies and other technologies.

In summary our contributions are:

- A classification of third party content that can and cannot be controlled by the website developer.
- An analysis of third party tracking capabilities – we analyze two mechanisms: recognition of a web user, and identification of the website she is visiting[2].
- A new architecture that allows to include third party content in web applications and eliminate stateful tracking.
- An implementation of our architecture, demonstrating its effectiveness at preventing stateful third party tracking in several websites.

---

[1] For example, see https://duckduckgo.com/.

[2] Tracking is often defined as the ability of a third party to recognize a user through different websites. However, being able to identify the websites a user is interacting with is equally crucial for the effectiveness of tracking.

2   Background and Motivation

Third party web tracking is the ability of a third party to re-identify users as they browse the web and record their browsing history [34]. Tracking is often done with the purpose of web analytics, targeted advertisement, or other forms of personalization. The more a third party is prevalent among the websites a user interacts with, the more precise is the browsing history collected by the tracker. Tracking has often been conceived as the ability of a third party to recognize the web user. However, for successful tracking, each user request should contain two components:

User recognition is the information that allows tracker to recognize the user;
Website identification is the website which the user is visiting.

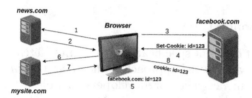

Fig. 1. Third party tracking

For example, when a user visits `news.com`, the browser may make additional requests to `facebook.com`. As a result, Facebook learns about the user's visit to `news.com`. Figure 1 shows a hypothetical example of such tracking where `facebook.com` is the third party.

Consider that a third party server, such as `facebook.com` hosts different content, and some of them are useful for the website developers. The web developer of another website, say `mysite.com`, would like to include such *functional* content from Facebook, such as Facebook "Like" button, an image, or a useful JavaScript library, but the developer does not want its users to be tracked by Facebook. If the web developer simply includes third party Facebook content in his application, all its users are likely to be tracked by cookie-based tracking. Notice that each request to `facebook.com` also contains an HTTP Referrer header, automatically attached by the browser. This header contains the website URL that the user is visiting, which allows Facebook to build user's browsing history profile.

The example demonstrates cookie-based tracking, which is extremely common [38]. Other types of third party tracking, that use client-side storage mechanisms, such as HTML5 LocalStorage, or cache, and device fingerprinting that do not require any storage capabilities, are also becoming more and more popular [29].

Web Developer Perspective. A web developer may include third party content in her webpages, either because this content *intentionally* tracks users (for example, for targeted advertising), or because this content is important for the functioning of the web application. We therefore distinguish two kinds of third party content from a web developer perspective: *tracking* and *functional*. *Tracking* content is *intentionally* embedded by website owner for tracking purposes. *Functional* content is embedded in a webpage for other purposes than tracking: for example, JavaScript libraries that provide additional functionality, such as jQuery, or other components, such as maps. In this work, we focus on *functional* content and investigate the following questions:

- What kind of third party content can be controlled from a server-side (web developer) perspective?
- How to eliminate the two components of tracking (user recognition and website identification) from functional third party content that websites embed?

2.1 Browsing Context

Browsers implement different specifications to securely fetch and aggregate third party content. One widely used approach is the *Same Origin Policy (SOP)* [15], a security mechanism designed for developers to isolate legacy content from potentially untrusted third party content. An origin is defined as scheme, host and port number, of the URL [21] of the third party content.

When a browser renders a webpage delivered by a first party, the page is placed within a *browsing context* [1]. A browsing context represents an instance of the browser in which a document such as a webpage is displayed to a user, for instance browser tabs, and popup windows. Each browsing context contains (1) a copy of the browser properties (such as browser name, version, device screen etc.), stored in a specific object; (2) other objects that depend on the origin of the document according to SOP. For instance, the object `document.cookie` gives the cookies related to the domain and path of the current context.

In-Context and Cross-Context Content. Certain types of content embedded in a webpage, such as images, links, and scripts, are associated with the context of the webpage, and we call them *in-context* content. Other types of content, such as `<iframe>`, `<embed>`, and `<object>` tags are associated with their own browsing context, and we call them *cross-context* content. Usually, cross-context content, such as `<iframe>` elements, cannot be visually distinguished from the webpage in which they are embedded, however they are as autonomous as other browsing contexts, such as tabs or windows. Table 1 shows different third party content and their execution contexts.

The Same Origin Policy manages interactions between different browsing contexts. In particular, it prevents in-context scripts from interacting with cross-context iframes in case their origins are different. To communicate, they may use inter-frame communication APIs such as `postMessage` [12].

Table 1. Third party content and execution context.

	HTML Tags	Third party content
in-context	`<link>`	Stylesheets
	`<img>`	Images
	`<audio>`	Audios
	`<video>`	Videos
	`<form>`	Forms
	`<script>`	Scripts
cross-context	`<(i)frame>`, `<frameset>`, `<a>`	Web pages
	`<object>`, `<embed>`, `<applet>`	Plugins and web pages

2.2 Third Party Tracking

In this work, we consider only stateful tracking technologies – they require an identifier to be stored client-side. The most common storage mechanism is cookies, but others, such as HTML5 LocalStorage and browser cache can also be used for stateful tracking. Figure 2 presents the well-known stateful tracking mechanisms. We distinguish two components necessary for successful tracking: user recognition and website identification. For each component, we describe the capabilities of in-context and cross-context. We also distinguish *passive tracking* (through HTTP headers) and *active tracking* (through JavaScript or plugin script).

	User Recognition		Website Identification	
	Passive	Active	Passive	Active

in-context	HTTP cookies
	Cache-Control
		–	Referer
			Origin
				`document.URL`
				`document.location`
				`window.location`

cross-context	Etag
	Last-Modified
		Flash LSOs
		`document.cookie`
		`window.localStorage`
		`window.indexedDB`
			Referer	`document.referrer`

Fig. 2. Stateful tracking mechanisms

In-Context Tracking. In-context third party content is associated with the browsing context of the webpage that embeds it (see Table 1).

Passively, such content may use HTTP headers to recognize a user and identify the visited website. When a webpage is rendered, the browser sends a request to fetch all third party content embedded in that page. The responses from the third party, along with the requested content, may contain HTTP headers that are used for tracking. For example, the *Set-cookie* HTTP header tells the browser to save third party cookies, that will be later on automatically attached to every request to that third party in the *Cookie* header. *Etag* HTTP header and other cache mechanisms like *Last-Modified* and *Cache-Control* HTTP headers may also be used to store user identifiers [39] in a browser. To identify the visited website, a third party can either check the *Referer* HTTP header, automatically attached by the browser, or an *Origin* header[3].

Actively, in-context third party content cannot use browser storage mechanisms, such as cookies or HTML5 Local Storage associated to the third party because of the limitations imposed by the SOP (see Sect. 2.1). For example, if a third party script from *third.com* uses `document.cookie` API, it will read the cookies of the main website, but not those of *third.com*. This allows tracking within the main website but does not allow tracking cross-sites [38]. For website identification, third party active content, such as scripts, can use several APIs, for example `document.location`.

Cross-Context Tracking. Cross-context content, such as iframe, is associated with the browsing context of the third party that provided this content.

Passively, the browser may transmit HTTP headers used for user recognition and website identification, just like in the case of in-context content. Every third-party request for cross-context content will contain the URL of the embedding webpage in its *Referer* header.

Requests to fetch third party content further embedded inside a cross-context (such as iframe) will carry, not the URL of the embedding webpage, but that of the iframe in their *Referer* or *Origin* headers (in the case of CORS requests). This prevents them from passively identifying the embedding webpage.

Actively, cross-context third party content can use a number of APIs to store user identifiers in the browser. These APIs include cookies (`document.cookie`), HTML5 LocalStorage (`document.localStorage`), IndexedDB, and Flash Local Stored Objects (LSOs). For website identification, `document.referrer` API can be used – it returns the value of the HTTP Referrer header transmitted in the request to the cross-context third party.

Combining In-Context and Cross-Context Tracking. Imagine a third party script from `third.com` embedded in a webpage – according to the context and to the SOP, it is in-context. If the same webpage embeds a third party iframe from `third.com` (cross-context), then because of SOP, such script and iframe cannot interact directly. However, the can still communicate through inter-frame communication APIs such as `postMessage` [12].

On one hand, the in-context script can easily identify the website using APIs such as `document.location`. On the other hand, the cross-context iframe can easily recognize the user by calling `document.cookie`. Therefore, if the iframe and the script are allowed to communicate, they can exchange those partial tracking information to fully track the user.

---

[3] Origin header is also automatically generated by the browser when the third party content is trying to access data using Cross-Origin Resource Sharing [4] mechanism.

For example, a social widget, such as Facebook "Like" button, or Google "+1" button, may be included in webpages as a script. When the social widget script is executed on the client-side, it loads additional scripts, and new browsing contexts (iframes) allowing the third party to benefit from both in-context and cross-context capabilities to track users.

3   Privacy-Preserving Web Architecture

For third party tracking to be effective, two capabilities are needed: (1) the tracker should be able to identify the website in which it is embedded, and (2) recognize the user interacting with the website. Disabling only one of these two capabilities for a given third party already prevents tracking. In order to mitigate stateful tracking (see Sect. 2), we make the following design choices:

1. **Preventing only user recognition for in-context.** As show in Table 2, in-context content cannot perform any active user recognition. We are left with passive user recognition and (active and passive) website identification. Preventing passive user recognition for such content (images, scripts, forms) is possible by removing HTTP headers such as *Cookie, Set-cookie, ETag* that are sent along with requests/responses to fetch those content.
   Note that it is particularly difficult to prevent active website identification because trying to alter or redefine `document.location` or `window.location` APIs, will cause the main page to reload. Therefore, in-context active content (scripts) can still perform active website identification. Nonetheless, since we remove their user recognition capability, tracking is therefore prevented for in-context content.
2. **Preventing only website identification for cross-context.** We prevent passive website identification by instructing the browser not to send the HTTP *Referer* header along with requests to fetch a cross-context content. Therefore, when the cross-context content gets loaded, the tracker is unable to identify the website in which it is embedded in. Indeed, executing `document.referrer` returns an empty string instead of the URL of the embedding page.
   Because of the limitations of the SOP, a website owner has no control over cross-context third party content, such as iframes. Therefore, active and passive user recognition can still happen in third party cross-context. We discuss other possibilities to block some active user recognition APIs in Sect. 4.1. Nonetheless, since website identification is not possible, tracking is therefore prevented for cross-context third party content.
3. **Prevent communication between in-context and cross-context content.** Our architecture proposes a way to block such communications that can be done by `postMessage` API. We discuss the limitations of this approach in Sect. 4.1.

To help web developers keep their promises of non-tracking and still include third-party content in their web applications, we propose a new web application

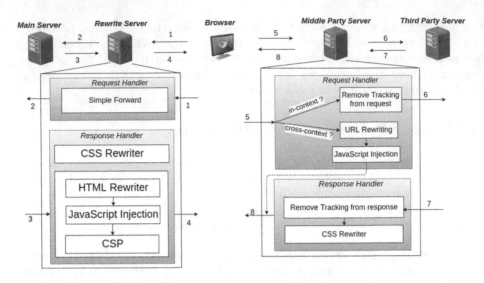

Fig. 3. Privacy-preserving web architecture

architecture. This architecture allows web developers to (1) automatically rewrite the URLs of all in-context third party content embedded in a web application, (2) redirect those requests to a trusted third party server which (3) remove/disable known *stateful* tracking mechanisms (see Sect. 2) for such content; (4) rewrite and redirect cross-context requests to the trusted third party so as to prevent website identification and communication with in-context scripts.

Figure 3 provides an overview of our web application architecture. It introduces two new components fully controlled by the website owner.

Rewrite Server (Sect. 3.1) acts like a reverse proxy [14] for the original web server. It rewrites the original web pages in such a way that all the requests to fetch all the third party content that they embed are redirected through the Middle Party Server before reaching the intended third party server.

Middle Party Server (Sect. 3.2) is at the core of our solution since it intercepts all browser third party requests, removes tracking, then forwards them to the intended third parties. From every response from a third party, the server removes tracking information and forwards the response back to the browser. For in-context content such as images and scripts, the Middle Party Server prevents user recognition and website identification, while for cross-context content such as iframes, it prevents website identification and communication with other in-context scripts.

3.1   Rewrite Server

The goal of the Rewrite Server is to rewrite the original content of the requested webpages in such a way that all third party requests will be redirected to the Middle Party Server. It consists of three main components: static HTML rewriter for

HTML pages, static CSS rewriter and JavaScript injection component. Into each webpage, we load a JavaScript code that insures that all dynamically generated third party content are redirected to the Middle Party Server as well.

HTML and CSS Rewriter rewrites the URLs of static third party content embedded in original web pages and CSS files in order to redirect them to the Middle Party Server. For example, the URL of a third-party script source `http://third.com/script.js` is written so that it is instead fetched through the Middle Party Server: `http://middle.com/?src=http://third.com/script.js`. The **HTML Rewriter** component is implemented using the Jsdom HTML parser [8], and **CSS Rewriter**, using the CSS parser [5] module for Node.js.

JavaScript Injection. The Rewrite Server also injects a script in all original webpages after they are rewritten. This script controls APIs used to dynamically inject content inside a webpage once the webpage is rendered in a browser. It is available at `https://webstats.inria.fr/sstp/dynamic.js`. Table 2 shows APIs that can be used to dynamically inject third party content within a webpage. They are controlled using the injected script.

Table 2. Injecting dynamic third party content

API	Content
`document.createElement`	Inject content from Table 1
`document.write`	Any content
`window.open`	Web pages (popups)
`Image`	Images
`XMLHttpRequest`	Any data
`Fetch, Request`	Any content
`EventSource`	Stream data
`WebSocket`	Websocket data

A **Content Security Policy (CSP)** [44] is injected in the response header of each webpage in order to prevent third parties from bypassing the rewriting and redirection to the Middle Party Server. A CSP delivered with the webpage controls the resources of that page by specifying which resources are allowed to be loaded and executed. By limiting the resource origins to only those of the Middle Party Server and the website own domain, we prevent third parties from bypassing the redirection to the Middle Party Server in order to load content directly from a third party server. Such attempts will get blocked by the browser upon enforcement of the CSP of the page. The following listing gives the CSP injected in all webpages, assuming that *middle.com* is the domain of the Middle Party Server.

```
1    Content-Security-Policy: default-src 'self'
         middle.com; object-src 'self';
```

3.2   Middle Party

The main goal of the Middle Party is to proxy the requests and responses between browsers and third parties in order to remove tracking information exchanged between them. It functions differently for in-context and cross-context content.

In-Context content are scripts, images, etc. (see Table 1). Since a third party script from `http://third.com/script.js` is rewritten by the Rewrite Server to `http://middle.com/?src=http://third.com/script.js`, it is fetched through the Middle Party Server. This hides the third party destination from the browser, and therefore prevents it from attaching third party HTTP cookies to such requests. Because the browser will still attach some tracking information to the requests, then when the middle party receives a request URL from the browser, it takes the following steps. **Remove Tracking from request** that are set by the browser as HTTP headers. Among those headers are *Etag, If-Modified-Since, Cache-Control, Referer*. Next, it makes a request to the third party in order to get the content of the script `http://third.com/script.js`. **Remove Tracking from response** returned by the third party. The headers that the third party may send are *Set-Cookie, Etag, Last-Modified, Cache-Control*. **CSS Rewriter** rewrites the response if the content is a CSS file, in order to also redirect to the Middle Party Server any third party content that they may embed. Finally, the response is returned back to the browser.

Cross-context content are iframes, links, popups, etc. (see Table 1). The Middle Party Server prevents website identification for cross-context content and communication with in-context scripts. This is done by loading cross-context content from another cross-context controlled by the Middle Party Server as illustrated by Fig. 4.

For instance, a third party iframe from `http://third.com/page.html` is rewritten to `http://middle.com/?emb=http://third.com/page.html`. When the Middle Party Server receives such a request URL from the browser, it takes the following actions: **URL Rewriting.** Instead of fetching directly the content of `http://third.com/page.html`, the Middle Party Server generates a content in which it puts the URL of the third party content as a hyperlink = `"http://third.com/page.html" rel = "noreferrer noopener"></a>`. The most important part of this content is in the `rel` attribute value. Therefore, `noreferrer noopener` instructs the browser not the send the *Referer* header

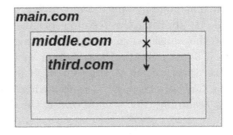

Fig. 4. Prevent combining in-context and cross-context tracking

when the link `http://third.com/page.html` is followed client-side. **JavaScript Injection** module adds a script to the content so that the link gets automatically followed once the content is rendered by the browser. Once the link is followed, the browser fetches the third party content directly on the third party server, without going through the Middle Party server anymore. Nonetheless, it does not include the *Referer* header for identifying the website. Therefore, the `document.referrer` API also returns an empty string inside the iframe context. This prevents it from identifying the website. The third party server response is placed within a new iframe nested within a context that belongs to the Middle Party, and not directly within the site webpage. This prevents in-context scripts and the cross-context content from exchanging tracking information as illustrated by Fig. 4.

HTTPS Content. We recommend deploying the Middle Party Server as an HTTPS server. Therefore, third party content originally served over HTTPS (before rewriting) still get served over HTTPS even in the presence of the Middle Party Server. Moreover, third party content originally served over HTTP would get blocked by current browsers according to the Mixed Content policy [43]. With an HTTPS Middle Party, HTTP third party requests will not be prevented from loading since they are fetched over HTTPS through the Middle Party.

Multiple Redirections. A third party may attempt to circumvent our solution by performing multiple redirections. This is commonly used in advertisements (though ads are not in scope of this paper).

When a (third party) web server wants to perform a redirection to another server, it usually does so by including in the response, a special HTTP *Location* that indicates the server to which the next request will be sent. The Middle Party Server prevents such circumvention by rewriting the *Location* header so that the browser sends the next redirection request to the Middle Party Server again. As a result, all the redirections pass via the Middle Party.

4 Implementation

We have implemented both the Rewrite Server and the Middle Party Server as full Node.js [10] web servers supporting *HTTP(S)* protocols and web sockets. Implementation details are available at `https://webstats.inria.fr/sstp/`.

Rewrite Server. In our implementation, we deploy the Rewrite Server on the same physical machine as the original web application server. In order to do so, we moved the original server on a different port number, and the Rewrite Server on the initial port of the original server. Therefore, requests that are sent by browsers reach first the Rewrite Server. It then simply forwards them to the original server, which handles the request as usual and return a response to the Rewrite Server. Then, HTML webpages, and CSS files are rewritten using the **HTML Rewriter** and **CSS Rewriter** components respectively. To handle dynamic third party content, we inject a script. And in order to prevent malicious third parties from bypassing the redirection, we inject a CSP (See Sect. 3.1).

Middle Party. All requests to load third party contents embedded in a website deploying our architecture will go through the Middle Party Server. In-Context and cross-context contents are handled differently.

In-Context Contents are simply stripped off tracking information that they carry from the browser to the third parties and vice versa. See Sect. 3 for the list of tracking information that are removed from third party requests and responses. In particular, third party CSS responses are rewritten, using the **CSS Rewriter** component, to redirect to the Middle Party Server any third party content that they may further embed. As in the case of the Rewrite Server, this component is implemented using a CSS parser [5] for Node.js.

Cross-Context contents are handled in a way that the original website identity is not leaked to them. They are also prevented from communicating with any in-context third party content to exchange tracking information. If the cross-context URL was `http://third.com/page.html`, instead of making a request to `third.com`, the Middle Party Server returns to the browser a response consisting of rewriting the URL to

```
1  <a href="http://third.com/page.html" rel="noreferrer
      noopener"></a>.
```

and injecting the following script:

```
1  var third_party = document.getElementsByTagName("a")[0];
2  if(window.top == window.self){
3    third_party.target = "_blank";
4    third_party.click();
5    window.close();
6  }else{
7    var iframe = document.createElement("iframe");
8      iframe.name = "iframetarget";
9    document.body.appendChild(iframe);
10   third_party.target = "iframetarget";
11   third_party.click();
12 }
```

Overall, when this response is rendered, the browser will not the *Referer* header to the third party, and the third party is prevented from communicating with in-context content, as explained in Sect. 3.2.

4.1   Discussion and Limitations

Our approach suffers from the following limitations. First, our implementation prevents cross-context and in-context contents from communicating with each other using `postMessage` API. However, in-context third party script can identify the website a user visits via `document.location.href` API. Then the script can include the website URL, say `http://main.com`, as a parameter of the URL of a third party iframe, for example `http://third.com/page.html?ref=http://main.com` and dynamically embed it in the webpage. In our architecture, this URL is rewritten and routed to the

Middle Party. Since, the Middle Party Server does not inspect URL parameters, this information will reach the third party even though the *Referer* is not sent with cross-context requests.

Another limitation is that of dynamic CSS changes. For instance, changing the background image via the *style* object of an element in the webpage is not captured by the dynamic rewriting script injected in webpages. Therefore, if the image was a third party image, the CSP will prevent it from loading.

Performance Overhead. There is a performance cost associated with the Rewrite Server, which can be evaluated as the cost of introducing any reverse proxy to a web application architecture (See Sect. 3.1). Rewriting contents server-side and browser-side is also expensive in terms of performance. We believe that server-side caching mechanisms, in particular for static webpages, may help speed up the responsiveness of the Rewrite Server.

The Middle Party Server may also lead to performance overhead especially for webpages with numerous third party contents. Therefore, it can be provided as a service by a trusted external party, as it is the case for Content Distribution Networks (CDNs) serving contents for many websites.

Extension to Stateless Tracking. Even though this work did not address stateless tracking, such as device fingerprinting, our architecture already hides several fingerprintable device properties and can be extended to several others: (1) The redirection to the Middle Party anonymizes the real IP addresses of users; (2) Some stateless tracking APIs such as `window.navigator`, `window.screen`, and `HTMLCanvasElement` can be easily removed or randomized from the context of the webpage to mitigate in-context fingerprinting.

Possibility to Blocking Active User Recognition in Cross-Context. With the prevalence of third party tracking on the web, we have shown the challenges that a developer will face towards mitigating that. The sandbox attribute for iframes help prevent access to security-sensitive APIs. As tracking has become a hot concern, we suggest that similar mechanisms can help first party websites tackle third party tracking. The sandbox attribute can for instance be extended with specific values to tackle tracking. Nonetheless, the sandbox attribute can be used to prevent cross-context from some stateful tracking mechanisms [9].

5   Evaluation and Case Study

Demo website. We have set up a demo website that embeds a collection of third party content, both in-context and cross-context. In-context content include images, HTML5 audio and video, and a Google Map which further loads dynamic content such as images, fonts, scripts, and CSS files. A Youtube video is embedded as cross-context content in an iframe. The demo website is deployed at `https://sstp-rewriteproxy.inria.fr`. With the deployment of our solution, there is no change from a user perspective on how the demo website is accessed. Indeed, it is still accessible at `https://sstp-rewriteproxy.inria.fr`. However from the server-side, it is the Rewrite Server which is now running at `https://sstp-rewriteproxy.inria.fr` instead of the original server. It then intercepts user requests and forwards them to the original server which has been moved on port 8080 (`http://sstp-rewriteproxy.inria.fr:8080`), hidden from users and the outside.

The Middle Party Server runs at `https://sstp-middleparty.inria.fr`. With our architecture deployed, all requests to fetch third party content embedded in the demo website are redirected to the Middle Party Server. For in-context content, its removes any tracking information in the requests sent by the browser. Then it forwards the requests to the third parties. Any tracking information set by the third parties in the responses are also removed before being forwarded to the browser. For the cross-context content (Youtube Video in our demo), it is not directly loaded as an iframe inside the demo page. Instead, an iframe from the Middle Party Server is created and embedded inside the demo webpage. Then the Youtube video is automatically loaded in another iframe inside this first iframe which context is that of Middle Party Server. During this process, the *Referer* header is not leaked to Youtube (Sect. 3.2), preventing it from identifying the demo website in which it is included. In the Appendix, we show a screenshot of redirection requests to the Middle Party Server.

Real websites. Since we did not have access to real websites, we could not install the Rewrite Server and evaluate our solution on them. We therefore implemented a browser proxy based on a Node.js proxy [11], and included all the logic of the Rewrite Server within the proxy. The proxy was deployed at `https://sstp-rewriteproxy.inria.fr:5555` and acts like the Rewrite Server for real websites intercepting and forwarding requests to them, and rewriting the responses in order to redirect them to our Middle Party Server deployed at `https://sstp-middleparty.inria.fr`.

We then evaluated our solution on different kinds of websites: a news website `http://www.bbc.com`, an entertainment website `http://www.imdb.com`, and a shopping website `http://verbaudet.fr`. All three websites load content from various third party domains. Visually, we did not notice any change in the behaviors of the websites. We also interacted with them in a standard way (clicking on links on a news website, choosing products and putting them in the basket on the shopping website) and the main functionalities of the websites were preserved.

Overall, these evaluation scenarios have helped us improve the solution, especially rewriting dynamically injected third party content. We believe that this implementation will get even mature in the future when we will be able to convince some website owners to deploy it.

Limitations of the evaluation on real websites. The evaluation on the real websites may break some features or introduce performances issues. Here, we discuss such problems and how to prevent them.

Third party identity (OpenID) providers such as Facebook or Google need to use third party cookies in order to be able to authenticate users to websites embedding them. Therefore, stripping off cookies can prevent users from successfully logging in to the related websites. In a deployment scenario, we make it possible for the developer to instruct the Rewrite Server not to rewrite such third party identity provider content so that users can still log in.

Furthermore, it is common for websites to rely on Content Distribution Networks (CDNs), from which they load content for performance purposes. Therefore, rewriting and redirecting CDNs requests to the Middle Party Server can introduce performance issues. In this case also, a developer can declare a list of CDNs which requests should not be rewritten by the Rewrite Server.

Finally, as one may have noticed, the real websites we have considered in our evaluation scenario are all HTTP websites. We could not evaluate our solution on real HTTPS websites because HTTPS requests and responses that arrive at the browser proxy are encrypted. Therefore, we could not be able to rewrite third party content that are embedded in such websites.

6 Related Work

A number of studies have demonstrated that third party tracking is very prevalent on the web today and analyzed the underlying tracking technologies [29,31,34,38]. Lerner et al. [33] analyzed how third party tracking evolved for a period of twenty years. Trackers have been categorized according to either their business relationships with websites [34], their prominence [29,31] or the user browsing profile that they can build [38]. Mayer and Mitchell [34] grouped tracking mechanisms in two categories called stateful (cookie-based and super-cookies) and stateless (fingerprinting). It is rather intuitive to convince ourselves about the effectiveness of a stateful tracking, since it is based on unique identifiers that are set in users browsers. Nonetheless, the efficacy of stateless mechanisms has been extensively demonstrated. Since the pioneer work of Eckersley [28], new fingerprinting methods have been revealed in the literature [22–24,26,27,29,36,40,41]. A classification of fingerprinting techniques is provided in [42]. Those studies have contributed to raising public awareness of tracking privacy threats. Mayer and Mitchell [34] have shown that users are very sensitive to their online privacy, thus hostile to third party tracking. Englehardt et al. [30] have demonstrated that tracking can be used for surveillance purposes. The success of anti-tracking defenses is yet another illustration that users are concerned about tracking [35].

There are a number of defenses that try to protect users against third party tracking. First, major browser vendors do natively provide mechanisms for users to block third party cookies or browse in private/incognito mode for instance. More and more browsers even take a step further, considering privacy as a design principle: Tor Browser [17], TrackingFree [37], Blink [32], CLIQZ [3].

But the most popular defenses are browser extensions. Being tightly integrated into browsers, they provide additional privacy features that are not natively implemented in browsers. Well known privacy extensions are Disconnect [6], Ghostery [7], ShareMeNot [38], which is now part of PrivacyBadger [13], uBlock Origin [20] and a relatively new MyTrackingChoices [25]. Merzdovnik et al. [35] provide a large-scale evaluation of these anti-tracking defenses. Well known trackers such as advertisers, which businesses heavily depend on tracking, have also been taking steps towards limiting their own tracking capabilities [34]. The W3C is pushing forward the Do Not Track standard [18,19] for users to easily express their tracking preferences so that trackers may comply with them. To the best of our knowledge, we are the first to investigate how a website owner can embed third party content while preventing them from accidentally tracking users. The idea of proxying requests within a webpage is inspired by web service workers API [16], though this API is still a working draft which is currently being tested in Mozilla Firefox and Google Chrome.

7   Conclusions

Most of the previous research analyzed third party tracking mechanisms, and how to block tracking from a user perspective. In this work, we classified third party tracking capabilities from a website developer perspective. We proposed a new architecture for website developers that allows to embed third party content while preserving users privacy. We implemented our solution, and evaluated it on real websites to mitigate stateful tracking.

Appendix

Screenshots of the demo website map console (Fig. 5).

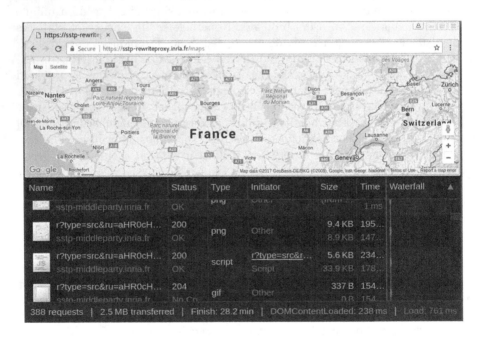

Fig. 5. A demo page displaying a Google Maps

References

1. Browsing Contexts. https://www.w3.org/TR/html51/browsers.html
2. Cascading Style Sheets. https://www.w3.org/Style/CSS/
3. CLIQZ. https://cliqz.com
4. Cross-origin-resource sharing. https://developer.mozilla.org/en-US/docs/Web/HTTP/Access_control_CORS
5. CSS Parser for Node.js. https://github.com/reworkcss/css
6. Disconnect. https://disconnect.me/
7. Ghostery. https://www.ghostery.com/
8. HTML Parser for Node.js. https://github.com/tmpvar/jsdom
9. Iframe Sandbox Attribute. https://www.w3.org/TR/2011/WD-html5-20110525/the-iframe-element.html#attr-iframe-sandbox
10. Node.js. https://nodejs.org/en/
11. Node.js Proxy. https://newspaint.wordpress.com/2012/11/05/node-js-http-and-https-proxy
12. PostMessage - Cross-Origin Iframe Secure Communication. https://developer.mozilla.org/en-US/docs/Web/API/Window/postMessage
13. Privacy Badger. https://www.eff.org/fr/privacybadger
14. Reverse Proxy. https://en.wikipedia.org/wiki/Revers_proxy
15. Same Origin Policy. https://www.w3.org/Security/wiki/Same_Origin_Policy
16. Service Worker API. https://developer.mozilla.org/en-US/docs/Web/API/Service_Worker_API
17. Tor Browser. https://www.torproject.org/projects/torbrowser/design/
18. Tracking Compliance and Scope. https://www.w3.org/TR/tracking-compliance/
19. Tracking Preference Expression. https://www.w3.org/TR/tracking-dnt/
20. uBlock Origin. https://www.ublock.org/
21. URL. https://www.w3.org/TR/url
22. Abgrall, E., Traon, Y.L., Monperrus, M., Gombault, S., Heiderich, M., Ribault, A.: XSS-FP: browser fingerprinting using HTML parser quirks. CoRR (2012)
23. Acar, G., Eubank, C., Englehardt, S., Juárez, M., Narayanan, A., Díaz, C.: The web never forgets: persistent tracking mechanisms in the wild. In: Proceedings of CCS 2014 (2014)
24. Acar, G., Juárez, M., Nikiforakis, N., Díaz, C., Gürses, S.F., Piessens, F., Preneel, B.: FPDetective: dusting the web for fingerprinters. In: Proceedings of CCS 2013 (2013)
25. Achara, J.P., Parra-Arnau, J., Castelluccia, C.: Mytrackingchoices: pacifying the ad-block war by enforcing user privacy preferences. CoRR (2016)
26. Boda, K., Földes, Á.M., Gulyás, G.G., Imre, S.: User tracking on the web via cross-browser fingerprinting. In: Laud, P. (ed.) NordSec 2011. LNCS, vol. 7161, pp. 31–46. Springer, Heidelberg (2012). doi:10.1007/978-3-642-29615-4_4
27. Cao, Y., Li, S., Wijmans, E.: (cross-)browser fingerprinting via os and hardware level features. In: Proceedings of the 24th NDSS (2017)
28. Eckersley, P.: How unique is your web browser? In: Atallah, M.J., Hopper, N.J. (eds.) PETS 2010. LNCS, vol. 6205, pp. 1–18. Springer, Heidelberg (2010). doi:10.1007/978-3-642-14527-8_1
29. Englehardt, S., Narayanan, A.: Online tracking: a 1-million-site measurement and analysis. In: Proceedings of the 2016 CCS, pp. 1388–1401 (2016)
30. Englehardt, S., Reisman, D., Eubank, C., Zimmerman, P., Mayer, J., Narayanan, A., Felten, E.W.: Cookies that give you away: The surveillance implications of web tracking. In: Proceedings of the 24th WWW, pp. 289–299 (2015)

31. Krishnamurthy, B., Wills, C.E.: Privacy diffusion on the web: a longitudinal perspective. In: Proceedings of the 18th WWW, pp. 541–550 (2009)
32. Laperdrix, P., Rudametkin, W., Baudry, B.: Beauty and the beast: diverting modern web browsers to build unique browser fingerprints. In: Proceedings of IEEE SP 2016 (2016)
33. Lerner, A., Simpson, A.K., Kohno, T., Roesner, F.: Internet jones and the raiders of the lost trackers: an archaeological study of web tracking from 1996 to 2016. In: Proceedings of the 25th USENIX Security, Austin, TX (2016)
34. Mayer, J.R., Mitchell, J.C.: Third-party web tracking: policy and technology. In: Proceedings of the 2012 IEEE SP, pp. 413–427 (2012)
35. Merzdovnik, G., Huber, M., Buhov, D., Nikiforakis, N., Neuner, S., Schmiedecker, M., Weippl, E.: Block me if you can: a large-scale study of tracker-blocking tools. In: Proceedings of the 2nd EuroSP, Paris, France (2017)
36. Nikiforakis, N., Kapravelos, A., Joosen, W., Kruegel, C., Piessens, F., Vigna, G.: Cookieless monster: exploring the ecosystem of web-based device fingerprinting. In: Proceedings of the 2013 IEEE SP, pp. 541–555 (2013)
37. Pan, X., Cao, Y., Chen, Y.: I do not know what you visited last summer: protecting users from stateful third-party web tracking with trackingfree browser. In: Proceedings of the 22nd NDSS (2015)
38. Roesner, F., Kohno, T., Wetherall, D.: Detecting and defending against third-party tracking on the web. In: Proceedings of the 9th NSDI, pp. 155–168 (2012)
39. Soltani, A., Canty, S., Mayo, Q., Thomas, L., Hoofnagle, C.J.: Flash cookies and privacy. In: AAAI Spring Symposium: Intelligent Information Privacy Management, pp. 158–163 (2010)
40. Starov, O., Nikiforakis, N.: Extended tracking powers: measuring the privacy diffusion enabled by browser extensions. In: Proceedings of the 2017 WWW (2017)
41. Takei, N., Saito, T., Takasu, K., Yamada, T.: Web browser fingerprinting using only cascading style sheets. In: Proceedings of the 10th BWCCA, pp. 57–63 (2015)
42. Upathilake, R., Li, Y., Matrawy, A.: A classification of web browser fingerprinting techniques. In: Proceedings of the 7th NTMS, pp. 1–5 (2015)
43. West, M.: Mixed Content (2016). https://www.w3.org/TR/mixed-content/
44. West, M., Barth, A., Veditz, D.: Content Security Policy Level 2 (2015)

Idea-Caution Before Exploitation: The Use of Cybersecurity Domain Knowledge to Educate Software Engineers Against Software Vulnerabilities

Tayyaba Nafees[(⊠)], Natalie Coull[(⊠)], Robert Ian Ferguson[(⊠)],
and Adam Sampson [(⊠)]

School of Arts, Media and Computer Games,
University of Abertay Dundee, Dundee DD1 1HG, UK
{1405357, N. Coull, ian. ferguson,
A. Sampson}@abertay.ac.uk,
http://www.abertay.ac.uk

Abstract. The transfer of cybersecurity domain knowledge from security experts ('Ethical Hackers') to software engineers is discussed in terms of desirability and feasibility. Possible mechanisms for the transfer are critically examined. Software engineering methodologies do not make use of security domain knowledge in its form of vulnerability databases (e.g. CWE, CVE, Exploit DB), which are therefore not appropriate for this purpose. An approach based upon the improved use of pattern languages that encompasses security domain knowledge is proposed.

Keywords: Software Development Lifecycle (SDLC) · Security Pattern (SP) · Software Fault Pattern (SFP) · Attack Pattern (AP) · Vulnerability DataBase (VDB)

1 Introduction

Programmers make mistakes. There are '15–50 errors per 1000 lines of delivered code' [1]. Much research effort has concentrated on addressing this problem [2]. Of particular concern are those software flaws that lead to security vulnerabilities. The deliberate misuse of such a vulnerability is termed an exploitation, resulting in information leaks, and reduce the value or usefulness of the system [3]. Generally, software developers do not understand the security as their focus is on delivering features, rather than on ensuring the software security, so it is often considered as something to be added to a system as a bolt-on component into later stages of development. However, the cost of fixing bugs post software release is estimated to be 30 times pre-release cost [4]. Testing has poor relation with security. It is unusual for the software developer to use testing approaches for finding vulnerabilities; this issue has not received the research attention it requires [5]. One implication of this is that security concerns should be embedded into the software development lifecycle (including the early phases) [6].

© Springer International Publishing AG 2017
E. Bodden et al. (Eds.): ESSoS 2017, LNCS 10379, pp. 133–142, 2017.
DOI: 10.1007/978-3-319-62105-0_9

90% of security incidents result from exploitation of flaws in software [7]. In reality, however, software developers struggle against recurring and consistent software flaws (i.e. buffer overflows and integer overflows), which are exploited daily by malicious hackers. Nonetheless, a large body of knowledge about software vulnerabilities exists within the cybersecurity community, in particular amongst penetration testers and ethical hackers. The term 'Ethical Hacker' (EH) will be used as a shorthand to denote this community. Currently ethical hackers put much effort into classifying discovered vulnerabilities and developing taxonomies of these vulnerabilities. Such vulnerabilities are then catalogued in publicly available vulnerability databases (VDBs) [8]. Software developers have worked to embed security within the software development lifecycle (SDLC) [9] in order to fix the deployment errors. The mechanism of knowledge transfers between the work on vulnerability databases (VDBs), developers' perceptions of security issues and the security development lifecycle (SDLC) is complex, which creates a distinct communication gap between ethical hackers and software engineers [10]. Interception of (knowledge) communication directs software developers to repeat persistent prevalent vulnerabilities and gives rise to software flaws exploitation. Various attempts to capture and formalize the transferring knowledge in a manner appropriate to software engineers have been made, including Misuse Patterns [11], Software Fault Patterns (SFP) [12], and Security Patterns (SP) [13]. The need for a better understanding of this mechanism and our proposed solution is the subject of remainder of this paper, which is structured as follows: Sect. 2 examines previous work in this area and leads the following hypotheses (Table 1).

Table 1. Proposed hypotheses

H-1	Software developers lack the conscious understanding to identify recurring software flaws during software development process due to stagnated and possibly degrading vulnerabilities' knowledge transfer
H-2	Patterns (anti-patterns, security patterns and attack patterns) are an appropriate means of communicating knowledge of vulnerabilities from ethical hackers to software engineers. However, existing applications of these pattern languages fail to do so

In Sect. 3, shortcomings of previous attempts are analyzed and in Sect. 4, proposals for a pattern-based approach (Vulnerability Anti-Pattern) to the problems are presented.

2   Background and Related Work

2.1   Building Security by Software Engineers

Other researchers had attempted addressing software developers' security concerns as part of the software development process. For example, earlier attempts have been conducted based upon improving libraries, implementation languages, and language processors [14, 15]. Approaches based on static and dynamic code analysis have been proposed by providing different guidelines, such as SDL banned functions [16]. Software engineers have attempted early exclusion of the vulnerabilities by considering

Table 2. Approaches to embed security in software development processes

Name	Description
Security development lifecycle (SDL)	SDL is proposed to reduce software maintenance costs and increase reliability of software with regards to software security related bugs. Cybersecurity standards, such as ISO 27001 are incorporated into the SDL to ensure that any software produced with this process complies with industry recognized standards. However, compliance with standards does not necessarily lead to all vulnerabilities being eliminated from software. The lacking of this model is discussed in Sect. 4.2
OWASP CLASP	OWASP Comprehensive, Lightweight Application Security Process includes a set of guidelines for web security requirements, cheat sheets, a development guide, a code review and a testing guide, tools and information about top web security vulnerabilities. This is explored further in Sect. 4.2
Security patterns (SP)	It defines as a solution to stop or mitigate a set of specified threats through certain security mechanisms, and designing to assist software developers who are not security experts with embedding security in their systems. It can also be a useful tool for teaching security concepts [18]. This is explored further in (Sect. 4.2). However, they are not based directly on the vulnerability knowledge stored in VDBs, which is necessary for achieving currency and a timely response to new threats [19]

security issues at all phases of the SDLC. Examples of these approaches are considered in Table 2: [13, 17].

2.2 Attempts by Ethical Hacker to Catalogue and Use Patterns to Communicate Vulnerabilities

The National Vulnerability Database (NVD) comprises CWE, CVE and CAPEC, which are the three most comprehensive vulnerability databases (VDBs). They are open-source and maintained by MITRE [20] as shown in Table 3.

Table 3. Attempts to catalogue vulnerabilities

Name	Description
CWE	The Common Weakness Enumeration database (CWE) catalogues weaknesses that can occur in software. These weaknesses are described as software bugs that can lead to vulnerabilities
CVE	The Common Vulnerabilities Enumeration database (CVE) catalogues specific examples of publicly known vulnerabilities that exist in software
CAPEC	The Common Attack Pattern Enumeration and Classification database (CAPEC) provides formal attack patterns, while considering the CVE examples and CWE information

In addition to the above VDBs, security experts have also endeavored to embed their knowledge of vulnerabilities in the form of patterns (as shown in Table 4) such as SFP, AP and Misuse pattern. This will be explored further in Sect. 3.4.

Table 4. Attempts to use patterns to communicate vulnerabilities

Name	Description
Software fault patterns (SFP)	SFP is aligned with the CWE database, whose contains a formal specification of weaknesses (vulnerabilities) and will be explored further in Sect. 3.4. However, a lack of detailed information about the structure and format of SFP presents a considerable obstacle for software developers
Attack patterns (AP)	AP is derived from CAPEC database, which describes a procedure of a particular vulnerability attack format. However, it is not intended as a source of design patterns (like standard software pattern) Generally, the complicated structure and understanding difficulty restrain developers in their usage. There is not much research done on usage of attack pattern by software developers due to their inherent complexity
Misuse patterns	It describes the malicious hacker generic prospect while considering sub-dimensions, which classifying into set of attack actions and enumerating with possible security patterns as a countermeasure [13]. Although, the misuse pattern groundwork clearly evidences the no usage of cybersecurity knowledge sources (i.e. VDBs) in defining attack action. Thus far, misuse patterns have certain construction deficiencies and lack considerable usage for developers

3 Analysis

3.1 Potential Causes of Poor Knowledge Sharing

The lack of a shared understanding between the Software Engineering and Ethical Hacking communities is well documented [21, 22]. Although there are exceptions, security testing typically takes place as an activity during the SDLC. Ethical Hackers communicate with and report to system administrators and IT managers. Although, there is some crossover between the ground knowledge and skill-set of a software engineer and an ethical hacker, they own some very distinct technical domains, with different educational paths, different technical languages and different professional bodies. Generally, a malicious hacker does not work under the same constraints of project schedules and deadlines as a software engineer does. If they wish to spend six months examining in minute detail of the state of stack under a particular attack condition, they will not have employers pressurizing employees, to deliver. Thus, they have the advantage of time. This coupled with the extensive knowledge sharing that takes place amongst the hacking community [23] means that a hacker may be more familiar with the weaknesses in a particular piece of software than those who created it.

3.2 Software Engineering Problems

The approaches from Sect. 3.1 are attempts by the software engineering community to enable the integration of security concerns into the process of developing software. The approaches, such as SDL, OWASP CLASP and SP, focus only on fulfilling security guidelines and standards rather than raising awareness of vulnerabilities. SDL does not embed any knowledge from cybersecurity experts and are challenging for those software developers who have limited awareness and understanding of the security vulnerabilities in order to apply the security guidelines effectively. The organizational emphasis of SDL may also be of limited applicability in the informal world of cross platform application deployment. OWASP CLASP implementation is limited to web-based systems. Furthermore, the value of SPs in order to provide usable and understandable documentation for developers is questionable due to their complexity [24], and they are generally not adopted by developers due to their poorly described implementation [25]. This can be attributed to the lack of an accepted standard catalogue and a lack of methodological support.

3.3 Cyber Security Problems

The various databases described are maintained by cybersecurity professionals to keep track of known vulnerabilities in the different versions of released software. It is clear that the intended audience for these databases is not software engineers involved in developing software but rather systems administrators looking to secure their existing systems. It might be possible that the information contained therein is simply not generalized enough to be directly relevant for software developers to use in the development process. Some of the difficulties that software developers face are enumerated in Table 5.

Table 5. VDBs issues

No standardization	No standard taxonomy/classification scheme for existing VDBs, thus each of them use their own approach, none of which were explicitly designed to use during SDLC. As such, these VDBs can typically appear complex and ambiguous to the software developer [26–28]
Limited knowledge	Closed source VDBs, such as the Carnegie-Mellon US Cert database and Secunia, are of necessity limited in the information that they can show concerning code-level errors
Complexed knowledge	It is clearly shown by many research studies, which have compared vulnerability information across the multiple VDBs that these repositories are deficient in providing interoperability, knowledge consistency and are not following standard classification schemes [29, 30]

3.4 Addressing Shortcomings of Previous Pattern-Based Attempts

Section 3.3 discussed previous attempts to use patterns/pattern languages in the cybersecurity context. These attempts highlighted the following shortcomings: a distinct communication gap between software developers and ethical hackers; software developers lack conscious understanding about prevalent vulnerabilities because of unusable and complicated knowledge sources, SDLC does not adequately address software security practices, and finally there are limited efforts from both the cybersecurity and software engineering communities to work together to address software vulnerabilities. It is clear that the use of patterns can only succeed in the context of an appropriate software development process, which must include knowledge from the VDBs. The author's future work will examine the way in which patterns can be used to capture VBDs knowledge in a usable format, the need to provide understandable vulnerabilities' awareness to developers is emphasized by Fahl et al. and Acar et al. work [31, 32]. The desirability of a methodology and tool is also support by McGraw [27] and Borstad [33].

4 Practical Proposition: Our Solution

To address these issues, our research has led to the creation of a set of 'Vulnerability Anti-Patterns', based on the OWASP Top 10 Vulnerabilities. Our anti-patterns have been constructed following two main stages: knowledge extraction (1-knowledge pulling process sourced from VDBs and security patterns) and knowledge provision (2-knowledge pushing process to educate developers through anti-patterns).

4.1 The Knowledge Extraction (1-Knowledge Pulling Process)

The knowledge pulling process sourced by cybersecurity community such as VDBs (CWE, CVE), security patterns and attack pattern databases (CAPEC), and collected essential information of the vulnerability. For example, general information, root-causes and attack procedures. This is the first step towards addressing the communication gap. The knowledge pulling process comprises two sub-parts: (1) Creating a taxonomy of vulnerabilities. The taxonomy includes vulnerability info, vulnerability footprints or characteristics and mitigation categories; (2) generating a decision tree which describes the vital VDBs information, and shows safeguard and injury paths that map security incidents with their low-level and high-level root-causes of vulnerabilities in respective phase of software development life cycle (SDLC).

4.2 Knowledge Provision (2-Knowledge Pushing Process)

Extracted knowledge passed to the knowledge pushing process, which captures previous process formalized information in the form of patterns, known as Vulnerability Anti-Patterns that is most appropriate mechanism to communicate knowledge of vulnerabilities to software developers.

4.2.1 The Notion of Vulnerability Anti-pattern (VAP)

A recurring error or vulnerability initiates an anti-pattern, which can occur due to any poor software design or implementation errors. Same in the case of vulnerabilities, which are, commonly reoccurring flaws, so why does not capture and address the fundamental problems of cybersecurity through anti-patterns. A VAP describes a problem, i.e. poor practice that negatively causes a security flaw, and a solution, i.e. a set of refactoring actions that can be carried out to mitigate or stop flaws. In contrast to SP, which are only designed to perceive a threat, not to repair a vulnerability, and VDBs that appear complicated for developers' understanding and are generally not considered as a part of developers' security practices. It has been argued [34] that the prevalent software errors occurred because of established software practices that actually have negative impact during SDLC. Such poor practices generally cause prevalent vulnerabilities. It can thus be suggested that these poor practices need to be identified and refactored so safe solutions can be generated [35]. The use of anti-patterns for finding and understanding vulnerabilities is understudied, particularly for software developers. VAP can describe poor practices or solutions, which aid in reasoning about and communicating unsuccessful design intent, and introduce refactored solutions, which suggests safe alternative procedures. The advantage of adopting VAP during software development process is that it bridges the knowledge gap between software developers and security experts about commonly occurring software flaws. This finding has important implications for developing security training methods. Therefore, an anti-pattern is suggested for the vulnerability that includes necessary vulnerability information in a well-defined and usable format for those inexperienced and naive developers who do not understand security and can be an effective way of communicating vulnerable poor practices, so developers can learn valuable lesson from other fellows' successes and failures. Without this wisdom, anti-patterns of prevalent vulnerabilities will continue to persist.

Vulnerability Anti-Pattern: A Proposed Solution. Authors propose a new refactored solution called 'Vulnerability Anti-Patterns' that are intended to provide the developers' security necessary awareness. Since the vulnerability anti-patterns' core objective is to highlight the entire software exploitation potential, each pattern has been written to describe the following: general practices of the anti-pattern (i.e. how it could be misused), examples such as CVE (real-world exploitation) and sample vulnerable code, and finally the footstep of risk patterns within SDLC, the refactored solution and related solutions in the form of security patterns. Ultimately, the anti-patterns should enable the developers to realize the root-cause of the vulnerability. In regards to the proposed solutions (or countermeasures to the vulnerabilities), we anticipate that the anti-patterns will encourage the developers to retain a deep understanding and conscious alertness of vulnerabilities in their future development practices. Our template for an anti-pattern is presented below. We have utilized this template and produced complete anti-patterns for 10 vulnerabilities to date. In addition to the complete pattern data outlined below, we have also produced an abridged version of each pattern, which describes, using languages from various different programming languages how each vulnerability can be exploited (Table 6).

Table 6. Vulnerability Anti-Pattern template.

Pattern main-division	Pattern sub-division
1. Vulnerability anti-pattern general info	1.1 Anti-pattern name:
	1.2 Also known as:
	1.3 Most frequent scale in SDLC: Requirement specification, Design, Implementation/Coding-phase
	1.4 Problem description:
	1.5 CWE mapping: CWE-ID, General name
	1.6 Related CWEs:
	1.7 CVE example:
2. Anti-pattern (Problematic solution)	2.1 Refactored solution name:
	2.2 Refactored solution type: Software pattern, Technology pattern, Process pattern, Role pattern
	2.3 Root causes (Context): Unbalanced Forces related to meeting requirements, controlling technology changes, controlling use and implementation of people
	2.4 Risk patterns and consequences:
	2.5 Typical causes
3. Problem fingerprints	3.1 Software Fault Pattern (SFP)
4. Known exploitation	4.1 Attack Pattern (Attack patterns-CAPEC)
5. Mitigation (Refactors the problem)	5.1 Refactored solutions:
	5.1.1 Solution steps SDLC, Description
	5.2 Examples: (Real-world Patch Example)
	5.3 Pen testing techniques
	5.4 Related Solutions(SP):
	5.4.1 General solution (All in one solution)
	5.4.2 Language solution

4.3   Evaluation

To evaluate the effectiveness of 'Vulnerability Anti-Patterns, we are in the process of conducting a series of experiments with software developers from two international organizations and computing students from our own university. **Stage-1:** Pre-assessment evaluation to measure participants' actual awareness about poor development practices. **Stage-2:** Participants are trained while using informal versions of the vulnerability anti-patterns. **Stage-3:** Post assessment evaluation to how much participants able to improve their understanding of vulnerabilities accompanied by the formal version of vulnerability anti-patterns. **Stage-4:** Comparative analysis performed between trained and untrained developers to measure the progression in developers' abilities to identify and understand the most commonly persistent software flaws regarding the efficiency of vulnerability anti-patterns.

5 Conclusion

Secure software development is one of the most challenging areas of cybersecurity. Although, the cybersecurity industry is mature and generates a wealth of resources on discovered software vulnerabilities in the form of VDBs, software developers are continuing to produce recurring and persistent software flaws at an alarming rate. The software engineering community has also worked to embed security into the SDLC; however, these independent efforts fail to provide effective solutions against prevalent vulnerabilities. Hackers on a daily basis exploit a large number of fatal development errors. Software developers are largely unaware of the design and implementation-level security flaws (poor development practices) which generally turn into fatal security weaknesses (vulnerabilities). There exists a big communication gap between the software developers and security experts, which does not help them to solve this problem. The research proposes a methodology to use a pattern for transferring a necessary vulnerabilities knowledge to software developers through 'Vulnerability Anti-Pattern', and considers the use of patterns to communicate knowledge of software vulnerabilities in usable format with the best means of avoiding their creation. It bridges the communication gap between them with assistance of classified cybersecurity knowledge sources such as VDBs, which ultimately share essential information about common errors and help to identify software developers' secure ideas to build secure software. We propose that one solution to this problem lies in the use of patterns languages (with appropriate methodological, tool and training support) to better capture and communicate the information currently held in VDBs to create a 'Safe Development Environment'. Therefore, knowledge of vulnerabilities can bridge the communication gap between cybersecurity and software engineering communities. It is toward this goal that our future work, based upon this initial study will be directed.

References

1. McConnell, S.: Code Complete: A Practical Handbook of Software Construction. Microsoft, Redmond (1993)
2. Todorov, A.: User guide for open source project bug submissions (2015). http://opensource.com/business/13/10/user-guide-bugs-open-source-projects
3. Leveson, N.: A new accident model for engineering safer systems. Saf. Sci. **42**, 237–270 (2004)
4. Cabinet Office: The cost of cybercrime (2011)
5. Bekrar, S., et al.: Finding software vulnerabilities by smart fuzzing, pp. 427–430 (2011)
6. Jorgensen, P.C.: Software Testing: A Craftsman's Approach. CRC Press, Boca Raton (2013)
7. DHS: Cyber incident response at DHS (2017)
8. Aslam, T., Krsul, I., Spafford, E.H.: Use of a taxonomy of security faults (1996)
9. Howard, M., Lipner, S.: The security development lifecycle: a process for developing demonstrably more secure software (2006)

142   T. Nafees et al.

10. Busch, M., Koch, N., Wirsing, M.: Evaluation of engineering approaches in the secure software development life cycle. In: Heisel, M., Joosen, W., Lopez, J., Martinelli, F. (eds.) Engineering Secure Future Internet Services and Systems. LNCS, vol. 8431, pp. 234–265. Springer, Cham (2014). doi:10.1007/978-3-319-07452-8_10
11. Fernandez, E.B., Yoshioka, N., Washizaki, H.: A worm misuse pattern, No. 2 (2010)
12. Mansourov, D.N.: Software fault patterns: towards formal compliance points for CWE (2011)
13. Schumacher, M., et al.: Security Patterns: Integrating Security and Systems Engineering. Wiley, Hoboken (2013)
14. Bourque, P., Fairley, R.E.: Guide to the Software Engineering Body of Knowledge (SWEBOK (R)): Version 3.0. IEEE Computer Society Press, Washington, D.C. (2014)
15. Shiralkar, T., Grove B.: Guidelines for secure coding (2009)
16. Howard, M.: Security development lifecycle (SDL) banned function calls (2012)
17. Howard, M., Lipner, S.: The Security Development Lifecycle. Microsoft Press, Redmond (2006)
18. Brenner, J.: ISO 27001: Risk management and compliance. Risk Manage. **54**, 24 (2007)
19. Halkidis, S., et al.: A qualitative analysis of software security patterns. Comput. Secur. **25**, 379–392 (2006)
20. MITRE Corporation: Common weakness enumeration (2015). http://cwe.mitre.org/
21. Van Wyk, K.R., McGraw, G.: Bridging the gap between software development and information security. IEEE Secur. Privacy **3**, 75–79 (2005)
22. Viega, J., McGraw, G.: Building Secure Software: How to Avoid Security Problems the Right Way Portable Documents. Pearson Education, Essex (2001)
23. Mansourov, N., et al.: Why hackers know more about our systems, pp. 1–21 (2011)
24. Bunke, M.: Software-security patterns: degree of maturity, p. 42 (2015)
25. Fernandez-Buglioni, E.: Security Patterns in Practice: Designing Secure Architectures Using Software Patterns. Wiley, Hoboken (2013)
26. Hui, Z., Huang, S., Ren, Z., Yao, Y.: Review of software security defects taxonomy. In: Yu, J., Greco, S., Lingras, P., Wang, G., Skowron, A. (eds.) RSKT 2010. LNCS, vol. 6401, pp. 310–321. Springer, Heidelberg (2010). doi:10.1007/978-3-642-16248-0_46
27. McGraw, G.: Software Security: Building Security In. Addison-Wesley Professional, Boston (2006)
28. Huang, C., Lin, F., Lin, F.Y., Sun, Y.S.: A novel approach to evaluate software vulnerability prioritization. J. Syst. Software **86**, 2822–2840 (2013)
29. Ghani, H., et al.: Predictive vulnerability scoring in the context of insufficient information availability, pp. 1–8 (2013)
30. Yun-hua, G., Pei, L.: Design and research on vulnerability database (2010)
31. Fahl, S., et al.: Rethinking SSL development in an appified world, pp. 49–60 (2013)
32. Acar, Y., et al.: You get where you're looking for: the impact of information sources on code security, pp. 289–305 (2016)
33. Borstad, O.G.: Finding security patterns to countermeasure software vulnerabilities (2008)
34. McGraw, G.: Software security. **36**, 662–665 (2012)
35. Julisch, K.: Understanding and overcoming cyber security anti-patterns. Comput. Netw. **57**, 2206–2211 (2013)

Defeating Zombie Gadgets by Re-randomizing Code upon Disclosure

Micah Morton[1]($\boxtimes$), Hyungjoon Koo[2], Forrest Li[1], Kevin Z. Snow[3],
Michalis Polychronakis[2], and Fabian Monrose[1]

[1] University of North Carolina at Chapel Hill, Chapel Hill, NC, USA
`micah@cs.unc.edu`
[2] Stony Brook University, Stony Brook, NY, USA
[3] ZeroPoint Dynamics, Cary, NC, USA

Abstract. Over the past few years, return-oriented programming (ROP) attacks have emerged as a prominent strategy for hijacking control of software. The full power and flexibility of ROP attacks was recently demonstrated using *just-in-time* ROP tactics (`JIT-ROP`), whereby an adversary repeatedly leverages a memory disclosure vulnerability to identify useful instruction sequences and compile them into a functional ROP payload at runtime. Since the advent of just-in-time code reuse attacks, numerous proposals have surfaced for mitigating them, the most practical of which involve the re-randomization of code at runtime or the destruction of gadgets upon their disclosure. Even so, several avenues exist for performing *code inference*, which allows `JIT-ROP` attacks to infer values at specific code locations without directly reading the memory contents of those bytes. This is done by reloading code of interest or implicitly determining the state of randomized code. These so-called *"zombie gadgets"* completely undermine defenses that rely on destroying code bytes once they are read. To mitigate these attacks, we present a low-overhead, binary-compatible defense which ensures an attacker is unable to execute gadgets that were identified through code reloading or code inference. We have implemented a prototype of the proposed defense for closed-source Windows binaries, and demonstrate that our approach effectively prevents zombie gadget attacks with negligible runtime overhead.

Keywords: Code reuse · `JIT-ROP` · Code inference · Destructive reads

1 Introduction

In recent years, memory corruption attacks have become increasingly sophisticated. For example, present day exploits on commodity systems must circumvent Address Space Layout Randomization (ASLR), a widely deployed defense which requires the adversary to use *memory disclosure* to compute the addresses of useful gadgets in a program before repurposing them for malicious means. Researchers and practitioners recently proposed further approaches to harden

© Springer International Publishing AG 2017
E. Bodden et al. (Eds.): ESSoS 2017, LNCS 10379, pp. 143–160, 2017.
DOI: 10.1007/978-3-319-62105-0_10

vulnerable applications against memory disclosure, through focusing on more fine-grained forms of code diversification [26,31]. In turn, attackers responded with the development of "just-in-time" ROP (JIT-ROP), a style of attack that leverages the dynamic scripting capabilities of document renderers and web browsers to repeatedly disclose memory in order to build exploit payloads at runtime, all the while making no assumptions about the layout of code and thus circumventing fine-grained ASLR [28].

Not willing to be outdone, defenders developed several new mechanisms in order to stay one step ahead of attackers armed with scripted memory disclosure capabilities. In this vein, proposed compile-time defenses [7,12] effectively mitigate JIT-ROP attacks by enforcing code memory to be executable but not readable—eliminating an attacker's ability to use memory disclosure to enumerate and read code pages. In an effort to be more readily deployable to closed-source software, other binary-compatible defenses have attempted to apply on-demand code randomization [6,10,33] or gadget destruction [30,32] at *runtime* in order to protect against JIT-ROP.

Unfortunately, the most promising JIT-ROP defenses either have major hurdles to overcome in achieving widespread deployability [29], due to their reliance on source code access and compiler support [7,12,13], or have been shown to be vulnerable to ingenious advancements in JIT-ROP capabilities. In particular, Snow et al. [27] demonstrated that existing execute-only memory protections applicable at the binary level based on the concept of destructive code reads [30,32] can be bypassed using code reloading, JIT code generation, or implicit code disclosure attacks. As explained in Sect. 4, these clever evasion techniques are made possible through the attacker's ability to re-load a given code module multiple times or to deduce the values of certain code bytes based on values of related instructions. That said, the shortcomings of previous binary-compatible defenses do not indicate that the task of defending against code reuse is insurmountable. Rather, in this work we propose further advancements to existing defense paradigms that aptly harden them against these powerful code reloading and code inference strategies.

In this paper, we identify two concepts as the pillars of any effective JIT-ROP defense that seeks to prevent the execution of disclosed gadgets. We refer to these as the *trigger* and *countermeasure* of a defense, respectively. These terms come from the fact that part of the defense must be *triggered* when an attacker has disclosed potentially useful executable bytes in memory, and some subsequent *countermeasure* must be taken to ensure those bytes cannot be leveraged by an attacker for hijacking control of the application. The purpose of this work is to adapt ideas put forth by existing defenses that implement runtime gadget destruction [30,32] by making novel extensions to both the trigger and countermeasure components. At its core, our defense features the ability to efficiently and robustly re-randomize program instructions in response to their code bytes being disclosed by an attacker. Specifically, to deal with code reloading attacks, our approach detects when code modules that could contain fresh usable copies of gadgets (that were previously disclosed and destroyed in another instance of that module) are about to be loaded, and replaces them with new randomized versions. In addition, to deal with the more sophisticated code inference attacks, our approach re-randomizes upon each destructive read the subset of the code that could potentially be implicitly disclosed.

2   Goals and Adversarial Model

Our goal is to provide a binary-compatible defense against just-in-time code reuse attacks [28]. We are particularly interested in sound defenses that have low runtime overhead and are applicable to real world programs and their complexities. We assume the attacker has full power of scripted arbitrary memory disclosure as well as the ability to cause arbitrary code modules to be loaded or unloaded, per the attacks recently presented by Snow et al. [27]. Specifically, we assume that *i.* Data Execution Prevention, *ii.* Fine-grained Address Space Layout Randomization (*e.g.,* [7,15,19,26,31]) and *iii.* Destructive read capabilities that leverage execute-only memory (*e.g.,* [8,30,32]) are in use. We also assume that adversary have at their disposal a memory disclosure vulnerability that allows them to read and write arbitrary memory locations. By now, these assumptions are commonly accepted as being no stronger than the capabilities already leveraged by skilled adversaries (*e.g.,* [6,9,12,18,28]) to defeat contemporary ASLR.

3   Background and Related Work

Over the past several years, a number of defenses (*e.g.,* [4,6,7,10–12,15,16,19–21,30,32,33]) have been suggested as ways to curtail the power of just-in-time code reuse attacks. Interested readers are referred to Crane et al. [13] for an excellent review of the current state of the art in return oriented programming attacks. Here, we instead focus on existing defensive strategies in terms of the *triggers* they utilize and their runtime *countermeasures*. To date, a myriad of triggers have been proposed, such as invoking countermeasures as a result of file I/O [6], process forking [24], or elapsed wall-time [10,33]. At the same time, the runtime countermeasures involve either re-randomizing code layout [6,10,24,33] or overwriting disclosed code bytes as a way to ensure they cannot be leveraged in a ROP payload [30,32].

Unfortunately, the existing approaches all have significant shortcomings. For example, Bigelow et al. [6] assumes that scripting environments are out of scope, and so their approach cannot protect widely used applications like modern browsers or document renderers; the work of Chen et al. [10] only offers a probabilistic defense, and the recent proposals of Tang et al. [30] and Werner et al. [32] have been undermined using only modest enhancements to the original JIT-ROP framework [27]. Additionally, many of these proposed defenses suffer from shortcomings in terms of real-world applicability (*e.g.,* such as poor performance guarantees or lack of compatibility with multi-threaded programs) or require the ability to re-compile code from source in order to enable the proposed protections [7,12,13]. Although the ability to recompile software for added security enforcement is often an ideal avenue for mitigating software threats, such defenses that require access to source code are not positioned for near-term deployability in the same way as binary-compatible defenses. Since binary-compatible defenses only require updating core system components rather than all commodity software running on a device, wide-spread deployability is more feasible. Our defense is motivated by the need to protect vulnerable systems in the near-term, and so many of our design choices prioritize deployability.

One related work which shares similar deployability goals is a defense proposed by Williams-King et al. [33] which offers a binary-compatible solution for constantly re-randomizing code at prescribed intervals (of wall-clock time) in order to break `JIT-ROP` payloads. Their approach requires relocating functions using complex pointer tracking techniques in order to avoid creating stale pointers that can no longer be safely dereferenced; however, such analysis is known to be an unsolvable problem in the general case, and raises a slew of challenges for real-world deployment. The approach of Williams-King et al. [33] makes strides in advancing the robustness of pointer tracking based defenses by leveraging program analysis and assuming access to debug symbols in order to bolster the accuracy of moving functions around at runtime within the address space of a protected process. Unfortunately, there are corner cases in deployable pointer tracking that are not handled by their work, thereby lessening the near-term deployability of the defense. For instance, even when instructing the compiler/linker to preserve as much information as possible, certain information is not retained, such as locations of static functions (for which the known offset within a module can be hard-coded by the compiler), alignment of jump tables, or existence of functions which implicitly fall through to the next function. This lack of information complicates the prospect of reordering functions in applications that feature these program constructs. Certain aspects of data flow tracking are also not supported (*e.g.,* when an object is initialized in one library and `memcpy`'d to a different library). Our work does not share these drawbacks, as we avoid pointer tracking altogether. In another related code-shuffling style approach, Chen et al. [10] attempt to provide a probabilistic defense against `JIT-ROP` attacks by applying time-based binary stirring [31] to a process in an attempt to re-randomize all code in the entire program. Unfortunately, since Chen et al. [10] provide no guidance on how to determine realistic intervals for triggering their defense, it remains unclear what the incurred overhead is for thwarting real-world `JIT-ROP` attacks that have a lifetime of a few seconds [28].

Destructive Reads. Of late, several defenses that rely on the notion of execute-only memory (*i.e.,* to enforce that any given location in a code section can be either read or executed—*but not both*) have been suggested as a mechanism for preventing code reuse attacks. Indeed, instead of attempting to solve the difficult problem of separating code and data and preventing code from being read recursively (*e.g.,* [4,5,19]), the idea behind *destructive reads* [30,32] is to allow all code to be disclosed, but to prevent any disclosed code from subsequently being executed. Sadly, while the notion of destructive reads was thought to be an effective technique for mitigating just-in-time code reuse attacks as originally proposed by Snow et al. [28], several ingenious attacks have surfaced that leverage the ability to load and unload modules at will—or for selectively disclosing bytes of memory as a means of inferring surrounding gadgets—to undermine any afforded protection [27].

Even with these attacks in mind, we show how the notion of destructive reads can be effectively combined with load-time randomization to provide strong protection against powerful code reuse attacks. Our solution for doing so is discussed next.

4   Approach

In what follows, we propose a practical defense against just-in-time code reuse attacks that take advantage of an adversary's ability to disclose and execute code bytes whose values were learned by loading and unloading code modules, or performing so-called *code inference attacks* like those recently presented by Snow et al. [27]. At a high level, our approach centers around the ability to place randomized versions of code in a process at key trigger points during the execution of a just-in-time code reuse attack. Specifically, we replace the code upon which an attack relies with logically equivalent code of a different form that will break the attacker's ROP payload. To achieve this, we apply binary-compatible *in-place* randomization to code modules in order to obtain multiple diversified copies of the code which are kept in kernel-space memory where they are not accessible to user-level processes. With swappable versions of a module available at our disposal, we can then efficiently replace disclosed code at runtime with minimal complexities while assuring correct program execution. Specifically, when a module is loaded into memory from disk, we ensure that a randomized copy of that module is mapped into the user-space process, thwarting code reloading attacks. Furthermore, individual reads to executable addresses in the module trigger our system to swap localized code sequences within functions for semantically-equivalent randomized code sequences from one of the alternate versions maintained in kernel-space. This technique prevents adversaries from making use of individually disclosed gadgets, while not requiring any re-routing of control flow or swapping of entire code modules.

Both `Heisenbyte` [30] and `NEAR` [32] provide solid foundations for detecting the most straightforward way an attacker can learn the values of code bytes— *i.e.*, by directly reading their values in memory—and are able to prevent the execution of those exact bytes at a later time. Unfortunately, attacks are still possible when scripting environments can be used to cause modules to be loaded or unloaded at will, exchanging destroyed gadgets for fresh versions of the previously disclosed bytes and thus rendering destructive code reads ineffective. Indeed, the most concerning attacks suggested by Snow et al. [27] involve the use of *implicit code reads* that allow an adversary to infer the values of code bytes *indirectly*, based on the directly read values of related code bytes. These

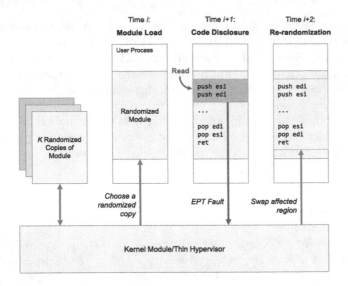

Fig. 1. At load time, one among many randomized versions of a module is picked at random. Whenever a potential code disclosure event occurs (due to a destructive read operation), the locally surrounding region is re-randomized by swapping it with a different randomized instance.

two orthogonal attack approaches necessitate two orthogonal components of our defense: one for thwarting *code reloading* and another for defending against *code inference.* Figure 1 shows an overview of the proposed approach, depicting how our defense ensures different randomized copies of code modules get mapped into memory on image load, as well as ensuring code bytes that are disclosed by an attacker get swapped for a different randomized version of those bytes before they can be leveraged in an exploit payload.

These two components of our defense extend destructive read capabilities presented in previous work, which we briefly explain before relaying the specifics of our contributions. Heisenbyte [30] and NEAR [32] both implement what is called a *thin hypervisor*, allowing them to leverage hardware virtualization support for Extended Page Tables (EPT) to intercept read accesses to executable sections of a given process. While this may seem like a drastic means by which to simply mark code pages as execute-only, at present, it is the only feasible approach for contemporary Intel processors.[1] In both Heisenbyte and NEAR, enforcing *destructive reads* involves registering an EPT fault handler that, when invoked, assures the byte values where a fault takes place can never be subsequently executed (*e.g.,* by overwriting the bytes with invalid opcodes). In addition, the byte values at those offsets must be preserved so that they can be made available in the event that an application wants to read the data again at a later time.

---

[1] That said, as hardware support [22] is added for more fine-grained control of the memory protections applied to individual pages, we expect the hypervisor component of execute-only-memory based defenses to become obsolete.

4.1   Defeating Code Reloading

The first of the two components of our defense aims to combat so called *code reloading* attacks. The approach we take here is straightforward: ensure that adversaries are faced with a different randomized copy of a module each time the module is loaded, thereby preventing them from disclosing gadgets in one copy of a module and executing them in a different identical copy. To do this, we apply in-place randomization (using the techniques of Pappas et al. [26]) to k distinct versions of the module and map the different versions into process memory on load. As shown on the left side of Fig. 1, this can be done by hooking the operating system functions that map executable images into memory and redirecting the associated *OpenFile* call to any of the k randomized versions of the binary that reside on disk. While this straightforward countermeasure by itself eliminates a significant subset of the attacks presented in the work by Snow et al. [27], additional special attention must be taken to avoid the pitfalls that opened the door to attacks based on code inference via *implicit* disclosure.

4.2   Defeating Code Inference

The idea behind code inference attacks is that in-place code randomization [26] applies code transformations at such a local level, that reading even one byte where randomization has been applied is often enough information to infer how other related nearby bytes (which may actually contain useful gadgets) have been randomized. The problem this poses for defenses that leverage destructive code reads is that simply destroying the code byte that was directly read does nothing to prevent an attacker from leveraging gadgets that were discovered through *implicit* code disclosure, enabled by *explicit* code disclosure [27].

   The ability of attackers to mount code inference attacks stems from the nature of the code transformations applied by binary-compatible fine-grained randomization techniques [23,26], and specifically their narrow scope. Specifically, in-place randomization [26] applies the following four code transformations: *instruction substitution*, which replaces existing instructions with functionally-equivalent ones; *basic block instruction reordering*, which applies a functionally equivalent instruction ordering within a basic block by maintaining any data dependencies; *register preservation code reordering*, which reorders the *push* and *pop* instructions of a function's prologue and epilogue; and *register reassignment*, which swaps register operands throughout overlapping live regions.

   By disclosing a few instructions, an attacker is able to infer the state of related instructions that are part of a ROP gadget. For example, an adversary could use code inference to implicitly learn the precise structure of a gadget that has been randomized using register preservation code reordering—which involves reordering the push and pop instructions of a function's prologue and epilogue. By (destructively) reading instructions in the prologue that are affected by the transformation, but which are not part of the actual gadget, an attacker can accurately infer the structure of the gadget in the function epilogue. Concretely, if the attacker knows that registers are saved onto the stack by a function, the order by which these registers are popped in the epilogue is the reverse order in which they were pushed during the prologue, so reading the prologue allows the adversary to infer the exact gadget contained in the function epilogue. Since the actual disclosure by the adversary was aimed at the prologue, destructive read enforcement will only protect those bytes, leaving the epilogue to be freely used as a useful gadget for the adversary. Similar code inference attacks against the rest of the transformations are discussed by Snow et al. [27], all of which are mitigated by our defense.

Crafting a countermeasure that renders implicit code reads ineffective turned out to be more difficult than it appeared on first blush. The reason is that an important criterion of ours was to allow for runtime re-randomization *without* having to deal with unsound and cumbersome pointer tracking. As noted in Sect. 3, other approaches to runtime re-randomization (*e.g.,* [6,24,33]) have also turned to ASLR-style code relocation at runtime, but these works needed to apply heuristics to deal with the problem of stale pointers. Re-randomization schemes can introduce stale pointers into a program if they do not carefully adjust every pointer that references a given code section when that section is relocated at runtime. The tracking of all pointers is rife with challenges and it remains an active area of research.

We choose not to introduce such complexity into our work. As an alternative to moving around large chunks of code in process memory, we opted for a more localized solution that guarantees that any—*explicitly* or *implicitly*—disclosed bytes are re-randomized in response to disclosure, while simplifying as much as possible the problem of ensuring correct program continuation. As shown on the right side of Fig. 1, we detect when a code disclosure occurs (causing an EPT fault, which is intercepted by our *thin hypervisor*) and replace only the part of the code that was disclosed with a different randomized version. As in our approach for combating code reloading attacks, we must maintain k different randomized versions of the program code, so we can randomly select from k different versions (which reside in kernel module memory) of the disclosed code to swap in at runtime. The intricacies of ensuring program correctness when swapping code ranges are discussed further in Sect. 5.

Critically, to deal with code inference attacks, we ensure that the part of code that is randomized includes not only the destructively read bytes, but also *all other instructions that could potentially be inferred.* The choice of using in-place randomization was a driving factor in simplifying our solution: with in-place randomization we can know the exact range of code that is vulnerable to implicit code disclosure for any given explicit code read. Importantly, we do not have to swap an entire randomized version of the program every time a disclosure happens, as the vast majority of randomized locations in a program cannot be inferred from a single disclosure. In other words, every explicit code read carries with it the potential to infer the values of other code bytes without actually reading them, but the range of code bytes that can be inferred is limited and is easy to compute in advance. We refer to this range of addresses as the *scope* of randomization, and return to a discussion thereof in Sect. 4.2.

What is important to understand at this stage is that through offline analysis we are able to compute the scope of randomization for each byte in a code module. Thus, when we intercept an explicit code read at a given location, we can look up the scope of randomization for that byte and swap the code in that range of addresses for a different randomized version. This necessitates only swapping out localized ranges of code, and in that way, we sidestep the issue of using broadly scoped runtime re-randomization techniques that incur a large overhead and rely on complex pointer tracking [6,10,33]. Moreover, in-place randomization guarantees that different randomized versions of the same code will always be the same size. Hence, these bytes can be interchanged without having to worry about making room for a larger version of logically equivalent code when the swap takes place.

Scope of In-place Randomization. The exact range of code that must be swapped out for a given EPT fault is directly dependent on type of transformation that was applied by in-place randomization to the surrounding code bytes. For the remaining discussion, we use the randomization technique of Pappas et al. [26] (called ORP) as an example since it is representative of the state of the art in this domain. The three possible scopes for a given transformation include randomizing at the opcode, basic block, or function level. Thus, if byte x in a module has to be randomized, the randomization may involve simply rewriting the opcode containing x, or could involve altering an entire function's worth of code that includes x.

There are two ways to think about the *scope of randomization* for a given byte in a code module. In one sense it can be considered the range of code bytes that are potentially vulnerable to implicit disclosure should that code byte be explicitly disclosed. In another sense this term represents the smallest range of code bytes that can be swapped for a different randomized version while still maintaining correct execution of the program. The three different scopes at which ORP applies code randomization determine the range of bytes that need to be swapped as a result of a given byte being directly read by an attacker. Note that we never have to swap out more than an entire function's worth of bytes for a single EPT violation, since no ORP transformations are applied at a broader scope than the function level. One caveat with using binary-compatible randomization techniques like ORP is that it may not always be possible to randomize all bytes in a given program. This is due to the fact that commodity binaries can include data in their executable code sections and disassembly of closed-source software can be imprecise. That said, the coverage of existing tools is high enough [23] that this limitation does not significantly weaken the security assurance that our defense offers. We discuss this further in Sect. 6.

Notice too that as long as we safely swap the correct amount of code (based on the type of randomization applied), we can ensure correct program execution. That said, the preceding discussion assumes that function in which we intend to replace code does not already have an activation record on the stack. In other words, if a function has been invoked but not yet returned at the time that a code disclosure targets that function, we cannot safely change the bytes of that function without potentially causing a crash when program execution returns to the function. For example, two different randomized versions of the same function could potentially save and restore registers to the stack in a different order for their respective function prologues/epilogues. If the registers are saved in one order during the function prologue and the code of the function gets randomized before that function invocation has returned, the newly randomized code may restore registers in a different order than they were saved in the prologue. If we allow this to happen, we could introduce failures into otherwise correct programs.

To ensure this does not happen, we take a conservative approach and do not randomize any span of bytes that are referenced by a pointer on one of the program stacks at the time of the disclosure. This simplification ensures that no functions where execution has already started but not yet completed will be randomized. The approach is conservative as it assumes that *every* word on each of the program stacks is a pointer, but in practice, this is certainly not the case. This conservative approach would seem to be a weakness, but it turns out not to be the case for two reasons: first, the code and data separation techniques we leverage from **NEAR** and **Heisenbyte** are highly effective in minimizing legitimate code reads that occur during normal program execution (*i.e.,* by moving data that does not need to be executed out of the code section of a binary). Second, code reads that cannot be eliminated by the "purification" steps of Werner et al. [32] or Tang et al. [30] are not likely to trigger a stack lookup because they will be referencing code bytes that cannot be randomized by our approach anyway.

To see why, it is important to keep in mind that the majority of reads directed at code sections by a program are for reading data that has been embedded in the code section, rather than reading actual machine instructions. But, as ORP's conservative offline disassembly should not identify this data as executable instructions, ORP will not randomize this data and our defense will, by extension, not be able to randomize data bytes in code sections. Our empirical analysis (Sect. 6) confirms that is the case. Nonetheless, this restriction could be relaxed by employing more accurate stack unwinding [17] or shadow stack techniques (implemented either in software or hardware) [2,14] that do not assume (as we do here for simplicity) that every word on the stack is a pointer.

5   Implementation

As a proof of concept, we chose to build this system for 32-bit x86 Windows, with all implementation contained in a single loadable kernel module.[2] The kernel module is comprised of code for setting up the *thin hypervisor* and reacting to EPT faults, as well as code for hooking operating system routines to ensure that each load results in a randomized copy of the image being mapped into a process' memory. In what follows, we discuss some key decisions we made during our design, as well as implementation challenges we encountered along the way.

---

[2] Our thin hypervisor and kernel module are built upon the code provided by [32] as part of their work on destructive reads.

5.1   Adapting Offline Randomization Techniques for Online Defense

One challenge we faced arose due to the fact that all the existing in-place randomization techniques we are aware of only work offline (*e.g.,* ORP randomizes code instructions in an executable file). Since swapping out code at runtime is central to our defense, we needed a way to access different randomized versions of a given range of program code when a destructive read occurs. Our solution was to create a single aggregate binary with k distinct randomized versions of the .text section. Thus, when the binary is loaded, multiple different randomized versions of the code for the module will be brought into memory and their instructions can be swapped into the executing .text section whenever necessary. This involves storing additional metadata specifying the ranges of swappable code that have been randomized, which is used to determine whether to swap out memory in response to a given EPT fault (*i.e.,* yes if the fault is in a range randomized by ORP, no otherwise).[3] On a final note, we must ensure that the extra .text sections maintained by our defense are only accessible to the operating system, so their contents cannot be disclosed by exploits as part of attacking a user space process. We achieve this by only mapping one of the k code sections as accessible to user space when the binary is loaded into memory.

5.2   Handling Relocatable Code

Another technical challenge is dealing with the problem of relocatable binaries. In Windows, for example, binaries are loaded into process memory in such a way that it not uncommon that hard-coded addresses in the binary must be adjusted before the module can execute properly. This absolute addressing (in contrast to Linux-style position-independent code) assumes a specific load address in process memory called the preferred offset. If the binary is loaded at an address other than the preferred offset, all hard-coded addresses in the executable need to be adjusted during the loading process. Our runtime re-randomization approach may introduce incorrect execution if we simply swap bytes of a program out for the corresponding bytes from a different randomized binary whose hard-coded addresses were not correctly adjusted.

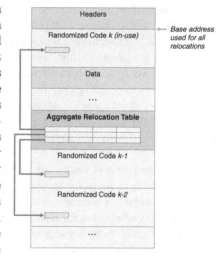

Fig. 2. Load time adjustments

---

[3] Failure of our system to swap a given range of code indicates that this range was not randomized through ORP, and thus is not vulnerable to inference attacks. Note that destructive read enforcement still protects these memory areas.

To address this problem, we coerce the loader to adjust all the hard-coded addresses in each of the k code sections *as if they are all being loaded at the same code section offset* within the module (*e.g.,* offset 0x1000 is typical in the PE format). In Windows, for example, each relocatable binary contains a table that specifies the hard coded addresses in the binary that need to be adjusted if it is not loaded at its preferred offset. As shown in Fig. 2, our approach takes executable file a and packages it with k randomized versions of a, so we also must combine the relocation tables from each randomized file into one large relocation table in the aggregate binary. In this way, we can safely start the module off executing from a randomly chosen version, i, of the binary, but when a destructive read is triggered, we then randomly select one of the other $k-1$ variants and swap the bytes that are in the scope of the destructive read.

6   Evaluation

To test the runtime overhead of our defense, we ran the same selection of SPEC benchmark programs that were used to evaluate the performance of destructive read enforcement [32]. Similar to Werner et al. [32], we compiled the CPU SPEC2006 benchmark programs with the Microsoft Visual Studio 2013 C/C++ compiler using the default compiler and linker options listed in the benchmark suite. We used the unoptimized "base" configuration.

The negligible performance penalty incurred by our solution on top of destructive read enforcement (shown in Table 1) can be attributed to the fact that for these benchmarks, all observed EPT faults were directed at data embedded in code sections, rather than actual code instructions that could be randomized. As such, a hash table lookup was enough to decide that these ranges could not be swapped, so no further action was necessary. Of course, as soon as an attacker starts disclosing actual machine instructions in the code, runtime overhead would likely increase due to the need to repeatedly unwind the program stacks and copy appropriate ranges of bytes surrounding the EPT faulting addresses.

As for memory overhead, our solution involves mapping k extra copies of the .text section into memory for each protected code module. To help understand the tradeoff between security assurance and memory overhead, we consider that the probability of success for a ROP exploit comprised of n gadgets that attempts to randomly guess which gadgets exist at given locations would be $1/k^n$. Thus, choosing a k value even as low as two or three can still provide strong assurance against ROP chains working as expected by the adversary. It may seem that storing the k additional .text sections in memory would incur a large memory overhead when considering that the .text sections of the benchmark programs we tested range from 65 KB to 2.4 MB. This is not the case, however, as in-place randomization only alters a small fraction of bytes in the code section (about 3% on average), and thus only these transformed bytes would need to be stored in memory to be swapped in as needed.

Table 1. End-to-end runtime overhead.

SPEC CPU benchmark	Destructive reads	Re-randomization	Total
400.perlbench	3.04%	0.1%	3.14%
401.bzip2	1.21%	0.03%	1.24%
403.gcc	19.88%	0.2%	20.08%
429.mcf	4.04%	0.3%	4.34%
445.gobmk	0.99%	0%	0.99%
456.hmmer	1.81%	0%	1.81%
458.sjeng	1.10%	0.09%	1.19%
464.h264ref	7.63%	0%	7.63%
417.omnetpp	2.32%	0.13%	2.45%
473.astar	2.13%	0.8%	2.83%
483.xalancbmk	5.51%	0.25%	5.76%
Average	4.51%	0.17%	4.68%

6.1   Security and Correctness

To show that we can reliably thwart code inference attacks without introducing incorrectness into programs, we ran a runtime stress test, forcing all possible randomizable code ranges to be swapped. This allows us to confirm that we can correctly swap in and out all parts of the program that are marked as randomizable. Our results confirm that in all cases swapping these code ranges worked as expected and did not alter the correctness of the code compared to the original binary. The average time to perform each swap incurred a low runtime overhead, at only 0.105 ms.

Moreover, to demonstrate that our solution thwarts code reloading attacks, we took the same approach outlined by Snow et al. [27] for generating exploit payloads from gadgets in commonly reloaded DLLs. We thoroughly inspected one of these DLLs (`vgx.dll`) to confirm that the constructed exploit payloads are broken by in-place randomization of the respective code modules, and consequently that the resulting payloads could not be reliably used in an attack. Indeed, approximately 70% (9,622 out of 13,729) of the gadgets in the module identified by the automated gadget finding tool ROPEME [1] were swappable. The remaining gadget discrepancy mainly arises from different parameter settings used by ROPEME and the build-in gadget discovery module in ORP (*e.g.,* the number of look-ahead bytes or gadget depth during the gadget generation process).

With k being a finite number of different program variations, the reader may be curious as to whether our system would be vulnerable to some type of fingerprinting attack that seeks to infer the version of code that has been swapped into user-space process memory. This would not be feasible, however, for a few reasons. First, since every randomizable gadget in a program is a degree of freedom for in-place randomization, an attacker would be forced to disclose all randomizable sections in order to uniquely identify one of the k versions. The footprint of such a brute-force probing attack would be so substantial that it would be trivially detectable and would constitute on its own a clear trigger for detection. Note that k can easily be tuned to make such an attack practically unrealistic. Furthermore, k can be increased to a much higher number than what is allowable by the available memory on the system. Indeed, rotating k randomized in-memory instances is only one option. The system could easily generate a higher number of new randomized instances in the background once the pool of ready-to-use instances in the kernel module is running low. We leave the implementation of this additional functionality for future work.

6.2   Function Randomization Variability and Coverage

The in-place code randomization of Pappas et al. [26] uses a combination of four different transformation techniques of different spatial granularity (instruction, basic block, and whole function) to generate alternative representations of a program's code. For a given code disclosure, multiple transformations may have been applied to the code area surrounding the address which caused an EPT fault. We use the coarsest randomization scope

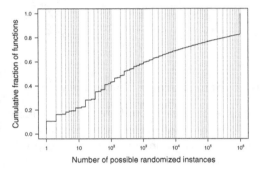

Fig. 3. Function randomization variability.

($i.e.$, the function that contains the disclosed code bytes) as the unit of re-randomization because function scope randomizations tend to offer the highest level of variability for a given range of code. That said, when we swap the bytes of a given function for a randomized copy, the contained bytes may have been altered by any combination of the four transformation techniques, so our solution still fully benefits from all four transformation tactics. It is crucial to evaluate whether re-randomization at the function level allows for enough randomization variability to prevent attackers from guessing or inferring the structure of the code to be swapped in. Specifically, according to the definition by Pappas et al. [26], we define *function randomization variability* to be the number of possible randomized instances that can be generated for a given function.

    To gain a better understanding of the resulting randomization variability, we performed an empirical evaluation based on more than 1.5 million functions from 2,566 PE files from both Windows 7 and Windows 8.1. Figure 3 shows the number of possible randomized instances of a function (including its original form), as a cumulative fraction of all 1.5 M functions contained in the analyzed PE files. Notice that 10% of the functions have a variability value of one (*i.e.*, just their original instance), meaning that in-place randomization cannot generate any variants for them. The next 4% have only two possible instances, and then the variability for the rest of the functions increases exponentially. For ease of exposition, we cap the calculation of all possible variants to 100,000. As explained in Sect. 6, note that just two versions of a function could be enough to foil an attacker, since randomly choosing which version of the code to swap at runtime means that the success rate for the attacker diminishes rapidly.

In general, these 10% of functions cannot be randomized due to their tiny size, often a consequence of compiler intricacies such as basic block sharing, wrapper functions, and other performance optimizations. In fact, our data on Windows binaries shows that about 15% of functions are at most 10 bytes in size, whereas only half of them are larger than 50 bytes. Moreover, 40% of functions consist of a single basic block, while 62% have five or fewer basic blocks. Our findings confirm the observations of Pappas et al. [26] in that the 10% of non-randomizable functions consists mostly of such tiny functions. Overall, we found that roughly 80% of gadgets can be probabilistically broken. Although the possibility remains that a functional payload might still be constructed based solely on non-randomizable gadgets, Pappas et al. [26] showed that this was not possible using state-of-the-art ROP compilers—even without considering recent work by Koo et al. [23] that increases gadget randomization coverage even further. Moreover, additional improvements to in-place randomization techniques could be easily adopted by our system, as this is an orthogonal research topic.

7 Limitations

One limitation of our approach is that it leaves open the possibility of code bytes being disclosed from functions currently on the call stack without those disclosed bytes being re-randomized immediately. In this restricted scenario, the JIT-ROP strategy of following code pointers to disclose code pages en masse (with hopes of leaking enough data to be able to compile a ROP payload on demand) can no longer be followed. Indeed, a completely different approach must be taken, involving somehow knowing which functions have been called but not yet returned at the time the exploit is underway—and then only disclosing code in those functions. While such an attack may be conceivable in theory, our expectation is that non-trivial enhancements to the principal of just-in-time code reuse would need to be made before such an attack vector would be feasible. Even if such attacks were possible, the fact that destructive reads targeted at randomizable ranges in a process are rare in normal programs[4] means it would be highly suspicious if one of these reads were to a function that has an activation record on the stack. Since an attacker would need to leverage this rare event many times during said hypothetical attack (*i.e.,* to be able to disclose the requisite amount of code in order to build a ROP payload), the repeated observance of this phenomena could signal that an attack is underway and the offending process would simply be terminated.

---

[4] In our evaluation with the benchmark programs there was not a single instance were there was an EPT fault in a range of code that was marked by ORP as randomizable code.

Finally, among the attacks against destructive code reads presented by Snow et al. [27], we currently do not deal with code cloning via JIT code generation, as this would require substantial changes into the JIT engine of each protected application. We do not consider this as a significant issue since modern browsers have already adopted constant blinding techniques [3, 25] to prevent the generation of malicious code or ROP gadgets, and thus thwart this type of attack.

8   Conclusion

Over the past year, defenses that leverage the concept of *destructive reads* (*e.g.,* [30, 32]) have been shown to offer a readily deployable mitigation against the threat of just-in-time code reuse attacks. The initial attraction of the promise of destructive reads as a defensive measure stems from the fact that it offers a solution that is compatible with closed-source applications, has low overhead, and has well-defined security properties—three factors that Szekeres et al. [29] argue promote wide-spread adoption of security technologies. Unfortunately, very recent attacks by Snow et al. [27] shed light on inherent weaknesses in adversarial assumptions that did not account for the possibility of *code re-loading* and *code inference* techniques, which can be used to undermine the security guarantees provided by destructive reads.

To address these weaknesses, we provide a solution that strengthens the applicability of destructive reads by eliminating the threats posed by code reloading and code inference attacks. Our defense includes two orthogonal components: one for mitigating code reloading and the other for preventing code inference. In particular, we demonstrate a novel solution for loading randomized copies of an executable any time the image is loaded, thereby preventing an entire class of code reloading attacks. In addition, we take advantage of the localized approach for code diversification used for in-place randomization [19, 26, 31] to enable efficient and robust runtime re-randomization of code that has been disclosed *implicitly* through code inference. Our solution is practical, and offers the first protection (we are aware of) against the ingenious use of zombie gadgets as disclosed by Snow et al. [27].

Acknowledgments. We are grateful to the anonymous reviewers and our shepherd, Stefan Brunthaler, for their insightful comments. This work was supported in part by the Office of Naval Research (ONR) under award no. N00014-15-1-2378, and the National Science Foundation (NSF) awards no. 1421703 and 1617902. Any opinions, findings, and conclusions or recommendations expressed in this paper are those of the authors and do not necessarily reflect the view of the US government, ONR or NSF.

References

1. ROPEME - ROP exploit made easy (2016). https://github.com/packz/ropeme
2. Control-flow enforcement technology preview (2016). https://software.intel.com/sites/default/files/managed/4d/2a/control-flow-enforcement-technology-preview.pdf

3. Athanasakis, M., Athanasopoulos, E., Polychronakis, M., Portokalidis, G., Ioannidis, S.: The devil is in the constants: bypassing defenses in browser JIT engines. In: Symposium on Network and Distributed System Security (2015)
4. Backes, M., Nürnberger, S.: Oxymoron: making fine-grained memory randomization practical by allowing code sharing. In: USENIX Security Symposium, pp. 433–447 (2014)
5. Backes, M., Holz, T., Kollenda, B., Koppe, P., Nürnberger, S., Pewny, J.: You can run but you can't read: preventing disclosure exploits in executable code. In: ACM Conference on Computer and Communications Security, pp. 1342–1353 (2014)
6. Bigelow, D., Hobson, T., Rudd, R., Streilein, W., Okhravi, H.: Timely rerandomization for mitigating memory disclosures. In: ACM Conference on Computer and Communications Security, pp. 268–279. ACM (2015)
7. Braden, K., Crane, S., Davi, L., Franz, M., Larsen, P., Liebchen, C., Sadeghi, A.-R.: Leakage-resilient layout randomization for mobile devices. In: Symposium on Network and Distributed System Security (2016)
8. Brookes, S., Denz, R., Osterloh, M., Taylor, S.: Exoshim: preventing memory disclosure using execute-only kernel code. In: International Conference on Cyber Warfare and Security (2016, to appear)
9. Chen, P., Xu, J., Wang, J., Liu, P.: Instantly obsoleting the address-code associations: a new principle for defending advanced code reuse attack. arXiv preprint arXiv:1507.02786 (2015)
10. Chen, Y., Wang, Z., Whalley, D., Lu, L.: Remix: on-demand live randomization. In: Proceedings of the Sixth ACM Conference on Data and Application Security and Privacy, pp. 50–61. ACM (2016)
11. Crane, S., Homescu, A., Brunthaler, S., Larsen, P., Franz, M.: Thwarting cache side-channel attacks through dynamic software diversity. In: Symposium on Network and Distributed System Security (2015)
12. Crane, S., Liebchen, C., Homescu, A., Davi, L., Larsen, P., Sadeghi, A.-R., Brunthaler, S., Franz, M.: Readactor: practical code randomization resilient to memory disclosure. In: IEEE Symposium on Security and Privacy, pp. 763–780 (2015)
13. Crane, S.J., Volckaert, S., Schuster, F., Liebchen, C., Larsen, P., Davi, L., Sadeghi, A.-R., Holz, T., De Sutter, B., Franz, M.: It's a trap: table randomization and protection against function-reuse attacks. In: ACM Conference on Computer and Communications Security, pp. 243–255 (2015)
14. Dang, T.H., Maniatis, P., Wagner, D.: The performance cost of shadow stacks and stack canaries. In: ACM Asia Conference on Computer and Communications Security, pp. 555–566 (2015)
15. Davi, L., Liebchen, C., Sadeghi, A.-R., Snow, K.Z., Monrose, F.: Isomeron: code randomization resilient to (just-in-time) return-oriented programming. In: Symposium on Network and Distributed System Security (2015)
16. Evans, D., Nguyen-Tuong, A., Knight, J.: Moving Target Defense: Creating Asymmetric Uncertainty for Cyber Threats. Springer, New York (2011)
17. Fu, Y., Rhee, J., Lin, Z., Li, Z., Zhang, H., Jiang, G.: Detecting stack layout corruptions with robust stack unwinding. In: Monrose, F., Dacier, M., Blanc, G., Garcia-Alfaro, J. (eds.) RAID 2016. LNCS, vol. 9854, pp. 71–94. Springer, Cham (2016). doi:10.1007/978-3-319-45719-2_4
18. Gawlik, R., Kollenda, B., Koppe, P., Garmany, B., Holz, T.: Enabling client-side crash-resistance to overcome diversification and information hiding. In: Symposium on Network and Distributed System Security (2016)

19. Gionta, J., Enck, W., Ning, P.: HideM: protecting the contents of userspace memory in the face of disclosure vulnerabilities. In: ACM Conference on Data and Application Security and Privacy, pp. 325–336 (2015)

20. Giuffrida, C., Kuijsten, A., Tanenbaum, A.S.: Enhanced operating system security through efficient and fine-grained address space randomization. In: USENIX Security Symposium, pp. 475–490 (2012). https://www.usenix.org/conference/usenixsecurity12/technical-sessions/presentation/giuffrida

21. Goues, C.L., Nguyen-Tuong, A., Chen, H., Davidson, J.W., Forrest, S., Hiser, J.D., Knight, J.C., Van Gundy, M.: Moving target defenses in the helix self-regenerative architecture. In: Jajodia, S., Ghosh, A., Subrahmanian, V., Swarup, V., Wang, C., Wang, X. (eds.) Moving Target Defense II. Advances in Information Security, vol. 100. Springer, New York (2013). doi:10.1007/978-1-4614-5416-8_7. ISBN:978-1-4614-5416-8. http://dx.doi.org/10.1007/978-1-4614-5416-8_7

22. Hansen, D.: [RFC] x86: Memory protection keys (2015). https://lwn.net/Articles/643617/

23. Koo, H., Polychronakis, M.: Juggling the gadgets: binary-level code randomization using instruction displacement. In: ACM Asia Conference on Computer and Communications Security, May 2016

24. Lu, K., Nürnberger, S., Backes, M., Lee, W.: How to make aslr win the clone wars: runtime re-randomization. In: Symposium on Network and Distributed System Security (2016)

25. Maisuradze, G., Backes, M., Rossow, C.: What cannot be read, cannot be leveraged? revisiting assumptions of JIT-ROP defenses. In: USENIX Security Symposium (2016)

26. Pappas, V., Polychronakis, M., Keromytis, A.D.: Smashing the gadgets: hindering return-oriented programming using in-place code randomization. In: IEEE Symposium on Security and Privacy, pp. 601–615 (2012)

27. Snow, K., Rogowski, R., Werner, J., Koo, H., Monrose, F., Polychronakis, M.: Return to the zombie gadgets: undermining destructive code reads via code inference attacks. In: IEEE Symposium on Security and Privacy (2016)

28. Snow, K.Z., Monrose, F., Davi, L., Dmitrienko, A., Liebchen, C., Sadeghi, A.-R.: Just-in-time code reuse: on the effectiveness of fine-grained address space layout randomization. In: IEEE Symposium on Security and Privacy, pp. 574–588 (2013)

29. Szekeres, L., Payer, M., Wei, T., Song, D.: SoK: eternal war in memory. In: IEEE Symposium on Security and Privacy, pp. 48–62 (2013)

30. Tang, A., Sethumadhavan, S., Stolfo, S.: Heisenbyte: thwarting memory disclosure attacks using destructive code reads. In: ACM Conference on Computer and Communications Security, pp. 256–267 (2015)

31. Wartell, R., Mohan, V., Hamlen, K.W., Lin, Z.: Binary stirring: self-randomizing instruction addresses of legacy x86 binary code. In: ACM Conference on Computer and Communications Security, pp. 157–168 (2012)

32. Werner, J., Baltas, G., Dallara, R., Otterness, N., Snow, K.Z., Monrose, F., Polychronakis, M.: No-execute-after-read: preventing code disclosure in commodity software. In: ACM Asia Conference on Computer and Communications Security (2016)

33. Williams-King, D., Gobieski, G., Williams-King, K., Blake, J.P., Yuan, X., Colp, P., Zheng, M., Kemerlis, V.P., Yang, J., Aiello, W.: Shuffler: fast and deployable continuous code re-randomization. In: USENIX Symposium on Operating Systems Design and Implementation, pp. 367–382 (2016)

KASLR is Dead: Long Live KASLR

Daniel Gruss[✉], Moritz Lipp, Michael Schwarz, Richard Fellner,
Clémentine Maurice, and Stefan Mangard

Graz University of Technology, Graz, Austria
daniel.gruss@iaik.tugraz.at

Abstract. Modern operating system kernels employ address space layout randomization (ASLR) to prevent control-flow hijacking attacks and
code-injection attacks. While kernel security relies fundamentally on preventing access to address information, recent attacks have shown that the
hardware directly leaks this information. Strictly splitting kernel space
and user space has recently been proposed as a theoretical concept to
close these side channels. However, this is not trivially possible due to
architectural restrictions of the x86 platform.

In this paper we present *KAISER*, a system that overcomes limitations
of x86 and provides practical kernel address isolation. We implemented
our proof-of-concept on top of the Linux kernel, closing all hardware
side channels on kernel address information. *KAISER* enforces a strict
kernel and user space isolation such that the hardware does not hold
any information about kernel addresses while running in user mode. We
show that *KAISER* protects against double page fault attacks, prefetch
side-channel attacks, and TSX-based side-channel attacks. Finally, we
demonstrate that *KAISER* has a runtime overhead of only 0.28%.

1 Introduction

Like user programs, kernel code contains software bugs which can be exploited to
undermine the system security. Modern operating systems use hardware features
to make the exploitation of kernel bugs more difficult. These protection mechanisms include making code non-writable and data non-executable. Moreover,
accesses from kernel space to user space require additional indirection and cannot be performed through user space pointers directly anymore (SMAP/SMEP).
However, kernel bugs can be exploited within the kernel boundaries. To make
these attacks harder, address space layout randomization (ASLR) can be used
to make some kernel addresses or even all kernel addresses unpredictable for
an attacker. Consequently, powerful attacks relying on the knowledge of virtual
addresses, such as return-oriented-programming (ROP) attacks, become infeasible [14,17,19]. It is crucial for kernel ASLR to withhold any address information
from user space programs. In order to eliminate address information leakage,

---

The stamp on the top of this paper refers to an approval process conducted by the
ESSoS artifact evaluation committee chaired by Karim Ali and Omer Tripp.

© Springer International Publishing AG 2017
E. Bodden et al. (Eds.): ESSoS 2017, LNCS 10379, pp. 161–176, 2017.
DOI: 10.1007/978-3-319-62105-0_11

the virtual-to-physical address information has been made unavailable to user programs [13].

Knowledge of virtual or physical address information can be exploited to bypass KASLR [7,22], bypass SMEP and SMAP [11], perform side-channel attacks [6,15,18], Rowhammer attacks [5,12,20], and to attack system memory encryption [2]. To prevent attacks, system interfaces leaking the virtual-to-physical mapping have recently been fixed [13]. However, hardware side channels might not easily be fixed without changing the hardware. Specifically side-channel attacks targeting the page translation caches provide information about virtual and physical addresses to the user space. Hund et al. [7] described an attack exploiting double page faults, Gruss et al. [6] described an attack exploiting software prefetch instructions,[1] and Jang et al. [10] described an attack exploiting Intel TSX (hardware transactional memory). These attacks show that current KASLR implementations have fatal flaws, subsequently KASLR has been proclaimed dead by many researchers [3,6,10].

Gruss et al. [6] and Jang et al. [10] proposed to unmap the kernel address space in the user space and vice versa. However, this is non-trivial on modern x86 hardware. First, modifying page table structures on context switches is not possible due to the highly parallelized nature of today's multi-core systems, e.g., simply unmapping the kernel would inhibit parallel execution of multiple system calls. Second, x86 requires several locations to be valid for both user space and kernel space during context switches, which are hard to identify in large operating systems. Third, switching or modifying address spaces incurs translation lookaside buffer (TLB) flushes [8]. Jang et al. [10] suspected that switching address spaces may have a severe performance impact, making it impractical.

In this paper, we present *KAISER*, a highly-efficient practical system for kernel address isolation, implemented on top of a regular Ubuntu Linux. *KAISER* uses a shadow address space paging structure to separate kernel space and user space. The lower half of the shadow address space is synchronized between both paging structures. Thus, multiple threads work in parallel on the two address spaces if they are in user space or kernel space respectively. *KAISER* eliminates the usage of global bits in order to avoid explicit TLB flushes upon context switches. Furthermore, it exploits optimizations in current hardware that allow switching address spaces without performing a full TLB flush. Hence, the performance impact of *KAISER* is only 0.28%.

KAISER reduces the number of overlapping pages between user and kernel address space to the absolute minimum required to run on modern x86 systems. We evaluate all microarchitectural side-channel attacks on kernel address information that are applicable to recent Intel architectures. We show that *KAISER* successfully eliminates the leakage in all cases.

Contributions. The contributions of this work are:

---

[1] The list of authors for "Prefetch Side-Channel Attacks" by Gruss et al. [6] and this paper overlaps.

1. *KAISER* is the first practical system for kernel address isolation. It introduces shadow address spaces to utilize modern CPU features efficiently avoiding frequent TLB flushes. We show how all challenges to make kernel address isolation practical can be overcome.
2. Our open-source proof-of-concept implementation in the Linux kernel shows that *KAISER* can easily be deployed on commodity systems, *i.e.*, a full-fledged Ubuntu Linux system.[2]
3. After KASLR has already been considered dead by many researchers, *KAISER* fully restores the former efficacy of KASLR with a runtime overhead of only 0.28%.

Outline. The remainder of the paper is organized as follows. In Sect. 2, we provide background on kernel protection mechanisms and side-channel attacks. In Sect. 3, we describe the design and implementation of *KAISER*. In Sect. 4, we evaluate the efficacy of *KAISER* and its performance impact. In Sect. 5, we discuss future work. We conclude in Sect. 6.

2 Background

2.1 Virtual Address Space

Virtual addressing is the foundation of memory isolation between different processes as well as processes and the kernel. Virtual addresses are translated to physical addresses through a multi-level translation table stored in physical memory. A CPU register holds the physical address of the active top-level translation table. Upon a context switch, the register is updated to the physical address of the top-level translation table of the next process. Consequently, processes cannot access all physical memory but only the memory that is mapped to virtual addresses. Furthermore, the translation tables entries define properties of the corresponding virtual memory region, e.g., read-only, user-accessible, non-executable.

On modern Intel x86-64 processors, the top-level translation table is the page map level 4 (PML4). Its physical address is stored in the CR3 register of the CPU. The PML4 divides the 48-bit virtual address space into 512 PML4 entries, each covering a memory region of 512 GB. Each subsequent level sub-divides one block of the upper layer into 512 smaller regions until 4 kB pages are mapped using page table (PTs) on the last level. The CPU has multiple levels of caches for address translation table entries, the so-called TLBs. They speed up address translation and privilege checks. The kernel address space is typically a defined region in the virtual address space, e.g., the upper half of the address space.

Similar translation tables exist on modern ARM (Cortex-A) processors too, with small differences in size and property bits. One significant difference to

---

[2] We are preparing a submission of our patches into the Linux kernel upstream. The source code and the Debian package compatible with Ubuntu 16.10 can be found at https://github.com/IAIK/KAISER.

x86-64 is that ARM CPUs have two registers to store physical addresses of translation tables (TTBR0 and TTBR1). Typically, one is used to map the user address space (lower half) whereas the other is used to map the kernel address space (upper half). Gruss et al. [6] speculated that this might be one of the reasons why the attack does not work on ARM processors. As x86-64 has only one translation-table register (CR3), it is used for both user and kernel address space. Consequently, to perform privilege checks upon a memory access, the actual page translation tables have to be checked.

Control-Flow Attacks. Modern Intel processors protect against code injection attacks through non-executable bits. Furthermore, code execution and data accesses on user space memory are prevented in kernel mode by the CPU features supervisor-mode access prevention (SMAP) and supervisor-mode execution prevention (SMEP). However, it is still possible to exploit bugs by redirecting the code execution to existing code. Solar Designer [23] showed that a non-executable stack in user programs can be circumvented by jumping to existing functions within libc. Kemerlis et al. [11] presented the *ret2dir* attack which redirects a hijacked control flow in the kernel to arbitrary locations using the kernel physical direct mapping. Return-oriented programming (ROP) [21] is a generalization of such attacks. In ROP attacks, multiple code fragments—so-called gadgets—are chained together to build an exploit. Gadgets are not entire functions, but typically consist of one or more useful instructions followed by a return instruction.

To mitigate control-flow-hijacking attacks, modern operating systems randomize the virtual address space. Address space layout randomization (ASLR) ensures that every process has a new randomized virtual address space, preventing an attacker from knowing or guessing addresses. Similarly, the kernel has a randomized virtual address space every time it is booted. As Kernel ASLR makes addresses unpredictable, it protects against ROP attacks.

2.2   CPU Caches

Caches are small memory buffers inside the CPU, storing frequently used data. Modern Intel CPUs have multiple levels of set-associative caches. The last-level cache (LLC) is shared among all cores. Executing code or accessing data on one core has immediate consequences for all other cores.

Address translation tables are stored in physical memory. They are cached in regular data caches [8] but also in special caches such as the translation lookaside buffers. Figure 1 illustrates how the address translation caches are used for address resolution.

2.3   Microarchitectural Attacks on Kernel Address Information

Until recently, Linux provided information on virtual and physical addresses to any unprivileged user program through operating system interfaces. As this information facilitates mounting microarchitectural attacks, the interfaces are

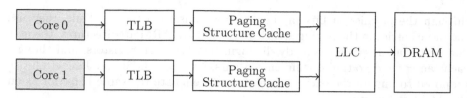

Fig. 1. Address translation caches are used to speed up address translation table lookups.

now restricted [13]. However, due to the way the processor works, side channels through address translation caches [4,6,7,10] and the branch-target buffer [3] leak parts of this information.

Address Translation Caches. Hund et al. [7] described a double page fault attack, where an unprivileged attacker tries to access an inaccessible kernel memory location, triggering a page fault. After the page fault interrupt is handled by the operating system, the control is handed back to an error handler in the user program. The attacker measures the execution time of the page fault interrupt. If the memory location is valid, regardless of whether it is accessible or not, address translation table entries are copied into the corresponding address translation caches. The attacker then tries to access the same inaccessible memory location again. If the memory location is valid, the address translation is already cached and the page fault interrupt will take less time. Thus, the attacker learns whether a memory location is valid or not, even if it is not accessible from the user space.

Jang et al. [10] exploited the same effect in combination with Intel TSX. Intel TSX is an extension to the x86 instruction set providing a hardware transactional memory implementation via so-called TSX transactions. If a page fault occurs within a TSX transaction, the transaction is aborted without any operating system interaction. Thus, the entire page fault handling of the operation system is skipped, and the timing differences are significantly less noisy. In this attack, the attacker again learns whether a memory location is valid, even if it is not accessible from the user space.

Gruss et al. [6] exploited software prefetch instructions to trigger address translation. The execution time of the prefetch instruction depends on which address translation caches hold the right translation entries. Thus, in addition to learning whether an inaccessible address is valid or not, an attacker learns its corresponding page size as well. Furthermore, software prefetches can succeed even on inaccessible memory. Linux has a kernel physical direct map, providing direct access to all physical memory. If the attacker prefetches an inaccessible address in this kernel physical direct map corresponding to a user-accessible address, it will also be cached when accessed through the user address. Thus, the attacker can retrieve the exact physical address for any virtual address.

All three attacks have in common that they exploit that the kernel address space is mapped in user space as well, and that accesses are only prevented through the permission bits in the address translation tables. Thus, they use the same entries in the paging structure caches. On ARM architectures, the user and kernel addresses are already distinguished based on registers, and thus no cache access and no timing difference occurs. Gruss et al. [6] and Jang et al. [10] proposed to unmap the entire kernel space to emulate the same behavior as on the ARM architecture.

Branch-Target Buffer. Evtyushkin et al. [3] presented an attack on the branch-target buffer (BTB) to recover the lowest 30 bits of a randomized kernel address. The BTB is indexed based on the lowest 30 bits of the virtual address. Similar as in a regular cache attack, the adversary occupies parts of the BTB by executing a sequence of branch instructions. If the kernel uses virtual addresses with the same value for the lowest 30 bits as the attacker, the sequence of branch instructions requires more time. Through targeted execution of system calls, the adversary can obtain information about virtual addresses of code that is executed during a system call. Consequently, the BTB attack defeats KASLR.

We consider the BTB attack out of scope for our countermeasure (*KAISER*), which we present in the next section, for two reasons. First, Evtyushkin et al. [3] proposed to use virtual address bits >30 to randomize memory locations for KASLR as a zero-overhead countermeasure against their BTB attack. Indeed, an adaption of the corresponding range definitions in modern operating system kernels would effectively mitigate the attack. Second, the BTB attack relies on a profound knowledge of the behavior of the BTB. The BTB attack currently does not work on recent architectures like Intel Skylake, as the BTB has not been reverse-engineered yet. Consequently, we also were not able to reproduce the attack in our test environment (Intel Skylake i7-6700K).

3   Design and Implementation of *KAISER*

In this section, we describe the design and implementation of *KAISER*[3]. We discuss the challenges of implementing kernel address isolation. We show how shadow address space paging structures can be used to separate kernel space and user space. We describe how modern CPU features and optimizations can be used to reduce the amount of regular TLB flushes to a minimum. Finally, to show the feasibility of the approach, we implemented *KAISER* on top of the latest Ubuntu Linux kernel.

3.1   Challenges of Kernel Address Isolation

As recommended by Intel [8], today's operating systems map the kernel into the address space of every user process. Kernel pages are protected from unwanted access by user space applications using different access permissions, set in the page table entries (PTE). Thus, the address space is shared between the kernel and the user and only the privilege level is escalated to execute system calls and interrupt routines.

---

[3] Kernel Address Isolation to have Side channels Efficiently Removed.

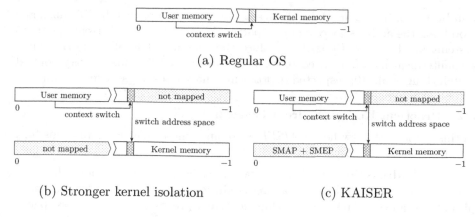

(a) Regular OS

(b) Stronger kernel isolation   (c) KAISER

Fig. 2. (a) The kernel is mapped into the address space of every user process. (b) Theoretical concept of stronger kernel isolation. It splits the address spaces and only interrupt handling code is mapped in both address spaces. (c) For compatibility with x86 Linux, KAISER relies on SMAP to prevent invalid user memory references and SMEP to prevent execution of user code in kernel mode.

The idea of *Stronger Kernel Isolation* proposed by Gruss et al. [6] (cf. Fig. 2) is to unmap kernel pages while the user process is in user space and switch to a separated kernel address space when entering the kernel. Consequently, user pages are not mapped in kernel space and only a minimal numbers of pages is mapped both in user space and kernel space. While this would prevent all microarchitectural attacks on kernel address space information on recent systems [6,7,10], it is not possible to implement *Stronger Kernel Isolation* without rewriting large parts of today's kernels. There is no previous work investigating the requirements real hardware poses to implement kernel address isolation in practice. We identified the following three challenges that make kernel address isolation non-trivial to implement.

Challenge 1. Threads cannot use the same page table structures in user space and kernel space without a huge synchronization overhead. The reason for this is the highly parallelized nature of today's systems. If a thread modifies page table structures upon a context switch, it influences all concurrent threads of the same process. Furthermore, the mapping changes for all threads, even if they are currently in the user space.

Challenge 2. Current x86 processors require several locations to be valid for both user space and kernel space during context switches. These locations are hard to identify in large operating system kernels due to implicit assumptions about the omnipresence of the entire kernel address space. Furthermore, segmented memory accesses like core-local storage are required during context switches. Thus, it must be possible to locate and restore the segmented areas without re-mapping the unmapped parts of the kernel space. Especially, unmapping the user space in the Linux kernel space, as proposed by Gruss et al. [6], would require rewriting large parts of the Linux kernel.

Challenge 3. Switching the address space incurs an implicit full TLB flush and modifying the address space causes a partial TLB flush [8]. As current operating systems are highly optimized to reduce the amount of implicit TLB flushes, a countermeasure would need to explicitly flush the TLB upon every context switch. Jang et al. [10] suspected that this may have a severe performance impact.

3.2   Practical Kernel Address Isolation

In this section we show how *KAISER* overcomes these challenges and thus fully revives KASLR.

Shadow Address Spaces. To solve challenge 1, we introduce the idea of *shadow address spaces* to provide kernel address isolation. Figure 3 illustrates the principle of the shadow address space technique. Every process has two address spaces. One address space which has the user space mapped but not the kernel (*i.e.*, the *shadow address space*), and a second address space which has the kernel mapped but the user space protected with SMAP and SMEP.

The switch between the user address space and the kernel address space now requires updating the CR3 register with the value of the corresponding PML4. Upon a context switch, the CR3 register initially remains at the old value, mapping the user address space. At this point *KAISER* can only perform a very limited amount of computations, operating on a minimal set of registers and accessing only parts of the kernel that are mapped both in kernel and user space. As interrupts can be triggered from both user and kernel space, interrupt sources can be both environments and it is not generally possible to determine the interrupt source within the limited amount of computations we can perform at this point. Consequently, switching the CR3 register must be a short static computation oblivious to the interrupt source.

With shadow address spaces we provide a solution to this problem. Shadow address spaces are required to have a globally fixed power-of-two offset between the kernel PML4 and the shadow PML4. This allows switching to the kernel PML4 or the shadow PML4 respectively, regardless of the interrupt source. For instance, setting the corresponding address bit to zero switches to the kernel PML4 and setting it to one switches to the shadow PML4. The easiest offset to implement is to use bit 12 of the physical address. That is, the PML4 for the kernel space and shadow PML4 are allocated as an 8 kB-aligned physical memory block. The shadow PML4 is always located at the offset +4 kB. With this trick, we do not need to perform any memory lookups and only need a single scratch register to switch address spaces.

The memory overhead introduced through shadow address spaces is very small. We have an overhead of 8 kB of physical memory per user thread for kernel page directories (PDs) and PTs and 12 kB of physical memory per user process for the shadow PML4. The 12 kB are due to a restriction in the Linux kernel that only allows to allocate blocks containing 2^n pages. Additionally, *KAISER* has a system-wide total overhead of 1 MB to allocate 256 global kernel page directory pointer table (PDPTs) that are mapped in the kernel region of the shadow address spaces.

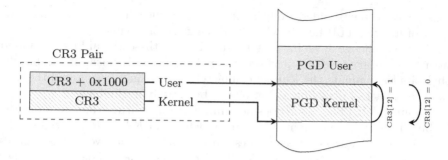

Fig. 3. Shadow address space: PML4 of user address space and kernel address space are placed next to each other in physical memory. This allows to switch between both mappings by applying a bit mask to the CR3 register.

Minimizing the Kernel Address Space Mapping. To solve challenge 2, we identified the memory regions that need to be mapped for both user space and kernel space, *i.e.*, the absolute minimum number of pages to be compatible with x86 and its features used in the Linux kernel. While previous work [6] suggested that only a negligible portion of the interrupt dispatcher code needs to be mapped in both address spaces, in practice more locations are required.

As x86 and Linux are built around using interrupts for context switches, it is necessary to map the interrupt descriptor table (IDT), as well as the interrupt entry and exit .text section. To enable multi-threaded applications to run on different cores, it is necessary to identify per-CPU memory regions and map them into the shadow address space. *KAISER* maps the entire per-CPU section including the interrupt request (IRQ) stack and vector, the global descriptor table (GDT), and the task state segment (TSS). Furthermore, while switching to privileged mode, the CPU implicitly pushes some registers onto the current kernel stack. This can be one of the per-CPU stacks that we already mapped or a thread stack. Consequently, thread stacks need to be mapped too.

We found that the idea to unmap the user space entirely in kernel space is not practical. The design of modern operating system kernels is based upon the capability of accessing user space addresses from kernel mode. Furthermore, SMEP protects against executing user space code in kernel mode. Any memory location that is user-accessible cannot be executed by the kernel. SMAP protects against invalid user memory references in kernel mode. Consequently, the effective user memory mapping is non-executable and not directly accessible in kernel mode.

Efficient and Secure TLB Management. The Linux kernel generally tries to minimize the number of implicit TLB flushes. For instance when switching between kernel and user mode, the CR3 register is not updated. Furthermore, the Linux kernel uses PTE global bits to preserve mappings that exist in every process to improve the performance of context switches. The global bit of a PTE marks pages to be excluded from implicit TLB flushes. Thus, they reduce the impact of implicit TLB flushes when modifying the CR3 register.

To solve challenge 3, we investigate the effects of these global bits. We found that it is necessary to either perform an explicit full TLB flush, or disable the global bits to eliminate the leakage completely. Surprisingly, we found the performance impact of disabling global bits to be entirely negligible.

Disabling global bits alone does not eliminate any leakage, but it is a necessary building block. The main side-channel defense in *KAISER* is based on the separate shadow address spaces we described above. As the two address spaces have different CR3 register values, *KAISER* requires a CR3 update upon every context switch. The defined behavior of current Intel x86 processors is to perform implicit TLB flushes upon every CR3 update. Venkatasubramanian et al. [25] described that beyond this architecturally defined behavior, the CPU may implement further optimizations as long as the observed effect does not change. They discussed an optimized implementation which tags the TLB entries with the CR3 register to avoid frequent TLB flushes due to switches between processes or between user mode and kernel mode. As we show in the following section, our evaluation suggests that current Intel x86 processors have such optimizations already implemented. *KAISER* benefits from these optimizations implicitly and consequently, its TLB management is efficient.

4   Evaluation

We evaluate and discuss the efficacy and performance of *KAISER* on a desktop computer with an Intel Core i7-6700K Skylake CPU and 16 GB RAM. To evaluate the effectiveness of *KAISER*, we perform all three microarchitectural attacks applicable to Skylake CPUs (cf. Sect. 2). We perform each attack with and without *KAISER* enabled and show that *KAISER* can mitigate all of them. For the performance evaluation, we compare various benchmark suites with and without *KAISER* and observe a negligible performance overhead of only 0.08% to 0.68%.

4.1   Evaluation of Microarchitectural Attacks

Double Page Fault Attack. As described in Sect. 2, the double page fault attack by Hund et al. [7] exploits the fact that the page translation caches store information to valid kernel addresses, resulting in timing differences. As *KAISER* does not map the kernel address space, kernel addresses are never valid in user space and thus, are never cached in user mode. Figure 4 shows the average execution time of the second page fault. For the default kernel, the execution time of the second page fault is 12 282 cycles for a mapped address and 12 307 cycles for an unmapped address. When running the kernel with *KAISER*, the access time is 14 621 in both cases. Thus, the leakage is successfully eliminated.

Note that the observed overhead for the page fault execution does not reflect the actual performance penalty of *KAISER*. The page faults triggered for this

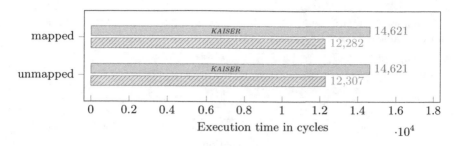

Fig. 4. Double page fault attack with and without *KAISER*: mapped and unmapped pages cannot be distinguished if *KAISER* is in place.

attack are never valid and thus can never result in a valid page mapping. They are commonly referred to as segmentation faults, typically terminating the user program.

Intel TSX-based Attack. The Intel TSX-based attack presented by Jang et al. [10] (cf. Sect. 2) exploits the same timing difference as the double page fault attack. However, with Intel TSX the page fault handler is not invoked, resulting in a significantly faster and more stable attack. As the basic underlying principle is equivalent to the double page fault attack, *KAISER* successfully prevents this attack as well. Figure 5 shows the execution time of a TSX transaction for unmapped pages, non-executable mapped pages, and executable mapped pages. With the default kernel, the transaction execution time is 299 cycles for unmapped pages, 270 cycles for non-executable mapped pages, and 226 cycles for executable mapped pages. With *KAISER*, we measure a constant timing of 300 cycles. As in the double page fault attack, *KAISER* successfully eliminates the timing side channel.

We also verified this result by running the attack demo by Jang et al. [9]. On the default kernel, the attack recovers page mappings with a 100% accuracy. With *KAISER*, the attack does not even detect a single mapped page and consequently no modules.

Prefetch Side-Channel Attack. As described in Sect. 2, prefetch side-channel attacks exploit timing differences in software prefetch instructions to obtain address information. We evaluate the efficacy of *KAISER* against the two prefetch side-channel attacks presented by Gruss et al. [6].

Figure 6 shows the median execution time of the `prefetch` instruction in cycles compared to the actual address translation level. We observed an execution time of 241 cycles on our test system for page translations terminating at PDPT level and PD level respectively. We observed an execution time of 237 cycles when the page translation terminates at the PT level. Finally, we observed a distinct execution times of 212 when the page is present and cached, and 515 when the page is present but not cached. As in the previous attack, *KAISER*

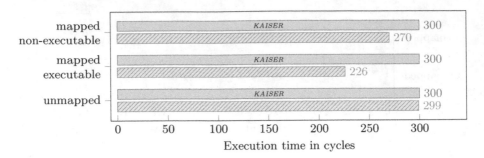

Fig. 5. Intel TSX-based attack: On the default kernel, the status of a page can be determined using the TSX-based timing side channel. *KAISER* completely eliminates the timing side channel, resulting in an identical execution time independent of the status.

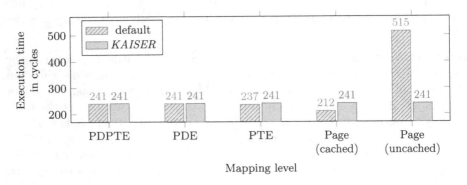

Fig. 6. Median prefetch execution time in cycles depending on the level where the address translation terminates. With the default kernel, the execution time leaks information on the translation level. With *KAISER*, the execution time is identical and thus does not leak any information.

successfully eliminates any timing differences. The measured execution time is 241 cycles in all cases.

Figure 7 shows the address-translation attack. While the correct guess can clearly be detected without the countermeasure (dotted line), *KAISER* eliminates the timing difference. Thus, the attacker is not able to determine the correct virtual-to-physical translation anymore.

4.2 Performance Evaluation

As described in Sect. 3.2, *KAISER* has a low memory overhead of 8 kB per user thread, 12 kB per user process, and a system-wide total overhead of 1 MB. A full-blown Ubuntu Linux already consumes several hundred megabytes of memory. Hence, in our evaluation the memory overhead introduced by *KAISER* was hardly observable.

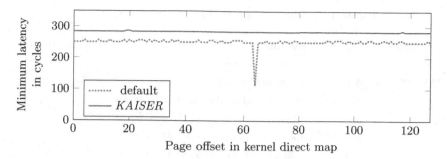

Fig. 7. Minimum access time after prefetching physical direct-map addresses. The low peak in the dotted line reveals to which physical address a virtual address maps (running the default kernel). The solid line shows the same attack on a kernel with *KAISER* active. *KAISER* successfully eliminates the leakage.

In order to evaluate the runtime performance impact of *KAISER*, we execute different benchmarks with and without the countermeasure. We use the PARSEC 3.0 [1] (input set "native"), the pgbench [24] and the SPLASH-2x [16] (input set "native") benchmark suites to exhaustively measure the performance overhead of *KAISER* in various different scenarios.

The results of the different benchmarks are summarized in Fig. 8 and Table 1. We observed a very small average overhead of 0.28% for all benchmark suites and a maximum overhead of 0.68% for single tests. This surprisingly low performance overhead underlines that *KAISER* should be deployed in practice.

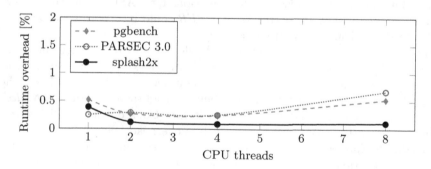

Fig. 8. Comparison of the runtime of different benchmarks when running on the *KAISER*-protected kernel. The default kernel serves as baseline (=100%). We see that the average overhead is 0.28% and the maximum overhead is 0.68%.

4.3   Reproducibility of Results

In order to make our evaluation of efficacy and performance of *KAISER* easily reproducible, we provide the source code and precompiled Debian packages compatible with Ubuntu 16.10 on GitHub. The repository can be found

Table 1. Average performance overhead of *KAISER*.

Benchmark	Kernel	Runtime				Average overhead
		1 core	*2 cores*	*4 cores*	*8 cores*	
PARSEC 3.0	default	27:56,0 s	14:56,3 s	8:35,6 s	7:05,1 s	0.37%
	KAISER	28:00,2 s	14:58,9 s	8:36,9 s	7:08,0 s	
pgbench	default	3:22,3 s	3:21,9 s	3:21,7 s	3:53,5 s	0.39%
	KAISER	3:23,4 s	3:22,5 s	3:22,3 s	3:54,7 s	
SPLASH-2X	default	17:38,4 s	10:47,7 s	7:10,4 s	6:05,3 s	0.09%
	KAISER	17:42,6 s	10:48,5 s	7:10,8 s	6:05,7 s	

at https://github.com/IAIK/KAISER. We fully document how to build the Ubuntu Linux kernel with *KAISER* protections from the source code and how to obtain the benchmark suites we used in this evaluation.

5   Future Work

KAISER does not consider BTB attacks, as they require knowledge of the BTB behavior. The BTB behavior has not yet been reverse-engineered for recent Intel processors, such as the Skylake microarchitecture (cf. Sect. 2.3). However, if the BTB is reverse-engineered in future work, attacks on systems protected by *KAISER* would be possible. Evtyushkin et al. [3] proposed to use virtual address bits >30 to randomize memory locations for KASLR as a zero-overhead countermeasure against BTB attacks. *KAISER* could incorporate this adaption to effectively mitigate BTB attacks as well.

Intel x86-64 processors implement multiple features to improve the performance of address space switches. Linux currently does not make use of all features, e.g., Linux could use process-context identifiers to avoid some TLB flushes. The performance of *KAISER* would also benefit from these features, as *KAISER* increases the number of address space switches. Consequently, utilizing these optimization features could lower the runtime overhead below 0.28%.

KAISER exploits very recent processor features which are not present on older machines. Hence, we expect higher overheads on older machines if *KAISER* is employed for security reasons. The current proof-of-concept implementation of *KAISER* shows that defending against the attack is possible. However, it does not eliminate all KASLR information leaks, especially information leaks that are not caused by the same hardware effects. A full implementation of *KAISER* must map any randomized memory locations that are used during the context switch at fixed offsets. This is straightforward, as we have already introduced new mappings which can easily be extended. During the context switch, kernel memory locations are only accessed through these fixed mappings. Hence, the offsets of the randomized parts of the kernel can not be leaked in this case.

6   Conclusion

In this paper we discussed limitations of x86 impeding practical kernel address isolation. We show that our countermeasure (*KAISER*) overcomes these limitations and eliminates all microarchitectural side-channel attacks on kernel address information on recent Intel Skylake systems. More specifically, we show that *KAISER* protects the kernel against double page fault attacks, prefetch side-channel attacks, and TSX-based side-channel attacks. *KAISER* enforces a strict kernel and user space isolation such that the hardware does not hold any information about kernel addresses while running user processes. Our proof-of-concept is implemented on top of a full-fledged Ubuntu Linux kernel. *KAISER* has a low memory overhead of approximately 8 kB per user thread and a low runtime overhead of only 0.28%.

Acknowledgments. We would like to thank our anonymous reviewers, Anders Fogh, Rodrigo Branco, Richard Weinbeger, Thomas Garnier, David Gens and Mark Rutland for their valuable feedback. This project has received funding from the European Research Council (ERC) under the European Union's Horizon 2020 research and innovation programme (grant agreement No 681402). This work was partially supported by the TU Graz LEAD project "Dependable Internet of Things in Adverse Environments".

References

1. Bienia, C.: Benchmarking Modern Multiprocessors. Ph.D. thesis, Princeton University, January 2011
2. Branco, R., Gueron, S.: Blinded random corruption attacks. In: IEEE International Symposium on Hardware Oriented Security and Trust (HOST 2016) (2016)
3. Evtyushkin, D., Ponomarev, D., Abu-Ghazaleh, N.: Jump over ASLR: attacking branch predictors to bypass ASLR. In: International Symposium on Microarchitecture (MICRO 2016) (2016)
4. Gras, B., Razavi, K., Bosman, E., Bos, H., Giuffrida, C.: ASLR on the line: practical cache attacks on the MMU. In: NDSS 2017 (2017)
5. Gruss, D., Maurice, C., Mangard, S.: Rowhammer.js: a remote software-induced fault attack in JavaScript. In: Caballero, J., Zurutuza, U., Rodríguez, R.J. (eds.) DIMVA 2016. LNCS, vol. 9721, pp. 300–321. Springer, Cham (2016). doi:10.1007/978-3-319-40667-1_15
6. Gruss, D., Maurice, C., Fogh, A., Lipp, M., Mangard, S.: Prefetch side-channel attacks: bypassing SMAP and kernel ASLR. In: CCS 2016 (2016)
7. Hund, R., Willems, C., Holz, T.: Practical timing side channel attacks against kernel space ASLR. In: S&P 2013 (2013)
8. Intel: Intel® 64 and IA-32 Architectures Software Developer's Manual, vol. 3 (3A, 3B & 3C): System Programming Guide 253665 (2014)
9. Jang, Y.: The DrK Attack - Proof of concept (2016). https://github.com/sslab-gatech/DrK. Accessed 24 Feb 2017
10. Jang, Y., Lee, S., Kim, T.: Breaking kernel address space layout randomization with intel TSX. In: CCS 2016 (2016)

11. Kemerlis, V.P., Polychronakis, M., Keromytis, A.D.: ret2dir: rethinking kernel isolation. In: USENIX Security Symposium, pp. 957–972 (2014)
12. Kim, Y., Daly, R., Kim, J., Fallin, C., Lee, J.H., Lee, D., Wilkerson, C., Lai, K., Mutlu, O.: Flipping bits in memory without accessing them: an experimental study of DRAM disturbance errors. In: ISCA 2014 (2014)
13. Shutemov, K.A.: Pagemap: Do Not Leak Physical Addresses to Non-Privileged Userspace. https://git.kernel.org/cgit/linux/kernel/git/torvalds/linux.git/commit/?id=ab676b7d6fbf4b294bf198fb27ade5b0e865c7ce. Accessed 10 Nov 2015
14. Levin, J.: Mac OS X and IOS Internals: To the Apple's Core. Wiley (2012)
15. Maurice, C., Weber, M., Schwarz, M., Giner, L., Gruss, D., Boano, C.A., Mangard, S., Römer, K.: Hello from the other side: SSH over robust cache covert channels in the cloud. In: NDSS 2017 (2017, to appear)
16. PARSEC Group: A Memo on Exploration of SPLASH-2 Input Sets (2011). http://parsec.cs.princeton.edu
17. PaX Team: Address space layout randomization (ASLR) (2003). http://pax.grsecurity.net/docs/aslr.txt
18. Pessl, P., Gruss, D., Maurice, C., Schwarz, M., Mangard, S.: DRAMA: exploiting DRAM addressing for cross-CPU attacks. In: USENIX Security Symposium (2016)
19. Russinovich, M.E., Solomon, D.A., Ionescu, A.: Windows Internals. Pearson Education (2012)
20. Seaborn, M., Dullien, T.: Exploiting the DRAM rowhammer bug to gain kernel privileges. In: Black Hat 2015 Briefings (2015)
21. Shacham, H.: The geometry of innocent flesh on the bone: Return-into-libc without function calls (on the x86). In: 14th ACM CCS (2007)
22. Shacham, H., Page, M., Pfaff, B., Goh, E., Modadugu, N., Boneh, D.: On the effectiveness of address-space randomization. In: CCS 2004 (2004)
23. Solar Designer: Getting around non-executable stack (and fix), August 1997. http://seclists.org/bugtraq/1997/Aug/63
24. The PostgreSQL Global Development Group: pgbench (2016). https://www.postgresql.org/docs/9.6/static/pgbench.html
25. Venkatasubramanian, G., Figueiredo, R.J., Illikkal, R., Newell, D.: TMT: a TLB tag management framework for virtualized platforms. Int. J. Parallel Program. **40**(3), 353–380 (2012)

JTR: A Binary Solution for Switch-Case Recovery

Lucian Cojocar(✉), Taddeus Kroes, and Herbert Bos

Vrije Universiteit Amsterdam, Amsterdam, Netherlands
{l.cojocar,t.kroes}@vu.nl, herbertb@cs.vu.nl

Abstract. Most security solutions that rely on binary rewriting assume a clean separation between code and data. Unfortunately, jump tables violate this assumption. In particular, switch statements in binary code often appear as indirect jumps with jump tables that interleave with executable code—especially on ARM architectures. Most existing rewriters and disassemblers handle jump tables in a crude manner, by means of pattern matching. However, any deviation from the pattern (e.g. slightly different instructions) leads to a mismatch.

Instead, we propose a complementary approach to "solve" jump tables and automatically find the right target addresses of the indirect jump by means of a tailored Value Set Analysis (VSA). Our approach is generic and applies to binary code without any need for source, debug symbols, or compiler generated patterns.

We benchmark our technique on a large corpus of ARM binaries, including malware and firmware. For gcc binaries, our results approach those of IDA Pro when IDA has symbols (which is generally not the case), while for clang binaries we outperform IDA Pro with debug symbols by orders of magnitude: IDA finds 11 of 828 switch statements implemented as jump tables in SPEC, while we find 763.

1 Introduction

Solving indirect control flow transfers such as jump tables in a disassembler is important for many applications—from binary rewriting to reverse engineering, and from malware analysis to code complexity metrics [21,37,47]—because it is essential to find some parts of the Control Flow Graph (CFG) of a program. Unfortunately, it is also very difficult and modern disassemblers frequently get it wrong in cases where code does not follow common, easy-to-fingerprint patterns, such as handwritten assembly or malware.

Extracting a reliable CFG requires the ability to *distinguish* between data and code and to *solve* the indirect control transfers—in the sense of finding the possible targets for such transfers. Any over-approximation adds spurious edges to the CFG, while under-approximations remove legitimate edges.

Unless they can extract the CFG reliably, many binary analysis techniques either no longer work at all, or with reduced accuracy. Besides reverse engineering in general, this includes the analysis of code complexity [21,37,47] and binary

© Springer International Publishing AG 2017
E. Bodden et al. (Eds.): ESSoS 2017, LNCS 10379, pp. 177–195, 2017.
DOI: 10.1007/978-3-319-62105-0_12

control flow testing [6,58]. Moreover, a reliable solution for jump tables also serves to detect the presence of custom protocol parsers [21].

If incorrect CFGs are a nuisance for software testers and reverse engineers, they can be downright catastrophic for binary rewriting solutions. Many software hardening approaches rely on binary rewriting [42] to offer security guarantees. Examples include control flow integrity (CFI) [6,22,26,50,52,58], sandboxing [18,25,27,36,38,45,55,57], static taint tracking [9,19,28,41,54]. An incomplete or incorrect CFG can void the security guarantees or even break legitimate software. Most binary rewriting solutions [8,12,42,49,51] are conservative when the CFG is incomplete, trading security guarantees for the overhead of the binary solution.

State-of-the-art disassemblers use pattern matching to solve complicated indirect control flow transfers. For instance, if a specific compiler generates a jump table to implement a switch statement in C, IDA Pro should know the precise template that the compiler will use *a priori*, so that it can search for exactly this pattern in the binary. Getting it right is important, as IDA uses the resulting jump targets to continue disassembly. Changing the code, however slightly, to not fit the template, results in a misclassification of the code. In practice, we found such cases in both benign and malicious software.

In this paper, we present a generic technique to solve indirect control transfers without pattern matching, to handle complicated cases—malware and handwritten code—for which templates are not available. We do not necessarily aim to outperform solutions based on pattern matching for "easy" cases (although we show that our solution is very competitive even for those). By means of a compiler-independent context-sensitive Value Set Analysis (VSA) tailored specifically to complicated indirect control transfers, we instead aim to help disassemblers handle complex and malicious code.

We compare our work against IDA Pro, a state-of-the-art pattern matching disassembler, and show that our analysis results are good and very robust. For instance, since IDA does not have good patterns for clang, our results are orders of magnitude better for clang and comparable for gcc even though we never embedded any compiler knowledge. In summary, our contributions are the following:

- We systematize how modern compilers implement switch statements by means of jump tables.
- We show that jump table detection by pattern matching is limited.
- We describe a context sensitive VSA suitable for recovering indirect jumps from binary code that outperforms powerful tools like IDA Pro and is compiler-independent.
- We evaluate our approach and show that it recovers complicated jump tables in binary code without access to source code or debug symbols.

2   The Problem with Patterns

Modern disassemblers commonly classify all sorts of code fragments by way of pattern matching—scanning the binary code for templates of known language constructs. For example, solutions like Jakstab and IDA Pro use well-known patterns for a variety of compilers to identify function entry points, function parameters, C++ virtual calls, switch statements, and many other constructs [1, 30, 32, 35]. Unfortunately, the effectiveness of pattern matching depends on the completeness and soundness of the templating for the code under analysis. For instance, Bao et al. [13] demonstrated the ineffectiveness of pattern matching for detecting function entry points. In general, pattern matching does not work well if the code deviates from the templates—a common phenomenon in hand-written assembly or malware.

In this section, we systematize how modern compilers implement switch statements by means of jump tables. We then show the limitations of pattern matching for identifying these jump tables.

2.1 Jump Tables in Practice

Instead of a straightforward if-then-else implementation, modern compilers frequently opt for jump tables to implement switch statements [44][1]. In practice, compilers generate three different types of jump table instances in terms of the control flow. These types are orthogonal to Cifuentes and Van Emmerik's expressions [20] and cover all jump tables that implement switch statements in compiler-generated code that we encountered, across hundreds of applications, a wide range of compilers, and various architectures.

```
1   // compare r3 with 10
2   cmp    r3, #10
3   // if less or same, load pc
4   // with pc + value in jump
5   // table, using r3<<2 as index
6   ldrls  pc, [pc, r3, lsl #2]
7   b      default
8   .word 0x20
9   .word 0x40
10  .word 0x80
11  .word 0x40
12  ...
```

Listing 1.1. jumpSIMPL: gcc implementation of switching. An alternative implementation replaces line 1 with **subs r4, r3, #10** which changes the pattern so that IDA cannot detect it.

```
1   add    r1, r1, #1
2   and    r3, r1, #0xff
3   cmp    r3, #0xB  // 12 cases
4   mov    r1, #6
5   strb   r3, [r4,#4]
6   addls  pc, pc, r3, lsl #2
7   b      loc_7d0c  //default case
8   b      loc_7d0c  //default case
9   b      loc_7c9c  //case 1
10  b      loc_7ccc  //case 2-9
11  ...
12  ---
```

Listing 1.2. jump2JUMP case. Line 7 computes he value of the target. Unlike jumpSIMPL, it uses unconditional relative jumps instead of jump tables (lines 7–11).

jumpSIMPL is the most common form of jump table. It uses a register as an index in the table and computes the value of that register using the switch input value. It then loads the value of an offset from the jump table, adjusts it and adds it to the program counter. An example of this idiom is shown in Listing 1.1.

jump2JUMP represents an implementation that is slightly less common, but still widely used. It first adds an offset based on the switched value to the current

---

[1] 23% of switch statements are lowered to jump tables by **gcc**. When compiling SPEC CPU 2006 with **clang** (for ARM), 21% of the switch statements are lowered to jump tables.

```
1   ldrb    r3, [r4, #7]                    // r3 is the index
2   adds    r0, #0x49
3   bl      rt_switch_stub                  // switch 7 cases
4
5   .byte 6                                 // item count
6   .byte 0x4, 0x8, 0xd, 0x12, 0x17, 0x20
7   .byte 0x1d                              // default offset
8
9   rt_switch_stub:                         // jt width = 8 bits
10  ldrb    r12, [lr, #-1]                  // load the item count
11  cmp     r3, r12                         // compare the index
12  ldrccb  r3, [lr, r3]                    // load case offset
13  ldrcsb  r3, [lr, r12]                   // load default offset
14  add     r12, lr, r3, lsl#1              // add the offset
15  bx      r12                             // jump to target
```

Listing 1.3. jump2STUB case. The stub uses the link register (lr) to access the jump table. The jump table contains the number of cases as the first entry. The default case is the last item in the jump table.

Program Counter (PC). The new PC will target another jump (forward) instruction. The offsets are not stored in code, but in the branch forward instructions. Even though it uses no jump table in the strict sense of the word, we still consider this case for our experiments, since the computation of PC represents a significant and similar hurdle for static disassemblers. Listing 1.2 shows an example of the jump2JUMP idiom.

jump2STUB, a less common implementation, makes the code to jump to a stub that takes as parameters the switched value and the jump table. The jump table is stored after the unconditional jump instruction. Listing 1.3 shows an example. While less common, we did encounter this switch statement implementation on multiple occasions in ARM Thumb code, in position independent code, and in firmware. The advantage of jump2STUB is its space efficiency—the rt_switch_stub is present only once in the binary regardless of the number of switch statements.

JTR is generic enough to recover all three cases even though we do not embed any logic that models these three types. As we shall see, we do use them for evaluation.

2.2   Pattern Matching Limitations

Disassemblers try very hard to detect switch statements (so they know which bytes to disassemble), by matching the bytes in binary code to well-known patterns that compilers are known to generate. Any deviation from the known patterns confuses the detection. Unfortunately, it is hard to find patterns that allow jump table detection to be both sound and complete. As a result, disassemblers can easily get it wrong. Consider Listing 1.1, which shows one of the idioms generated by gcc to implement switch statements. A mere replacement of the cmp compare instruction with any semantically similar instruction such as sub breaks the pattern recognition even though the program semantics remain unchanged. State-of-the-art disassemblers such as IDA miss the modified jump table entirely and interpret all the data in lines 6–10 as instructions instead.

As shown in Table 1, it is quite easy to fool modern disassemblers and decompilers by deviating from such well-known patterns, but the question is whether such cases also occur in real-world code. Unfortunately, they do. For instance, the last column of Table 1 contains code that is generated by `clang`. Moreover, Listing 1.4 displays a real-world (hand optimized) implementation of the `memcpy` function in `glibc`. Note that link-time optimisation (LTO) may easily inline such highly optimized code in several places in a program. As explained in the figure, state of the art disassemblers cannot compute the target address at line 5 and line 10, because they expect the calculation of jump targets immediately before the jump itself.

As a result, the analysis generates an incomplete CFG which renders subsequent analysis techniques less effective—hurting, for instance, the strength of security measures that rely on binary rewriting. Likewise, reverse engineering the code now requires significant manual annotation and analysis. In the remainder of this paper, we show that *JTR* can complement pattern matching approaches and solve these cases.

Table 1. *JTR* Pattern matching failures. In all cases except the baseline, IDA fails to detect the switch statement ("IDA sw"). Often, this leads to an incomplete CFG also ("IDA CFG"). *JTR* always recovers the correct targets of the switch statement. The last and first column of the table is code generated by compilers.

	`// gcc`
	`// default`
	`cmp r3, #11`
	`ldrls pc,`
	`  [pc,r3,lsl #2]`
	`b __default`
		`// cmp->subs`
		`subs r0, r3, #11`
		`ldrls pc,`
		`  [pc,r3,lsl #2]`
		`b __default`
			`cmp r3, #11`
			`// pc alias`
			`addls r3, r3, #1`
			`ldrls r0,`
			`  [pc,r3,lsl #2]`
			`movls pc, r0`
			`b __default`
				`cmp r3, #11`
				`// redundant`
				`// cond. jump`
				`bhi __default`
				`ldrls pc,`
				`  [pc,r3,lsl #2]`
				`b __default`
					`//clang`
					`//default`
					`add r0, r0, #9`
					`cmp r0, #6`
					`bhi __default`
					`lsl r0, r0, #2`
					`add r1, pc, #0`
					`ldr pc, [r0, r1]`

IDA sw	✓	✗	✗	✗	✗
IDA CFG	✓	✓	✗	✓	✗
JTR	✓	✓	✓	✓	✓

3   Tailored Value Set Analysis for Solving Indirect Jumps

As shown in Fig. 1, our analysis starts by lifting the binary to LLVM intermediate code using a home-grown translator[2], much like PIE [21] and LLBT [46], but slightly more advanced. As we do not consider it a contribution of this paper, will not discuss it further. Next, in Step 2, we apply a variety of optimizations, in particular aggressive inlining. As we will discuss later, without it LLVM does

---

[2] https://github.com/cojocar/bin2llvm.

```
1   2:  subs    r2, r2, #96
2       [...]
3   5:  ands    ip, r2, #28   // set flags
4       rsb     ip, ip, #32   // no flag change
5       addne   pc, pc, ip    // flags are tested
6       b       7f
7   6:  nop
8       ldr     r3, [r1], #4  // r3=*r1; r1 += 4
9       [...]                 // load 6 more regs
10      add     pc, pc, ip    // ip from line 5
11      nop
12      nop
13      str     r3, [r0], #4  // [r0]=r3; r0 += 4
14      [...]                 // store 6 more regs
15      bcs     2b            // jump to loop entry
```

Listing 1.4. Code snippet of the implementation of `memcpy` in glibc. Note that (a) both conditional and unconditional instructions compute the targets (lines 5 and 10), (b) the condition of the **add** on line 5 is determined by the **and** instruction on line 3), and (c) the target computed on line 10 depends on a value computed 11 instructions earlier. Since most disassemblers assume locality (the calculation of jump targets right before the jump), they fail to recover this case. In contrast, *JTR* successfully computes the possible values written to the PC on lines 5 and 10.

not inline some of the more intricate examples of `jump2STUB`. We now describe the main analysis steps of *JTR*—Steps 3–5 in Fig. 1. Analogous to how bounded address tracking [32, 33, 43] targets VSA [10] at binaries, we compute a list of all possible values a register may contain at specific points in *any* program—with an emphasis on indirect control transfers.

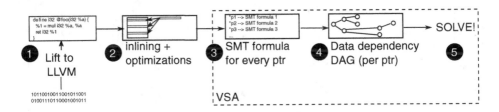

Fig. 1. High-level overview of the approach

To analyse all the indirect control transfers of interest (i.e., jump tables and complex arithmetic computations on the PC), we need only consider a program's non-constant writes to the program counter. In Step 3 in Fig. 1, after identifying all such indirect writes (stores) to PC, *JTR* goes through every function containing them to determine all possible paths from the store instruction back to the start of the function. For each path, we build a set $\mathscr{C}$ that represents the specific path constraints in SMT expressions form. Specifically, we go back along the paths to discover where this value originated and stop when we encounter a memory read or the start of the function. If the memory access itself depends on an indirect memory access, we recursively trace that back also, ensuring that we handle cases where, say, the program computes a pointer p by adding pointer q and index i.

To do so, *JTR* computes a *data dependency Directed Acyclic Graph (DAG)* to capture the relation between the memory pointers:

1. A node in the graph corresponds to a memory pointer access in its SMT expression form. Because the SMT formula stops when we encounter a memory read, the expression kept in non-root nodes always contains a memory read. The SMT expression captures any complex expression between nodes.
2. An edge in the graph captures the dependency between nodes. Given two nodes p and q, an edge from p to q means that p depends on the value pointed by q. In other words, to solve pointer p, we must compute the value pointed by q. In this way, the expression of p can easily emulate (but is not limited to) an indirect memory load with a base (node q) and an offset which can be a constant or another node.
3. The root of the dependency graph represents the pointer used in the targeted indirect write and the root expression will give us the possible values of PC.

For the final step, solving the DAG, the naive approach is to invoke the Satisfiability Modulo Theories (SMT) solver for the expression of the leaves, constrained by $\mathscr{C}$. Using the obtained values, we can then subsequently load the values pointed to and solve the rest of the tree. Doing so always gives results that are an overapproximation of the real jump targets, but with a high false positive rate in case of translation imprecision.

The key observation for improving the naive solution is that the possible values of a pointer are a limited subset of all possible memory addresses and $\mathscr{C}$ and some expressions of the nodes from the DAG *must* have a common expression. Let $\mathscr{N}$ be the set of the expressions of all nodes in the DAG. We denote $\mathscr{M}$ the set of common non-constant expressions between $\mathscr{C}$ and $\mathscr{N}$. We now construct $\mathscr{M} \leftarrow [m_0, ..., m_k]$ as a sorted set, with m_0 the *largest* expression in the set. We define the size of an expression as the number of nodes needed to represent the expression as a tree.

We now ask the Z3 [40] SMT solver for concrete values for m_0 while obeying the path constraints (see Algorithm 1). Using the concrete values, we recursively solve the DAG by temporarily expanding $\mathscr{C}$ with constraints that capture the concrete values. In the second part of Algorithm 1, we start from the leaves of the DAG and we simplify each node expression using the accumulated constraints. If a node's expression becomes constant, we load its corresponding memory pointer, otherwise we continue with the simplified expression. If the memory pointer is invalid, we abandon m_i and we move to m_{i+1} and restart the process. If the expression of the root node becomes constant then we successfully solved the DAG for one value. We continue the process until all the values of m_0 are tested.

If we explored all paths but found no solution, our analysis fails. In Sect. 4, we will see that despite its simplicity this method is quite effective in solving jump tables (and other indirect jumps).

Algorithm 1. DAG solving

```
Require: 𝒞, ℳ                                    1: procedure RecursiveDAGSolve(Node, 𝒞)
1: procedure Solve_DAG                           2:   expressions = {}
2:   for m ∈ ℳ do        ▷ ℳ is an ordered set   3:   for child←Node.children do
3:     for value∈ SMTSolve(m, 𝒞) do              4:     childExpr←RecursiveDAGSolve(child, 𝒞)
4:       constraint←m≡value                       5:     expressions←expressions∪(child, childExpr)
5:       𝒞 ← 𝒞∪constraint                         6:   for child, childExpr←expressions do
6:       rootExpr←RecursiveDAGSolve(DAG.root, 𝒞)  7:     if isConstantAndLoadable(childExpr) then
7:       if isConstant(rootExpr) then             8:       value←LoadPointer(childExpr)
8:         appendSolution(rootExpr)               9:       constraint←childExpr≡value
9:       𝒞 ← 𝒞\constraint                         10:      𝒞 ← 𝒞∪constraint
                                                  11:  return simplifyExpression(Node.expr, 𝒞)
```

Recovered Code Preparation. As LLVM optimizations may influence our results, we evaluated the effect of important optimizations that we applied to the lifted LLVM code. As a baseline, we used the same level of optimization as in PIE [21] which already provides common optimizations such as memory to register promotion, global value numbering, and dead code elimination. Next, we added a custom pass to replace the intricate control flow of the select instruction with a simpler if-then-else sequence. Finally, we turned on aggressive inlining.

In practice, presumably because the select instructions does not affect the control flow of the code of interest, we could not observe any change in the solving capabilities of *JTR*. Becuase *JTR* analysis is intra-procedural, aggressive inlining, *improved* our results overall as subtler jump2STUB were inlined and, in consequence, analyzed. We therefore turn on aggressive inlining in Step (2) of Fig. 1 and in all experiments in Sect. 4.

4   Evaluation

We evaluate our solution on 109 coreutils programs compiled for ARM, 4 firmwares, 17 malware samples, a synthetic set of 210 binaries, and the SPEC CPU 2006 test suite. We believe that this is a meaningful set to evaluate *JTR*, as it is large-scale, contains binaries generated with different (known and unkwon) compilers, while SPEC is commonly used by the security community for benchmarking. We summarize the results in Table 2 and discuss them in detail below.

Coreutils Binaries. It is a clear that if accurate patterns *are* available, we cannot beat pattern matching, but we show that we are competitive still with the most important state-of-the-art dissambler. As mentioned, we intend *JTR* to *complement* rather than *compete* with traditional jump target detectors—to resolve the complicated cases that pattern matching cannot handle. Nevertheless, it is interesting to evaluate our solution by itself. To show the limitations of pattern matching and the genericity of *JTR*, we use two different compilers, namely Clang (version 3.5) and GCC (version 4.9.2). We use the debug symbols in combination with IDA to generate a "ground truth".

In the absence of debug information, IDA recovers 77% of all the switch statements. The missing 23% are either due to failed function detection, or misinterpretation of jump tables as instructions (as is the case for each of our synthetic test programs). In contrast, *JTR* recovers 98%. However, we will compare *JTR* solely with our ground truth, so as to measure against the best of what IDA could do (when IDA has the debug symbols). We believe that comparing IDA's results on stripped binaries, even though the results look better, is less meaningful. We run our analysis on an Intel(R) i7-3770 CPU based machine with 20 GB of RAM on which *JTR* took 7 s on average per input binary and 755 seconds in total.

The results in Table 2 show that regardless of the compiler in use, *JTR* yields good results. *JTR* outperforms IDA when the `Clang` compiler is used. This is mainly because IDA uses a pattern that is usually generated by `gcc`. Specifically, the code commonly generated by `clang` for a jumptable is `ldr pc, [rX, rY]`, which is different from Listing 1.1. Moreover, `rX` and `rY` can be any general purpose register and the index value can reside in either. Coming up with a pattern that matches `Clang`'s behavior and has a low false positive rates is difficult, demonstrating the benefits of *JTR*'s generic technique.

Table 2. *JTR* results for different test sets. The ratios in the last rows relate to the ground truth when available, and to the "IDA + symbols" row otherwise.

Compiler	Coreutils		SPEC		Firmware	Malware	Synthetic
	gcc	clang	gcc	clang	unknown	unknown	various
Input binaries	109	109	12	16	4	17	210
Ground truth	–	–	–	828	–	–	80
IDA + symbols	642	0	655	11	66	205	80
JTR	629 (97.98%)	295	573 (87.48%)	763 (92.14%)	65 (98%)	166 (81%)	80 (100%)

Results on SPEC CPU Test Suite. We again compiled SPEC with both `clang` and `gcc`. The missing cases from the SPEC benchmark are either due to compilation errors (`perlbench`, `omnetpp` and `dealII` with `clang`), or to translation errors. We instrument the `clang` compiler to generate the ground truth. However, due to code inlining after the instrumentation, this ground truth is an underapproximation of the number of switch statements actually generated. For the testcases compiled with `gcc`, we rely on IDA's output for the ground truth (given the debug symbols).

We observe the same behavior as in the case of coreutils: *JTR* succeeds both on `clang` and on `gcc` and pattern matching yields poor results on SPEC with `clang`.

To show the impact of our analysis on the quality of the CFG, for the `clang` test set, we incorporate the recovered switch statements in IDA. Due to the 9097 new edges in the CFG discovered by *JTR*, we add a cumulated 2523 basic blocks to the CFGs. The detailed results are given in Table 4 (Appendix 1).

```
1   memset:
2       mov     r3, r0
3       cmp     r2, #8
4       blt     2f:     // branch if < signed
5       ...
6   2:
7       movs    r2, r2
8       moveq   pc, lr
9       rsb     r2, r2, #7
10      add     pc, pc, r2,lsl#2
11  // IDA dissasembler stops here
12      nop
13      strb    r1, [r3],#1 // repeated 8 times
14      ...
```

Listing 1.5. A real-world bug found by *JTR*. This code is handcoded assembly and part of the `memset` function in uClibc. It treats the length parameter (`r2`) as a signed value. If `r2` is interpreted as a negative number, the value written to the PC is outside of the mapped memory.

Firmware. Next, we evaluate *JTR* on the firmware of four different devices: a smart meter, a boot-ROM used by LPC214, a GPS stick and a GSM modem. The firmwares were manually reverse engineered in IDA, no symbols were available for this test. The ground truth is represented by the manual reverse engineering process. Our translator covered 66 switch statements that were implemented with jump tables, of which *JTR* identified all but one in the unoptimised LLVM bitcode. The missing jump table is recovered when aggressive inlining is enabled. We found 4 `jump2STUB` switch statement implementations in this set.

Malware. In this experiment, we used 17 malware binaries from 7 different families: AESddos, GoARM, PnScan, Taidra, Tsunami, Elknot and LightTaidra. We manually unpacked each of the samples and then fed them to *JTR*. In practice, none of the malware samples seemed to use control flow obfuscation.

Out of the 205 switch statements identified by IDA in the translated functions, the translator *JTR* recovered 166 (81%). The main cause for this modest result is the translator: several indirect jumps are wrongly translated or completely missed, therefore the input LLVM code for *JTR* is inaccurate. Interestingly, while investigating the results on this set, we also found the bug listed in Listing 1.5. The bug was confirmed by the developers of the uClibc library[3].

Synthetic Binaries. In our next experiment, we again demonstrate that our solution is compiler agnostic by running *JTR* on 210 binaries generated from 10 C source code files that contain switch statements or control flow based on jump table. We generate the binaries using 20 different compilers and compiler optimization levels from 6 different toolchains and IDEs.

In addition, we evaluated 10 cases of *hand-coded assembly*, which are not reported in Table 2 all of which were successfully recovered. *JTR* successfully recovers all of the 70 switch statements generated by the various compilers and reproduced by the translator.

---

[3] "bugfix: ARM: memset.S: use unsigned comparisons"–http://goo.gl/5NiXJq.

4.1   Detailed Analysis Results

Jump table types distribution. We show the distribution of the different types of jump table, as identified by IDA, in Table 3. The `jumpSIMPLE` type is the one that is by far the most popular on ARM, regardless of the test set. `jump2STUB` is rare on normal binaries but much less so in the firmware test set. In the synthetic set, we generated the `jump2STUB` cases by selecting Thumb mode and Cortex-M0 as the target platform. This CPU is often used in embedded devices, therefore compiler flags play an important role in evaluation of tools alike *JTR*. Table 3 shows that the performance of *JTR* is similar, regardless of the jump table type.

Table 3. Results of *JTR* on different jump table types. IDA is used to categorize the jump tables whenever possible.

Test set	Total	jumpSIMPLE	jump2JUMP	jump2STUB
Coreutils-gcc IDA	642	642	0	0
Coreutils-gcc *JTR*	629	629	0	0
Coreutils-clang IDA	0	0	0	0
Coreuitls-clang *JTR*	295	N/A	N/A	N/A
SPEC-gcc IDA	655	655	0	0
SPEC-gcc *JTR*	573	573	0	0
SPEC-clang IDA	11	11	0	0
SPEC-clang *JTR*	763	>11	N/A	N/A
Firmware IDA (translated)	66	58	4	4
Firmware *JTR*	65	58	3	4
Malware IDA	205	152	53	0
Malware *JTR*	166	120	46	0
Synthetic binaries IDA	80	59	21	20
Synthetic binaries *JTR*	77	56	21	20

Completeness and bug finding. On the ARM processor architecture, the code transitions between ARM mode and Thumb mode by means of a jump to an odd address with a specific instruction. Depending on the path, the address computed at runtime can be odd or even. When *JTR* computes the possible address value, the reported value can therefore also be either odd or even, depending on the path. The two results are essentially the same (modulo the mode) and we ignore the last bit. The computation is not ARM specific, but rather arises from the generality of the solution, as *JTR* explores both paths (ARM and Thumb).

As shown in Listing 1.5, *JTR* helps to find memory access violations. However, this is not its main objective and care must be taken when applying it naively. Specifically, because our method is (a) conservative – any pointer that fails to load on a specific path invalidates that path, and (b) intra-procedural, the false positive rate for a bug finding strategy that uses *JTR naively* will be high. However, one may augment *JTR* with model checking techniques (e.g., specify a range of values that one register can have) to reduce the false positive rate or target only a specific family of bugs, such as stack-based buffer overflows.

4.2 Comparing *JTR* with Other Solutions

We tried to compare *JTR* with a variety of other solutions.

Angr. The Angr framework [48] supports ARM architecture and uses static analysis to solve some jump table. Its public version (48998c5) does not work with switch statements implemented with jump tables [2]. Again, Angr generates an incomplete CFG, as the jump table targets are missing.

Jakstab. While JakStab [32] does not support ARM, we tried to compare *JTR* with JakStab's public version by adapting our examples to the x86 architecture. Instead of using a switch statement, we used a table of pointer to functions. With optimizations turned off, Jakstab recovers the targeted functions. When we turn on optimizations (−O2 or −O3), its analysis fails to recover the targets.

RetDec. The Retargetable decompiler [5, 24, 34] which does not use any VSA techniques, fails to retrieve targets in the absence of debug symbols. The decompiler either interprets the jump table as code or it does not reference it at all.

Radare2. Radare2's [4] support for switch statement implemented with jump tables is work in progress [3]. Note, however, that the implementation is based on pattern matching and therefore will have similar issues as IDA Pro.

REV.NG. Concurrent work from Di Federico et al. [23] use VSA to analyze LLVM code to recover a complete CFG. Even so, on ARM architectures, IDA's Jackard index on CFG matching consistently outperforms REV.NG's. The results on SPEC show that *JTR* improves the quality of the CFG generated by IDA. In our experience, REV.NG performed well on simple files, but none of the configurations[4] of SPEC binaries could currently be handled by REV.NG.

5 Related Work

Jump Tables and Switch Statements. Cifuentes and Van Emmerik [20] propose a solution based on lifting the binary code to Register Transfer List (RTL) expressions. Code slicing is used to extract the expression. Next the expression

---

[4] We compiled SPEC with Clang and with GCC. We tried static and dynamic linking.

are substituted until any of three known patterns are reached. The summarised patterns give enough information for recovering the possible targets of the jump table. However, the recovery of jump table's targets fails when the expression does not match one of the known patterns. Holsti [31] shows how to recover switch-case tables' targets when a Read-Only Memory (ROM) table is present. They use partial evaluation (e.g. run the program snippet with concrete input) to generate possible outputs. For this the state of the registers is modeled and loops are unrolled. This solution does not take into account the content of the memory and is dependant on detecting switch statement implementation patterns.

Meng and Miller [39] observe the difficulty of recovering an accurate CFG because of jump tables. They define three models for jump tables usage and populate these models by means of static analysis. We believe that these models are a form of pattern matching and that are not effective on ARM architecture, for example the `jump2STUB` case would require information about the where in the code the stub is. Gedich and Lazdin [29] uses the linearity property of jump tables' contents to detect them. Their solution assumes that the position of the jump table is roughly known. Once few targets are discovered, *JTR* can make use of this heuristic to accelerate the full jump table discovery.

Wang et al. [53] propose a solution to find data to code references. Their solution is working only when pointers to functions are stored in the jump table, in a data section. The compiler stores offsets rather than function pointer in the jump tables used by switch statements.

CFG Recovery. Reinbacher and Brauer [43] introduce a method based on SMT for generic control flow graph recovery. They leverage forward and backward abstract program interpretation to recover indirect jump targets. As opposed to *JTR*, they do not take advantage of the program's memory contents but rather use pre- and post-conditions for program's registers which are further refined by the algorithm process. JakStab [32] uses code inlining, abstract interpretation and local constant propagation to solve jump targets. It does not work on ARM. JakStab uses Bounded Address Tracking [43] and tracks every memory access and register assignment. Updates in the abstract domain are explicitly propagated. JakStab makes a distinction between memory regions. *JTR* relies on expressions and it does not need this tracking. Moreover, in *JTR* the case when a pointer points to an unknown region is captured by the SMT expressions rather than being explicitly accounted for.

Brumley et al. [17] proposes a decompiler that uses BAP's [16] VSA to recover the CFG from the tested binary. Their focus is different that *JTR*. *JTR* focuses in recovering the target of indirect control flows while Phoenix focuses on recovering high level semantics (e.g. switch statments) once the CFG is known.

Value Set Analysis. Balakrishnan and Reps [11] introduce a binary static analysis technique called VSA. They show both limitations and strengths of VSA when applied to binary reverse engineering. The method used by *JTR* extends their VSA by means of the SMT solving technique.

Brauer et al. [15] argues that SMT solving is effective to do VSA but they do not leverage the memory contents'. To achieve good performance they perform liveness analysis of the Intermediate Representation (IR). This is not required by *JTR* as the expression set contains at any time the optimal set. Bounded values and k-set analysis were previously used by Bardin et al. [14] to recover indirect jumps. They exploit the locality of the indirect target computation.

6   Limitations

Path Explosion. A large number of paths may exist from the targeted pointer to the start of the function. Building a dependency graph for each of them and subsequently solving it could lead to resource exhaustion. The deeper into the function's CFG the program uses the pointer, the higher the chances of running into this problem. We find that in practice, limiting the size of each path to 5 LLVM basic blocks yields good results. To further optimize the running time, *JTR* solves the paths in ascending order: from the shortest to the longest.

Code Discovery. The accuracy of the translator, although not a real contribution of this paper, directly influences the results of *JTR*. For instance, because the translator currently uses a static view of the program, it misses jump tables that the program populates at runtime. This is not a fundamental limitation and in future work, we will fix it by feeding back the *JTR* results. Note that dynamic jump tables are not common in benign software, but it is not hard to imagine that future malware will make use of it, as an additional defense.

Memory Layout and Program Correctness. *JTR* assumes that the input code is correct and that a memory map is available. While we can extract the memory map automatically using heuristics (e.g., read/write ordering [56]), guaranteeing the correctness of the program is hard. Conversely, *JTR* can be instructed to find bugs. For instance, in Listing 1.5 we show one example in which *JTR* finds a previousely unreported bug (see also Sect. 4). We are confident that we can extend *JTR* to find good candidates for memory violation errors.

During the analysis, we should take special care when loading pointers that point to Input/Output (IO) memory. We cannot predict the value returned by load from an IO memory. The naive solution is to ignore the memory accesses to IO memory and treat them as invalid accesses. However, doing so may have a negative impact on the true positive rate of *JTR* in case an IO value is used to index a jump table.

Memory Aliasing. Finally, the memory accesses generated by the LLVM translator can alias. When this happens the accuracy of the expressions stored in the nodes of the graph and of the path constraints decreases. The underlying reason is that *JTR* does not capture the aliasing information in SMT expressions. As future work, we will leverage the alias analysis already provided by LLVM to detect these cases.

LLVM Translator. Like SecondWrite [7] and PIE [21], *JTR* builds on top of a binary-to-LLVM translator. The translator lifts the code to LLVM in a straight-forward manner and *JTR* then analyzes the resulting code together with the memory image of the binary. Specifically, it uses weak heuristics for determining whether a function is in ARM mode or Thumb mode and occasionally misclassifies them. In addition, the translator does not itself resolve the indirect jump targets and its recursive descent disassembly therefore misses code fragments. The solution for the latter problem would be to feed the results of the *JTR* analysis back to the translator to discover the targeted code, but doing so is a major engineering task, and we leave this for future work.

Misclassifying a fragment's mode (ARM or Thumb) and missing code fragments in the recursive descent both cause *JTR* to miss indirect jumps and hence the appropriate targets. We stress that these issues are a problem of the translator only and not of the *JTR* analysis. By construction, *JTR* will generate a solution for the targets of every indirect jump in its input.

7 Conclusion

Jump tables on RISC architectures lead to frequent interleavings of (jump table) data and code in binaries. Most disassembler use pattern matching to detect such jump tables in binary code, which easily fails for complicated indirect control transfers. We argue that in specific security-relevant domains (handwritten code, firmware and malware), we need a more generic technique to handle the cases that elude common pattern matching. This paper proposed such a technique for "solving" jump targets for indirect control transfers. By transforming the targets to formulas that we solve in an SMT solver, we remove dependencies on templates, compilers, and processor architectures. The results show that our technique approaches and sometimes improves that of popular disassemblers that use pattern matching. *JTR* is available as an open source project: https://github.com/cojocar/jtr.

Acknowledgments. We thank the anonymous reviewers for their feedback. This work was supported by the Netherlands Organisation for Scientific Research through the grant NWO 628.001.005 CYBSEC "OpenSesame" and through the grant NWO 639.023.309 VICI "Dowsing".

1   SPEC Result Details

Table 4. IDA results on SPEC binaries compiled with `clang` are depicted in the first 5 columns. The first column represents the number of switch statement as reported by `clang`. We instrumented `clang` to tell if a switch statement was lowered to a jump table before code inlining takes place, thus the above 100% success rate on some cases for *JTR*. IDA misses most of the jump tables on `clang`. Column 3 and 4 show how the CFG benefits from the newly discovered targets. The percentages are relative to the total number of edges and basic blocks. The results for SPEC when compiled with `gcc` are shown in the last two columns. Here *JTR* performs better than IDA on `soplex`.

Testcase	Clang	IDA	*JTR*	Edges added	BBs added	IDA	*JTR*
namd	1	0	0 (0.00%)	0 (0.000%)	0 (0.000%)	1	1 (100.00%)
sphinx3	2	0	2 (100.00%)	9 (0.139%)	0 (0.000%)	2	2 (100.00%)
bzip2	5	0	7 (140.00%)	17 (0.502%)	2 (0.084%)	3	3 (100.00%)
milc	2	0	3 (150.00%)	23 (0.675%)	3 (0.113%)	4	4 (100.00%)
sjeng	13	0	10 (76.92%)	262 (4.248%)	126 (3.000%)	–	–
h264ref	26	0	25 (96.15%)	142 (0.794%)	10 (0.079%)	17	17 (100.00%)
soplex	27	0	40 (148.15%)	241 (1.641%)	20 (0.183%)	36	40 (111.11%)
cactusADM	36	0	34 (94.44%)	1399 (6.819%)	766 (5.116%)	34	29 (85.29%)
gromacs	40	0	40 (100.00%)	367 (1.685%)	30 (0.192%)	43	41 (95.35%)
calculix	8	1	12 (150.00%)	72 (0.141%)	0 (0.000%)	–	–
hmmer	41	0	39 (95.12%)	298 (2.327%)	60 (0.658%)	30	26 (86.67%)
wrf	10	10	74 (740.00%)	355 (0.433%)	1 (0.002%)	–	–
povray	126	0	97 (76.98%)	767 (2.153%)	17 (0.064%)	95	75 (78.95%)
gcc	361	0	320 (88.64%)	3467 (2.045%)	1038 (0.928%)	484	419 (86.57%)
xalancbmk	111	0	140 (126.13%)	1459 (1.265%)	414 (0.444%)	–	–
gobmk	19	0	17 (89.47%)	219 (0.666%)	36 (0.151%)	–	–
omnetpp	–	–	–	–	–	15	10 (66.67%)

References

1. IDA F.L.I.R.T. Technology: Overview
2. Angr, Switch Statement Analysis 106, June 2016. https://github.com/angr/angr/issues/106
3. Radare2, Analyze jump tables 3201, June 2016. https://github.com/radare/radare2/issues/3201
4. Radare2, Portable reversing framework, June 2016. https://radare.org
5. Retargetable Decompiler, June 2016. https://retdec.com/decompilation-run/
6. Abadi, M., Budiu, M., Erlingsson, U., and Ligatti, J. Control-flow integrity. In: CCS12 (2005)

7. Anand, K., Smithson, M., Elwazeer, K., Kotha, A., Gruen, J., Giles, N., Barua, R.: A compiler-level intermediate representation based binary analysis and rewriting system. In: ECCS8, pp. 295–308 (2013)
8. Anand, K., Smithson, M., Kotha, A., Elwazeer, K., Barua, R.: Decompilation to compiler high IR in a binary rewriter. Technical report, University of Maryland (2010)
9. Arzt, S., Rasthofer, S., Fritz, C., Bodden, E., Bartel, A., Klein, J., Le Traon, Y., Octeau, D., McDaniel, P.: Flowdroid: Precise context, flow, field, object-sensitive and lifecycle-aware taint analysis for android apps. In: ACM SIGPLAN (2014)
10. Balakrishnan, G., Reps, T.: Analyzing memory accesses in x86 executables. In: Duesterwald, E. (ed.) CC 2004. LNCS, vol. 2985, pp. 5–23. Springer, Heidelberg (2004). doi:10.1007/978-3-540-24723-4_2
11. Balakrishnan, G., Reps, T.: What you see is not what you execute. ACM Trans. Program. Lang. Syst. **32**(6), 23:1–23:84 (2010)
12. Bansal, S., Aiken, A.: Binary translation using peephole super optimizers. In: OSDI 2008 (2008)
13. Bao, T., Burket, J., Woo, M., Turner, R., Brumley, D. Byteweight: learning to recognize functions in binary code. In: USENIX Security 2014 (2014)
14. Bardin, S., Herrmann, P., Védrine, F.: Refinement-based CFG reconstruction from unstructured programs. In: Jhala, R., Schmidt, D. (eds.) VMCAI 2011. LNCS, vol. 6538, pp. 54–69. Springer, Heidelberg (2011). doi:10.1007/978-3-642-18275-4_6
15. Brauer, J., Hansen, R.R., Kowalewski, S., Larsen, K.G., Olesen, M.C.: Adaptable value-set analysis for low-level code. In: SSV 2012 (2012)
16. Brumley, D., Jager, I., Avgerinos, T., Schwartz, E.J.: BAP: a binary analysis platform. In: Gopalakrishnan, G., Qadeer, S. (eds.) CAV 2011. LNCS, vol. 6806, pp. 463–469. Springer, Heidelberg (2011). doi:10.1007/978-3-642-22110-1_37
17. Brumley, D., Lee, J., Schwartz, E.J., Woo, M.: Native x86 decompilation using semantics-preserving structural analysis and iterative control-flow structuring. In: USENIX SEC 2013 (2013)
18. Castro, M., Costa, M., Martin, J.-P., Peinado, M., Akritidis, P., Donnelly, A., Barham, P., Black, R.: Fast byte-granularity software fault isolation. In: SIGOPS 2009 (2009)
19. Cha, S.K., Woo, M., Brumley, D.: Program-adaptive mutational fuzzing. In: S&P 2015 (2015)
20. Cifuentes, C., Van Emmerik, M.: Recovery of jump table case statements from binary code. In: Program Comprehension (1999)
21. Cojocar, L., Zaddach, J., Verdult, R., Bos, H., Francillon, A., Balzarotti, D.: Parser identification in embedded systems. In: ACSAC 2015 (2015)
22. Davi, L., Lehmann, D., Sadeghi, A.-R., Monrose, F.: Stitching the gadgets: on the ineffectiveness of coarse-grained control-flow integrity protection. In: USENIX SEC 2014 (2014)
23. Di Federico, A., Payer, M., Agosta, G.: Rev.Ng: a unified binary analysis framework to recover CFGs and function boundaries. In: Proceedings of the 26th International Conference on Compiler Construction, CC 2017, pp. 131–141. ACM (2017)
24. Durfina, L., Křoustek, J., Zemek, P., Kolávr, D., Hruska, T., Masarík, K., Meduna, A.: Design of a retargetable decompiler for a static platform-independent malware analysis. Int. J. Secur. Its Appl. **5**(4), 91–106 (2011)
25. Erlingsson, U., Abadi, M., Vrable, M., Budiu, M., Necula, G.: Software guards for system address spaces. In: OSDI 2006 (2006)

26. Evans, I., Long, F., Otgonbaatar, U., Shrobe, H., Rinard, M., Okhravi, H., Sidiroglou-Douskos, S.: Control jujutsu: on the weaknesses of fine-grained control flow integrity. In: CCS 2015 (2015)
27. Ford, B., Cox, R.: Vx32: lightweight user-level sandboxing on the x86. In: USENIX Annual Technical Conference
28. Ganesh, V., Leek, T., Rinard, M.: Taint-based directed whitebox fuzzing. In: ICSE 2009 (2009)
29. Gedich, A., Lazdin, A.: Improved algorithm for identification of switch tables in executable code. In: FRUCT 2015 (2015)
30. Harris, L.C., Miller, B.P.: Practical analysis of stripped binary code. ACM SIGARCH Comput. Archit. News **33**(5), 63–68 (2005)
31. Holsti, N.: Analysing switch-case tables by partial evaluation. In: WCET (2007)
32. Kinder, J., Veith, H.: Jakstab: a static analysis platform for binaries. In: Gupta, A., Malik, S. (eds.) CAV 2008. LNCS, vol. 5123, pp. 423–427. Springer, Heidelberg (2008). doi:10.1007/978-3-540-70545-1_40
33. Kinder, J., Veith, H.: Precise static analysis of untrusted driver binaries. In: FMCAD 2010 (2010)
34. Křoustek, J.: Retargetable Analysis of Machine Code. PhD thesis, Faculty of Information Technology, Brno University of Technology, CZ (2015)
35. Kästner, D., Wilhelm, S.: Generic Control Flow Reconstruction from Assembly Code
36. Li, Y., McCune, J., Newsome, J., Perrig, A., Baker, B., Drewry, W.: Minibox : a two-way sandbox for x86 native code. In: USENIX ATC 2014 (2014)
37. McCabe, T.J.: A complexity measure. IEEE Softw. Eng. (1976)
38. McCamant, S., Morrisett, G.: Evaluating SFI for a CISC architecture. In: USENIX-SS 2006 (2006)
39. Meng, X., Miller, B.: Binary code is not easy. In: ISSTA 2016 (2016)
40. Microsoft. The Z3 Theorem Prover, February 2016. https://github.com/Z3Prover/z3
41. Ming, J., Wu, D., Xiao, G., Wang, J., Liu, P. TaintPipe: pipelined symbolic taint analysis. In: USENIX SEC 2015 (2015)
42. O'Sullivan, P., Anand, K., Kotha, A.: Retrofitting security in COTS software with binary rewriting. In: IFP SEC 2011 (2011)
43. Reinbacher, T., Brauer, J.: Precise control flow reconstruction using boolean logic. In: EMSOFT 2011 (2011)
44. Sayle, R.A.: A superoptimizer analysis of multiway branch code generation. In: Proceedings of the GCC Developers Summit (2008)
45. Sehr, D., Muth, R., Biffle, C. L., Khimenko, V., Pasko, E., Yee, B., Schimpf, K., Chen, B.: Adapting software fault isolation to contemporary CPU architectures. In: USENIX SEC 2010 (2010)
46. Shen, B.-Y., Chen, J.-Y., Hsu, W.-C., Yang, W.: An LLVM-based static binary translator. In: Proceedings of the 2012 International Conference on Compilers, Architectures and Synthesis for Embedded Systems, CASES 2012, pp. 51–60. ACM, New York (2012)
47. Shin, Y., Williams, L.: An empirical model to predict security vulnerabilities using code complexity metrics. In: ESEM 2008 (2008)
48. Shoshitaishvili, Y., Wang, R., Salls, C., Stephens, N., Polino, M., Dutcher, A., Grosen, J., Feng, S., Hauser, C., Kruegel, C., Vigna, G.: SoK: (State of) the art of war: offensive techniques in binary analysis. In: S&P 2016 (2016)
49. Smithson, M., Anand, K., Kotha, A.: Binary rewriting without relocation information. Technical report. University of Maryland, November 2010

50. Tice, C., Roeder, T., Collingbourne, P., Checkoway, S., Erlingsson, U., Lozano, L., Pike, G.: Enforcing forward-edge control-flow integrity in GCC & LLVM. In: USENIX SEC 2014 (2014)
51. Tikir, M. M., Laurenzano, M., Carrington, L., Snavely, A.: PMaC binary instrumentation library for PowerPC/AIX. In: Workshop on Bin. Inst. and App. (2006)
52. van der Veen, V., Andriesse, D., Göktaş, E., Gras, B., Sambuc, L., Slowinska, A., Bos, H., Giuffrida, C.: Practical context-sensitive cfi. In: CCS 2015 (2015)
53. Wang, S., Wang, P., Wu, D.: Reassembleable disassembling. In: USENIX SEC 2015 (2015)
54. Wang, X., Jhi, Y.-C., Zhu, S., Liu, P. Still : Exploit code detection via static taint and initialization analyses. In: ACSAC 2008 (2008)
55. Yee, B., Sehr, D., Dardyk, G., Chen, J., Muth, R., Ormandy, T., Okasaka, S., Narula, N., Fullagar, N.: Native client: a sandbox for portable, untrusted x86 native code. In: S&P 2009 (2009)
56. Zaddach, J., Bruno, L., Francillon, A., Balzarotti, D.: A framework to support dynamic security analysis of embedded systems' firmwares. In: NDSS 2014 (2014)
57. Zeng, B., Tan, G., Morrisett, G.: Combining control-flow integrity and static analysis for efficient and validated data sandboxing. In: CCS18, pp. 29–40. ACM (2011)
58. Zhang, M., Sekar, R.: Control flow integrity for COTS binaries. In: USENIX SEC 2013 (2013)

A Formal Approach to Exploiting Multi-stage Attacks Based on File-System Vulnerabilities of Web Applications

Federico De Meo[1](✉) and Luca Viganò[2]

[1] Dipartimento di Informatica, Università degli Studi di Verona, Verona, Italy
federico.demeo@univr.it
[2] Department of Informatics, King's College London, London, UK

Abstract. We propose a formal approach that allows one to (i) reason about file-system vulnerabilities of web applications and (ii) combine file-system vulnerabilities and SQL-Injection vulnerabilities for complex, multi-stage attacks. We have developed an automatic tool that implements our approach and we show its efficiency by discussing four real-world case studies, which are witness to the fact that our tool can generate, and exploit, attacks that, to the best of our knowledge, no other tool for the security of web applications can find.

1 Introduction

Context and motivations. Modern web applications (*web apps*, for short) often make intensive use of functionalities for reading and writing content from the *web app's file-system* (i.e., the file-system of the web server that hosts the web app). *Reading* from and *writing* to the file-system are routine operations that web apps perform for different tasks. For instance, the option of dynamically loading resources based on runtime needs is commonly adopted by developers to structure the web app's source code for stronger reusability. Similarly, several web apps allow users to upload (write) content that can be shared with other users or can be available from a web browser as in a cloud service. Reading and writing functionalities are offered by most server-side programming languages for developing web apps such as PHP [20], JSP [18] or ASP [3]. Modern database APIs also provide a convenient way to interact with the file-system (e.g., backup or restore functionalities), but they also increase the attack surface an attacker could exploit. Whenever an attacker finds a way to exploit vulnerabilities that allow him to gain access to the web app's file-system, the security of the whole web app is put at high risk. Indeed, both OWASP [19] and MITRE [7] list vulnerabilities that compromise the file-system among the most common and dangerous vulnerabilities that afflict the security of modern software.[1]

---

[1] The Top 10 compiled by OWASP is a general classification and it does not include a specific category named "file-system vulnerability"; however, "Injections", "Broken Authentication and session Management", "Security misconfiguration" (just to name a few) can all lead to a vulnerability related to the file-system.

© Springer International Publishing AG 2017
E. Bodden et al. (Eds.): ESSoS 2017, LNCS 10379, pp. 196–212, 2017.
DOI: 10.1007/978-3-319-62105-0_13

Vulnerability assessment and penetration testing are the two main steps that security analysts typically undertake when assessing the security of a web app and other computer systems [6,16,23]. During a *vulnerability assessment*, automatic scanning tools are used to search for common vulnerabilities of the system under analysis (Wfuzz [26] and DotDotPwn [13] are the main tools for file-system-related vulnerabilities). However, it is well known [14] that state-of-the-art scanners do not detect vulnerabilities linked to the logical flaws of web apps. This means that *even if a vulnerability is found, no tool can link it to logical flaws leading to the violation of a security property.* The result of the vulnerability assessment is thus used to perform the second and more complicated step: during a *penetration test (pentest)*, the analyst defines an attack goal and manually attempts to exploit the discovered vulnerabilities to determine whether the attack goal he defined can actually be achieved. A pentest is meant to show the real damage on a specific web app resulting from the exploitation of one or more vulnerabilities. Consider the following example, which is simple but also fundamental to understand the motivation for the approach that we propose.

Trustwave SpiderLabs found a SQL injection vulnerability in Joomla! [17], a popular Content Management System (CMS). In [24], Trustwave researchers show two things: the code vulnerable to SQL injection and how the injection could have been exploited for obtaining full administrative access. The description of the vulnerable code clearly highlights an inadequate filtering of data when executing a SQL query. The description of the damage resulting from the exploitation of the SQL injection shows that an attacker might be able to perform a session hijacking by stealing session values stored as plain-text in the database. The result of this analysis points out two problems: Joomla! is failing in (1) properly filtering data used when performing a SQL query and (2) securely storying session values. Problem (1) could have been identified by vulnerability scanners (e.g., sqlmap is able to identify the vulnerability), but *no automatic vulnerability scanner can identify Problem (2) and only a manual pentesting session is effective.* However, manual pentesting relies on the security analyst's expertise and skills, making the entire pentesting phase easily prone to errors. An analyst might underestimate the impact of a certain vulnerability leaving the entire web app exposed to attackers. *This is why we can't stop at the identification of a SQL injection or file-system-related vulnerability, and why we can't address the ensuing attacks with a manual analysis.* Our approach addresses this by automating the identification of attacks that exploit such multi-stage vulnerabilities.

Contributions. Our contributions are two-fold. First, we formally define file-system vulnerabilities and how to exploit them to violate security properties of web apps. A number of formal approaches based on the *Dolev-Yao (DY) attacker model* [12] have been developed for the security analysis of web apps, e.g., [1,2,4, 9,22,25]. However, file-system vulnerabilities of web apps have never been taken into consideration by formal approaches before. In this paper, we define how web apps interact with the file-system and show how the DY model can be used to exploit file-system vulnerabilities. Moreover, we extend our previous work on the exploitation of SQL-Injection (SQLi) vulnerabilities [9] by showing how to combine file-system vulnerabilities and SQLi vulnerabilities for the identification of complex, multi-stage attacks commonly identified only by manual analysis during the pentesting phase. It is crucial to point out that we do not search for payloads that can be used to exploit a particular vulnerability, but rather we exploit file-system vulnerabilities.

Second, to show that our formalization can effectively generate multi-stage attacks where file-system and SQLi vulnerabilities are exploited, we have developed a prototype tool called *WAFEx (Web Application Formal Exploiter,* [10]*)* and we discuss here its application to four real-world case studies. WAFEx can generate, and exploit, complex attacks that, to the best of our knowledge, no other state-of-the-art-tool for the security analysis of web apps can find. In particular, we show how WAFEx can automatically generate different attack traces violating the same security property, a result that only a manual analysis performed by a pentester can achieve. In each attack trace, multiple vulnerabilities are used in combination.

Organization. In Sect. 2, we give a classification of file-system-related vulnerabilities. In Sect. 3, we provide our formal approach. In Sect. 4, we describe the WAFEx tool and discuss its application to four real-world case studies. In Sect. 5, we draw conclusions and discuss related work and future work.

2   A Classification of File-System-Related Vulnerabilities

To provide a coherent and uniform starting point for reasoning about file-system-related vulnerabilities, we give a classification of the vulnerabilities of web apps that lead to compromise the file-system. The two security properties that we consider are: *authentication* (the attacker gets unauthorized access to a restricted area) and *confidentiality* (the attacker gets access to content stored in the web app's file-system that isn't meant to be publicly available). We have identified five vulnerability categories, which we describe below, focusing on the main details of the attacks that are relevant for our formalization.

(1) Directory Traversal (DT) (a.k.a. *Path Traversal*). Operations on files (reading and writing) performed by a web app are intended to occur in the *root directory* of the web app, a restricted directory where the web app actually resides. A *DT vulnerability* refers to a lack of authorization controls when an attacker attempts to access a location that is intended to identify a file or directory stored in a restricted area outside the web app's root directory. Whenever the access permissions of a web app are not restricted in such a way that they only allow users to access authorized files, an attacker might be able to craft a payload that allows him to access restricted files located outside the web app's root directory.

(2) SQL-Injection (SQLi). Most modern DMBSs provide APIs that extend SQL's expressiveness by allowing SQL code to access a web app's file-system for reading and writing purposes. Reading APIs allow developers to produce code that retrieves content stored in the web app's file-system and loads it in

the database. Writing APIs allow developers to produce code that saves content from the database to the web app's file-system. Attackers mainly exploit SQLi to bypass authentication mechanisms or to extract data from the database, but, as there is no limit on the SQL syntax that could be injected, it is also possible to exploit reading and writing APIs to access the underlying file-system [8].

(3) File Inclusion (FI). All programing languages for the development of web apps support functionalities for structuring code into separate files so that the same code can be reused at runtime by dynamically including files whenever required. A *FI vulnerability* refers to a lack of proper sanitization of user-supplied data during the creation of a file location string that will be used to locate a resource meant to be included in a web page. When the file location depends on user-supplied data, an attacker can exploit it and force the inclusion of files different from the ones intended by the developers. FI might allow an attacker to access arbitrary resources stored on the file-system and to execute code.

(4) Forced Browsing (FB) (a.k.a. *Direct Request*) refers to a lack of authorization controls when a resource is directly accessed via URLs. This lack of authorization might allow an attacker to enumerate and access resources that are not referenced by the web app (thus not directly displayed to the users through the web app) or that are intended to be accessed only as a result of previous HTTP requests. By making an appropriate HTTP request, an attacker could access resources with a direct request rather than by following the intended path. The lack of authorization controls comes from the erroneous assumption that resources can only be reached through a given navigation path. This mis-assumption leads developers to implementing authorization mechanisms only at certain points along the way for accessing a resource, leaving no controls when a resource is directly accessed.

(5) Unrestricted File Upload (UFU). A widespread feature provided by web apps is the possibility of uploading files that will be stored on the web app's file-system. An *UFU vulnerability* refers to a lack of proper file sanitization when a web app allows for uploading files. The consequences can vary, ranging from complete takeover with remote arbitrary code execution to simple defacement, where the attacker is able to modify the content shown to users by the web app.

3   A Formalization to Reason About File-System Vulnerabilities

We will now describe how we formally represent the behavior of a file-system and of a web app that interacts with it. We also show how our formalization allows the DY attacker to successfully exploit file-system vulnerabilities. In our formalization, we used ASLan++, the formal specification language of the AVANTSSAR Platform [2], but in fact our approach is general and for the sake of readability we give here pseudo-code rather than ASLan++.

Our approach doesn't search for payloads that can be used to exploit file-system vulnerabilities, but rather analyzes the security of web apps by exploiting

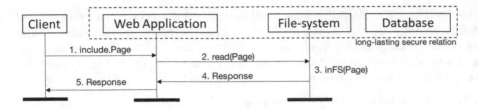

Fig. 1. MSC of a FI vulnerability.

vulnerabilities that lead attackers to have unauthorized access to the file-system. To deal with such vulnerabilities, we need to represent the *behavior of the*

(i) *web app*, which defines the interaction with client, file-system and database,
(ii) *file-system*, which interacts with the web app and the database for reading and writing content,
(iii) *database*, which can also interact with the file-system,
(iv) *attacker*, who interacts only with the web app.

We do not formalize the behavior of honest clients since we assume the DY attacker to be the only agent to communicate with the web app, i.e., we are only interested in dishonest interactions. This is because the exploitation of file-system vulnerabilities doesn't require interaction with the honest users.

To explain how our formalization works, we will use a simple FI example depicted in Fig. 1 as a *Message Sequence Chart (MSC)* in which there are three entities: client, web app and file-system (the fourth entity, database, does not send messages and will be discussed later). In this example and, in general, in our formalization, we assume the web app and the file-system (and the database) to have a long-lasting secure relation, i.e., no attacker can read or modify the communication between them.[2] As is standard, constants begin with a lower case character (e.g., `filePath`), variables with an upper case one (e.g., `Page`).

In step (1), the client sends to the web app a message containing the variable `Page`, representing the page to be included. In step (2), the web app performs a read operation by issuing a `read(Page)` request. In step (3), the file-system checks if the requested page points to an existing file and, in step (4), it replies to the web app with a variable `Response` that represents the result of the read operation. In step (5), the web app forwards the response to the client.

Definition 1. Messages *consist of* variables V, constants c, concatenation $M.M$, function application $f(M)$ *of uninterpreted function symbols* f *to messages* M, *and* encryption $\{M\}_M$ *of messages with public, private or symmetric keys that are themselves messages.*[3] *We define that* M_1 *is a submessage of* M_2

---

[2] We assume the communication with the file-system to be secure since the file-system actually is not a real network node, and thus no attacker can put himself between the communication with the file-system, i.e., man-in-the-middle attacks are not possible.

[3] In this paper, we need not distinguish between different kinds of encrypted messages, but we could do it by following standard practice. Here we don't even need to consider explicitly encrypted messages, but we add them for completeness.

as is standard (e.g., M_1 is a submessage of $M_1.M_3$, of $f(M_1)$ and of $\{M_1\}_{M_4}$) and, abusing notation, we then write $M_1 \in M_2$.

3.1   The DY Attacker as a Web Attacker

The DY model [12] defines an attacker that has total control over the network but cannot break cryptography: he can intercept messages and decrypt them if he holds the corresponding keys for decryption, he can generate new messages from his knowledge and send messages under any agent name. Message generation and analysis are formalized by derivation rules, expressing how the attacker can derive messages from his knowledge in order to use them for performing attacks.

Suppose that we want to search for a FI vulnerability possibly leading the attacker to access resources stored outside the root folder of the web app (DT). As described in Sect. 2, the attacker can try to access resources by injecting a payload used for accessing a file that will be included in the current page. However, it is important to point out two fundamental aspects of our work: (1) as stated, we are not interested in generating the payloads that will exploit vulnerabilities, but rather we want to represent that a vulnerability can be exploited and what happens when it is exploited, and (2) we want to avoid state-space explosion by making the models as simple as possible. We have thus introduced the constant `fsi` that represents any and all payloads for exploiting file-system vulnerabilities (e.g., `../../../` for DT). By using `fsi` and the definition of the file-system entity (Sect. 3.2), we allow the DY attacker to deal with file-system vulnerabilities.

3.2   File-System

We will now give a formalization of the file-system entity that can be used in any specification when searching for attacks related to file-system vulnerabilities of web apps. As depicted in Fig. 1, the file-system can be seen as a network node always actively listening for incoming connections, and the web app sends reading and writing requests to the file-system.

Our formalization aims to abstract away as many concrete details as possible, while still being able to represent the exploitation of file-system vulnerabilities, and so we do not represent the file-system structure but rather formalize messages sent and received along with reading and writing behavior. This allows us to give a compact formalization so as to avoid state-space explosion problems when carrying out the analysis with the model checker.

Incoming messages. As incoming messages for the file-system entity, we consider only reading and writing requests, for which we use the uninterpreted functions `readFile()` and `writeFile()`, both taking a generic variable `Filepath` that represents a file location in the file-system.

Reading and writing behavior. To exploit vulnerabilities related to reading and writing operations, we need to represent the available files in addition to the behavior of the two operations. We represent the existence of a file by means of the predicate inFS(), i.e., inFS(filePath) means that the file represented by the constant filePath is stored in the file-system.

When the file-system entity receives a reading request readFile(filePath), it checks, by means of inFS(), whether the file exists: if so, then it answers to the request with file(filePath), i.e., wrapping the file being read with the uninterpreted function file(), else the constant no_file is returned.[4]

When the file-system entity receives a writing request writeFile(file), it uses inFS() to mark the file as part of the file-system but it need not return a result to the web app (as explained in Footnote 4).

To represent an attacker's attempt to access files, we include the Horn clause

```
fs_hc_evil(M):inFS(fsi.M)
```

that states that the predicate inFS() holds for a message whenever it is of the form fsi.M, i.e., a message that is a concatenation including the constant fsi that represents a payload to exploit file-system vulnerabilities. More specifically, this states that the attacker has injected a malicious payload fsi into the parameters (expressed as a variable) M. In case of a DT attack, one may think of fsi as the ../../../ payload that escapes from the web app's root folder.

The specification. Summarizing, the pseudo-code representing the file-system behavior is in Listing 1.1 (the full ASLan++ specification is in [11]. We represent the file-system as a network node always actively listening for incoming messages. More specifically, we define the file-system by two mutually exclusive branches of an if-elseif statement: in the guard in line (1) the file-system receives (expressed in Alice&Bob notation) a reading request and in (4) it receives a writing request. For the reading request, the file-system verifies the existence of the file (2): if the file exists, then the file-system returns the variable Filepath wrapped with the uninterpreted function file() (2), else the constant no_file is returned instead (3, where ! formalizes negation). As we assume that writing operations always succeed, when a writing request is received, the file-system marks the new file as "existing" by means of inFS() and need not return (4).

Listing 1.1. Pseudo-code representing the behavior of the file-system; we write FS for the file-system and Entity as a general entity (either web app or database).

```
1  if(Entity -> FS: readFile(Filepath)){
2   if(inFS(Filepath)){
3    FS -> Entity : file(Filepath);
4   } elseif(!(inFS(Filepath))){
5    FS -> Entity : no_file;
6   } elseif(Entity -> FS: writeFile(Filepath)){
7    inFS(Filepath);
8   }
```

---

[4] We don't need to consider access control policies/models as they are external to the web app. Hence, we assume that every file that is in the file-system can always be read and that every writing operation will always succeed..

3.3 Database

To cover all file-system vulnerabilities (Sect. 2), we need to formalize a database that can interact with the file-system. We can adapt the basic formalization we gave in [9] for the case of SQLi vulnerabilities by including interaction with the file-system (and thus to also be able to cover file-system access through SQLi vulnerabilities, see Sect. 2). We can see the database, like the file-system, as a network node that interacts with the web app and the file-system. The idea behind the extension is to make the database able to perform a reading or writing request to the file-system whenever a query is valid. We also modified how sanitized queries are handled by removing the sanitization function `sanitizedQuery()` from the database specification of [9] and introducing a new uninterpreted function `sanitized()` that represents a general sanitization function (see Sect. 3.4 for further details).

The pseudo-code of the extension is shown in Listing 1.2. We focus only on the new part and refer to [9] for the main behavior. The database entity is still represented by an if-elseif statement. The main if branch (1) handles sanitized queries, represented with the new sanitization function, whereas the second branch (3) handles raw queries. Within the raw query branch, we have defined two additional behaviors. The first new branch performs a read operation on the file-system (5) and, if the file-system sends back a file (6), the database wraps the answer from the file-system with `tuple()` and sends it back to the web app (6). The second new branch (7) handles writing operations performed by the database, for which the answer to the web app will be a message of the form `tuple(newFile(filePath))`, where `newFile()` is an uninterpreted function stating that a file has been written as a result of a SQL query.

Listing 1.2. Pseudo-code representing the behavior of the extended database.

```
1  if(WebApp -> DB: query(sanitized(SQLquery))){
2   if(SQLquery == tuple(*)){
3    DB -> WebApp: no_tuple;
4  }} elseif(WebApp -> DB: query(SQLquery)){
5   if(inDB(sqlquery)){
6    DB -> WebApp: tuple(SQLquery);
7   } elseif(inDB(SQLquery)){
8    DB -> FS: read(SQLquery);
9    if(FS -> DB: file(SQLquery)){
10     DB -> WebApp: tuple(file(SQLquery));
11  }} elseif(inDB(SQLquery)){ DB -> FS: write(SQLquery);
12    DB -> WebApp: tuple(new_file(SQLquery));
13  } elseif(!(inDB(SQLquery))){
14    DB -> WebApp: no_tuple;
15  }}
```

3.4 Web Application

The web app is another node of the network that can send and receive messages. In our formalization, the web app can communicate with client, file-system and database. In [9] we also provided some guidelines on how to represent web apps, however, they were limited to basic interaction with the database. In this paper we provide extended guidelines that also take the file-system into consideration.

The file-system and the database entities don't depend on the web app and thus we can reuse them in every model. The web app formalization does depend on the scenario being modeled, but we give a series of guidelines on how to represent the web app's behavior for testing the interaction with the file-system and the database.

If statements. HTTP is a stateless protocol, which means that each pair request-response is considered as an independent transaction that is not related to any previous request-response. We use if statements to define that a web app can answer different requests without following a specific sequence of messages, thus representing the stateless nature of HTTP. The web app's model is thus a sequence of if statements defining all the requests the web app can handle.

Client communication. A general HTTP request (and response) header comprises different fields that are needed for the message to be processed by the browser. In our formalization, we don't need to represent all the fields of a real request (or response) header as they are not relevant to the analysis, and thus we limit to: a variable representing the sender, a variable representing the receiver, and a concatenation of constants and variables representing the message.

In case of a request, the message would be represented by the HTTP query string containing parameters and values. For example, a request to the URL `http://example.com/index.php?page=menu.php` can be represented as `Client -> WebApp : index.Page`, where `index` is a constant representing a web page and `Page` is a variable representing an HTTP query value. We proceed similarly to formalize a response from the web app to the client. We only represent the details needed for the analysis: a constant representing the returned page (e.g., `admin`, `dashboard`, ...), the function `file()` when the web app performs a reading operation on the file-system, and the function `tuple()` that is returned only if the executed query is `SELECT`, `UPDATE` or `DELETE` (see [9] for further details). For example, the response `WebApp -> Client : dashboard.file(fsi)` can be used to represent the result of a successful request where the client receives the `dashboard` page. The message `file(fsi)` is returned to express that a file was retrieved from the file-system.

File-system and database communication. As already stated in Sect. 3.2, whenever the web app has to read content from the file-system, it sends a `readFile()` request and whenever it has to write to the file-system, it sends a `writeFile()` request. When the web app has to perform a SQL query on the database, it sends a `query()` request to the database (see Sect. 3.3). To allow the web app to represent sanitized input, we introduced an uninterpreted function `sanitized()` that allows the modeler to "switch on" or "switch off" the possibility of exploiting a vulnerability either of the file-system or of the database, letting the model-checker analyze the web app for possible attacks. The web app has to check the response coming from the file-system or the database in order to behave properly. For example, if a file is being read, the web app has to check that the file-system is answering with the uninterpreted function file() before proceeding further.

Remote code execution. Our formalization can represent scenarios where the attacker is able to write arbitrary files into the web app's file-system leading to arbitrary remote code execution. As described earlier, a web app model is a sequence of if statements defining the requests the web app responds to. The possibility of uploading a file that leads to code execution can be seen as a way of increasing the number of requests the web app responds to. We then include into the model of the web app a series of predefined if branches representing the behavior of common malicious code an attacker might try to upload. We define that these malicious if branches can be used by the attacker only if the file exists in the file-system (i.e., inFS() is valid for that file). This will ensure that the attacker finds a way of writing the malicious file before actually using it.

Sessions. As already mentioned, HTTP is a stateless protocol. In order for the user to experience a stateful interaction with a web app (e.g., the web app recognizes when a user is logged-in when he changes page), developers make use of sessions. A *session* allows a web app to store information into a memory area in order to have it accessible across multiple pages. When a request is made to a web page that creates a session, the web page allocates a memory area and assigns to that area a session identifier. The same session identifier is sent back to the client (generally as a cookie value) within the response for that request. When a cookie is received, a web browser automatically sends it back to the web app when a new request is made. The web app receives the session identifier and uses it to retrieve the information stored within the associated memory area.

In order to represent sessions, we introduced the predicate sessionValue() to state that a variable is a session value. Whenever a request is made to a page that creates a session value, a new variable is created, marked as a session value and returned to the client. Whenever a page requires a session prior to performing any further step, the page needs to verify that one of the variables sent to the web app is indeed a session value.

Taking stock. Listing 1.3 can now finally formalize the FI example of Fig. 1. The web app accepts a request for include.Page, where include is a constant representing the web page being requested and Page is a variable representing the page to include (1). The web app sends a reading request with the page received by the client (1). The file-system checks if the file is stored in the file-system and then sends a response to the web app (2): if the response is of the form file(Page) (3), then the web app sends back to the client include (representing an included web page) along with file(Page) (representing the content of the included file), else it sends include without further details (4).

Listing 1.3. Pseudo-code representing the behavior of FI example of Fig. 1.

```
1  if(Client -> WebApp: include.Page){
2    WebApp -> FS : read(Page);
3    FS -> WebApp: Response;
4    if(Response == file(Page)){
5      WebApp -> Client: include.file(Page);
6    }else{
7      WebApp -> Client: include;
8    }}
```

3.5 Goals

The last component of the formalization is the goal (or security property) that should be verified. As we discussed in Sect. 2, we are not interested in finding file-system vulnerabilities but rather we want to exploit them. In particular, we define security properties related to authentication bypass and confidentiality breach, which, respectively, express that the attacker can access some part of the web app that should be protected with some sort of authorization mechanisms, or obtain information that is "leaked" from the web app (such "leakage" can happen from either the file-system or the database).

We use the LTL "globally" operator [], which defines that a formula has to hold on the entire subsequent temporal path, and the iknowledge predicate, which represents the knowledge of the attacker. We can then represent authentication goals by stating that the attacker will never have access to some specific page, and confidentiality goals by stating that the attacker will never increase his knowledge with parts coming from the file-system or the database, i.e., file(). The confidentiality goal for the FI example in Fig. 1 is shown in Listing 1.4, stating that the attacker will never know something of the form file().

Listing 1.4. Confidentiality goal for the FI example in Fig. 1.

```
[](!(iknowledge(file(*))))
```

4   Our Tool WAFEx and Its Application to Case Studies

In this section, we show how our formalization can be used effectively for representing and testing attacks involving the exploit of file-system vulnerabilities. We have developed a prototype tool, called *WAFEx*, that shows how the *abstract attack trace (AAT)* generated from our models can be concretized and tested over the implementations of the real web apps. We have tested WAFEx on *Damn Vulnerable Web Application (DVWA)* [15] and on *Multi-Stage*, a web app we wrote for security testing and freely available at [10]. DVWA is a vulnerable web app that provides an environment in which security analysts can test their skills and tools. DVWA is divided in examples implementing web pages vulnerable to the most common web app vulnerabilities. We selected three relevant exercises from DVWA: FI, UFU and SQLi. WAFEx was able to identify the intended vulnerability on all the case studies and was also able to identify an unintended vulnerability of SQLi for file reading in the SQLi exercise of DVWA.

In the remainder of this section, we will describe WAFEx and present the Multi-Stage case study that shows how file-system vulnerabilities and SQLi can be combined for the generation of multi-stage attack on the same web app.

Our pool of case studies might look small and trivial at first, but it is worth noting that DVWA is a state-of-the-art testing environment used for teaching the security of web apps to pentesters and the case studies represent real scenarios that might be implemented by many web apps. Moreover, ethical aspects prevented us from blindly executing WAFEx on the Internet since our implementation makes use of brute-forcing tools such as Wfuzz and sqlmap, whose unauthorized usage must be approved by the owner of the web app. Finally, we didn't test the latest release of any free CMSs as that would require a first phase of vulnerability assessment, which is out of the scope of this work.

We give here only the pseudo-code specification of the web apps and the goals; full models in pseudo-code and ASLan++ can be found in [11].

4.1 WAFEx: A Web Application Formal Exploiter

WAFEx takes in input an ASLan++ specification together with a concretization file that contains information such as the real URL of the web app and the name of the real parameters used for making requests. We have chosen ASLan++ so to apply the model-checkers of the AVANTSSAR Platform [2] (in particular, CL-AtSe), but our approach is general and could be used with other specification languages and/or other reasoners implementing the DY attacker model.

To aid the security analyst in the model creation, we have written a Python script that allows him to first use the Burp proxy [21] to record a trace of HTTP requests/responses generated by interacting with the web app, and then use our script to convert this trace into an ASLan++ model. The analyst has to specify the behavior for the HTTP requests and the security goal he wants to test.

WAFEx is also able to automatically use information it extracts during an attack (e.g., as a result of FI) to proceed further with the execution of an AAT. We have run WAFEx on our case studies using a Mac Book laptop (Intel i5-4288U with 8 G RAM and Python3.5). The execution time of the model-checking phase ranges from 30 ms to 50 ms, while the overall process (from MSC generation to concretization) depends on the external tools Wfuzz and sqlmap.

4.2 Case Study: The Multi-stage Web App

Multi-Stage is a web app that we specifically wrote in order to show how file-system and SQLi vulnerabilities can be combined together to generate multiple attack traces. We designed Multi-Stage to ensure that it is realistic and representative of software that could indeed be deployed.

Multi-Stage implements a typical HTTP login phase in which users can log into the system by providing username and password. The web app performs a query to the database in order to verify the credentials and grant access to a restricted area. The restricted area allows users to view other users' profiles and modify their own personal information (Name, Surname, Phone number), and it allows for the upload of a personal image to use as avatar. We check the web app for file reading attacks, i.e., we want to generate multi-stage attack traces showing how an attacker can exploit file-system and SQLi vulnerabilities to get read access to the web app's file-system. A detailed description of the model can be found in [10,11].

We ran this model with WAFEx in order to test the security of Multi-Stage. Unfortunately, the model-checker CL-AtSe that we use inside WAFEx does not allow for generating multiple attack traces (nor do the other back-ends of the AVANTSSAR Platform). Thus, whenever a trace was found, we disabled the branch corresponding to the attack and run WAFEx again to generate another trace different from the previous one. This process does, of course, miss some traces since by disabling a branch we prevent any other trace to use that branch in a different step of the attack trace.[5] However, it shows that multiple traces can actually be generated. We generated three different AATs: #1, #2 and #3.

AAT #1. This first AAT shows how an attacker might be able to exploit an SQLi in the login phase to directly read files from the file-system (Listing 1.5). The attacker i sends to the web app a request for login by sending the payload sqli.fsi (1). The web app sends a query to the database entity (2), which forces the database into sending a read request to the file-system entity with value fsi (3). The file-system checks if the provided file is part of the file-system and answers to the database with that file (4). The database forwards the response from the file-system to the web app (5), which, finally, sends to the attacker the dashboard page along with the result from the database (6).

Listing 1.5. AAT #1 for accessing the file-system in Multi-stage.

```
1  i -> WebApp : login.sqli.fsi.Password
2  WebApp -> DB: query(sqli.fsi)
3  DB -> FS : readFile(fsi)
4  FS -> DB : file(fsi)
5  DB -> WebApp : tuple(file(fsi))
6  WebApp -> i : dashboard.AuthCookie.tuple(file(fsi))
```

AAT #2. We disabled the branch that allows the database to read from the file-system and ran the model again in order to generate a different AAT (Listing 1.6). The attacker i tries to exploit a SQLi in order to write a malicious file so to exploit a remote code execution. i sends to the web app a request for login by sending the payload sqli.evil_file (1). The web app sends a query to the database entity (2), which forces the database into sending a writing request with value evil_file to the file-system (3). The file-system marks the new file as available in the file-system and the database sends a response to the web app

---

[5] We plan to extend CL-AtSe or replace it with a tool capable of generating multiple attack traces.

with the file just created (4). The web app responds to i with the `dashboard` page along with a newly generated cookie and the result of the creation of a new file (5). The attacker i now exploits the `evil_file` by sending the payload `fsi` to the web app (6). The web app will now perform a `readFile()` operation on the file-system and will send the retrieved file back to the attacker (7–9).

Listing 1.6. AAT #2 for accessing the file-system in Multi-Stage.

```
1   i -> WebApp : login.sqli.evil_file.Password
2   WebApp -> DB: query(sqli.evil_file)
3   DB -> FS : writeFile(evil_file)
4   DB -> WebApp : tuple(new_file(evil_file))
5   WebApp -> i : dashboard.AuthCookie.tuple(new_file(
        evil_file))
6   i -> WebApp : file.fsi
7   WebApp -> FS : readFile(fsi)
8   FS -> WebApp : file(fsi)
9   WebApp -> i : file(fsi)
```

AAT #3. We disabled the branch that allows the database to both read and write from the file-system, and ran the model again to generate a different AAT (Listing 1.7). The attacker i bypasses the authentication mechanism by sending the `sqli` payload (1). This allows him to have access to the web app, which responds with a valid authentication cookie value (2–4). The attacker can now take advantage of the profile edit page in order to upload a malicious file by sending the SQLi payload `sqli` and the `evil_file` payload (5). The web app sends a query request to the database and the database answers (6–7). The web app now sends a writing request to the file-system in order to store the newly uploaded avatar `evil_file` (8), and finally the web app responds back to the attacker with the `profileid` page and the `tuple(sqli)` resulting from exploiting a SQLi in the editing request (9). The attacker exploits the `evil_file` created in (8), to read content from the file-system. The web app receives a request for the `evil_file` with payload `fsi` (10) and makes a request to the file-system for reading `fsi` (11–12). Finally, the web app sends the file back to the attacker (13).

It is worth remarking what happened in steps (6–7). Since we assumed that all requests made by the attacker are malicious actions, the only way the attacker has to proceed is performing a SQLi attack in the edit request. However, by reading the trace it can be easily seen that the SQLi is not used to bypass an authentication or extract information.

Listing 1.7. AAT #3 for accessing the file-system in Multi-stage.

```
1   i -> WebApp : login.sqli.Password
2   WebApp -> DB: query(sqli)
3   DB -> WebApp: tuple(sqli)
4   WebApp -> i : dashboard.Cookie.tuple(sqli)
5   i -> WebApp : edit.Name.Surname.sqli.evil_file.Cookie
6   WebApp -> DB: query(sqli)
7   DB -> WebApp: tuple(sqli)
```

```
 8  WebApp -> FS:  writeFile(evil_file)
 9  WebApp -> i :  profileid.tuple(sqli)
10  i -> WebApp :  file.fsi
11  WebApp -> FS:  readFile(fsi)
12  FS -> WebApp:  file(fsi)
13  WebApp -> i :  file(fsi)
```

4.3 Concretization Phase

We configured a safe environment where we ran DVWA and our Multi-Stage case study. We ran WAFEx and concretized the AATs it generated. The concretization was successful for all our case studies, actually showing how the attacker would perform the real attacks on both DVWA and Multi-Stage. The only example that WAFEx could not concretize is the AAT#2 in Multi-Stage. In that case, the attacker is supposed to exploit a SQLi for writing to the file-system. WAFEx was not able to concretize the trace since the user executing the database did not have the privileges to write to the file-system, which highlights, as we already stated, that the presence of a vulnerability does not imply its exploitability and that only a penetration testing phase can analyze such scenarios.

5 Concluding Remarks, Related Work and Future Work

Our approach is able to find multi-stage attacks to web apps that involve the combined exploit of file-system and SQLi vulnerabilities. To the best of our knowledge, no other tool can find the attacks that WAFEx can find. Some related works are, however, worth discussing in more detail.

Pentesting remains the leading methodology for the security analysis of web apps. This is because the human component is crucial in evaluating the security of the web app. Tools like Wfuzz [26] or DotDotPwn [13] support the security analyst in finding the presence of vulnerabilities, but they do not give any clue on how a vulnerability can be used nor they say if an attack that uses that vulnerability can actually be carried out.

The idea underlying the methodology for modeling web apps given in [1] is similar to our approach, but they defined three different attacker models that should find web attacks, whereas we show how the standard DY attacker can be used. They also represent a number of HTTP details that we do not require that eases the modeling phase. Most importantly, they don't take combination of attacks into consideration.

The model-based security testing tool SPaCiTE [4] starts from a secure (ASLan++) specification of a web app and, by mutating the specification, automatically introduces security flaws. SPaCiTE implements a mature concretization phase, but it mainly finds vulnerability entry points and tries to exploit them, whereas our main goal is to consider how the exploitation of one or more vulnerabilities can compromise the security of the web app.

The "Chained Attack" approach of [5] considers multiple attacks to compromise a web app, but it does not consider file-system vulnerabilities nor interactions between vulnerabilities, which means that it can't reason about using a SQLi to access the file-system. Moreover, it requires an extra effort of the security analyst, who should provide an instantiation library for the concretization phase, while we use well-known external state-of-the-art tools.

The analysis in [9] was limited to SQLi for authentication bypass and data extraction attacks, which we used in this paper as the basis for considering SQLi for accessing the file-system and for modeling the Multi-Stage case study. In [22], Rocchetto et al. model web apps to search for CSRF attacks. While they limit the analysis to CSRF, there could be useful interactions with our approach.

We plan to extend WAFEx (i) with stronger functionalities for the automatic creation of the web app model and (ii) to cover other complex web app vulnerabilities like Cross-Site Scripting and sophisticated multi-stage attacks involving the exploitation of multiple vulnerabilities.

References

1. Akhawe, D., Barth, A., Lam, P., Mitchell, J., Song, D.: Towards a formal foundation of web security. In CSF. IEEE (2010). doi:10.1109/CSF.2010.27
2. Armando, A., et al.: The AVANTSSAR platform for the automated validation of trust and security of service-oriented architectures. In: Flanagan, C., König, B. (eds.) TACAS 2012. LNCS, vol. 7214, pp. 267–282. Springer, Heidelberg (2012). doi:10.1007/978-3-642-28756-5_19
3. ASP documentation: Including Files in ASP Applications. https://msdn.microsoft.com/en-us/library/ms524876(v=vs.90).aspx
4. Büchler, M., Oudinet, J., Pretschner, A.: Semi-automatic security testing of web applications from a secure model. In: SERE. doi:10.1109/SERE.2012.38
5. Calvi, A., Viganò, L.: An automated approach for testing the security of web applications against chained attacks. In: 31st ACM/SIGAPP Symposium on Applied Computing (SAC). ACM Press (2016). doi:10.1145/2851613.2851803
6. Carey, M.: Penetration Testing vs. Vulnerability Scanning - What's the Difference? https://www.alienvault.com/blogs/security-essentials/penetration-testing-vs-vulnerability-scanning-whats-the-difference
7. Christey, S.: The 2009 CWE/SANS top 25 most dangerous programming errors. http://cwe.mitre.org/top25
8. Damele, B., Guimarães, A.: Advanced SQL injection to operating system full control. In: BlackHat EU (2009)
9. De Meo, F., Rocchetto, M., Viganò, L.: Formal analysis of vulnerabilities of web applications based on SQL injection. In: Barthe, G., Markatos, E., Samarati, P. (eds.) STM 2016. LNCS, vol. 9871, pp. 179–195. Springer, Cham (2016). doi:10.1007/978-3-319-46598-2_13
10. De Meo, F., Viganò, L.: WAFEx: Web Application Formal Exploiter. http://regis.di.univr.it/wafex/
11. De Meo, F., Viganò, L.: A Formal Approach to Exploiting Multi-Stage Attacks based on File-System Vulnerabilities of Web Applications (Extended Version) (2017). https://arxiv.org/abs/1705.03658

12. Dolev, D., Yao, A.C.: On the security of public key protocols. IEEE Trans. Inf. Theory **29**, 198–208 (1983). doi:10.1109/TIT.1983.1056650

13. DotDotPwn - The Directory Traversal Fuzzer. https://github.com/wireghoul/dotdotpwn

14. Doupé, A., Cova, M., Vigna, G.: Why johnny can't pentest: an analysis of black-box web vulnerability scanners. In: Kreibich, C., Jahnke, M. (eds.) DIMVA 2010. LNCS, vol. 6201, pp. 111–131. Springer, Heidelberg (2010). doi:10.1007/978-3-642-14215-4_7

15. DVWA: Damn Vulnerable Web Application. http://www.dvwa.co.uk/

16. Glynn, F.: Vulnerability Assessment and Penetration Testing. http://www.veracode.com/security/vulnerability-assessment-and-penetration-testing

17. Joomla! https://www.joomla.org

18. The Java EE 5 Tutorial: Reusing Content in JSP Pages. http://docs.oracle.com/javaee/5/tutorial/doc/bnajb.html

19. OWASP. Top 10 for 2013. https://www.owasp.org/index.php/Category:OWASP_Top_Ten_Project

20. PHP documentation: include. http://php.net/manual/it/function.include.php

21. Postswigger. Burp Proxy (2014). https://portswigger.net/burp/proxy.html

22. Rocchetto, M., Ochoa, M., Torabi Dashti, M.: Model-based detection of CSRF. In: Cuppens-Boulahia, N., Cuppens, F., Jajodia, S., Abou El Kalam, A., Sans, T. (eds.) SEC 2014. IFIP AICT, vol. 428, pp. 30–43. Springer, Heidelberg (2014). doi:10.1007/978-3-642-55415-5_3

23. SANS Institute. Penetration Testing: Assessing Your Overall Security Before Attackers Do. https://www.sans.org/reading-room/whitepapers/analyst/penetration-testing-assessing-security-attackers-34635

24. Trustwave SpiderLabs. Joomla SQL Injection Vulnerability Exploit Results in Full Administrative Access (2015). https://www.trustwave.com/Resources/SpiderLabs-Blog/Joomla-SQL-Injection-Vulnerability-Exploit-Results-in-Full-Administrative-Access

25. Viganò, L.: The SPaCIoS project: secure provision and consumption in the internet of services. In: Software Testing, Verification and Validation (ICST) (2013). doi:10.1109/ICST.2013.75

26. Wfuzz: The Web Bruteforcer. https://github.com/xmendez/wfuzz

A Systematic Study of Cache Side Channels Across AES Implementations

Heiko Mantel[1(✉)], Alexandra Weber[1(✉)], and Boris Köpf[2]

[1] Computer Science Department, TU Darmstadt, Darmstadt, Germany
mantel@cs.tu-darmstadt.de, weber@mais.informatik.tu-darmstadt.de
[2] IMDEA Software Institute, Madrid, Spain
boris.koepf@imdea.org

Abstract. While the AES algorithm is regarded as secure, many implementations of AES are prone to cache side-channel attacks. The lookup tables traditionally used in AES implementations for storing precomputed results provide speedup for encryption and decryption. How such lookup tables are used is known to affect the vulnerability to side channels, but the concrete effects in actual AES implementations are not yet sufficiently well understood. In this article, we analyze and compare multiple off-the-shelf AES implementations wrt. their vulnerability to cache side-channel attacks. By applying quantitative program analysis techniques in a systematic fashion, we shed light on the influence of implementation techniques for AES on cache-side-channel leakage bounds.

1 Introduction

The Advanced Encryption Standard (AES) is a widely used symmetric cipher that is approved by the U.S. National Security Agency for security-critical applications [8]. While traditional attacks against AES are considered infeasible as of today, software implementations of AES are known to be highly susceptible to cache side-channel attacks [5,15,18,19,32]. While such side channels can be avoided by bitsliced implementations [6,24], lookup-table-based implementations, which aim at better performance, are often vulnerable and wide spread.

To understand the vulnerability to cache side-channel attacks, recall that the 128 bit version of AES relies on 10 rounds of transformations. The first nine rounds consist of the steps *SubBytes*, *ShiftRows*, *MixColumns*, and *AddRoundkey*. The last transformation round is similar but skips the step *MixColumns*. Many cryptographic libraries, such as LibTomCrypt [37], mbed TLS [3], Nettle [28] and OpenSSL [30], precompute the results of applying *SubBytes*, *ShiftRows*, and *MixColumns* for all possible inputs. They store the precomputed results in four 1KB lookup tables with entries of 32 bit each. With this, the AES rounds can be implemented by simple table lookups to indices depending on the current state – which is beneficial for performance but introduces the cache side channel.

While the table organization of the first nine rounds specified by [10] is used as the default in most implementations, there is a variety of approaches for implementing the last round of AES:

© Springer International Publishing AG 2017
E. Bodden et al. (Eds.): ESSoS 2017, LNCS 10379, pp. 213–230, 2017.
DOI: 10.1007/978-3-319-62105-0_14

- mbed TLS and Nettle rely on an additional 0.25 KB table with 8 bit entries to store the S-Box for *SubBytes*.
- OpenSSL computes the results of *SubBytes* and *ShiftRows* based on the lookup tables for the main rounds.
- LibTomCrypt uses four additional 1 KB lookup tables with 32 bit entries for the last round.

The organization of the lookup tables affects the vulnerability of AES implementations to cache side-channel attacks. While this effect was observed early on [32, 34] and studied based on an analytical model [39], it has not yet been analyzed based on the actual target of the attack, which is the executable code.

In this article, we use program analysis techniques for a systematic, quantitative study of cache-side-channel leakage across AES implementations. We analyze executable code of AES implementations from LibTomCrypt, mbed TLS, Nettle, and OpenSSL. More concretely, we systematically derive upper bounds for the leakage of these executables to a number of adversaries that are commonly considered in the literature. We also describe the effects of table preloading and of varying the cache configuration (i.e. cache size and replacement strategy) across implementations. By our study, it becomes clear how the usage of lookup tables in AES implementations influences the height of leakage bounds within the same cache size and across cache sizes. For instance, the leakage bounds for the lookup-table-based implementations stabilize with increasing cache size. The stabilization occurs once the cache is large enough for the mapping from AES memory blocks (dominated by the lookup tables) to cache sets to be injective.

We used the CacheAudit static analyzer [12] as a starting point for our study. Analyzing the AES executables in their original form required us to extend the tool's scope in terms of, both supported x86 instructions and CPU flags. This required significant engineering effort. The extended CacheAudit is available under www.mais.informatik.tu-darmstadt.de/cacheaudit-essos17.html.

2   Preliminaries

In this section, we review the necessary background on AES, caches, and cache side-channel attacks.

AES. AES is a widely used symmetric block cipher proposed by Daemen and Rijmen (originally as "Rijndael") [10]. The AES algorithm operates in multiple transformation rounds. It depends on the AES key's size, how many rounds are performed. The inputs to each round are the current state of the transformed message or ciphertext and a *round key* that is generated from the AES key by a key expansion. Each round consists of multiple steps, including a substitution step that can be implemented using a lookup table of size 0.25 KB, called *S-Box*. Lookup tables of size 1 KB are often used to store precomputed results of entire transformation rounds for all possible inputs to speed up the computation. The result for a given input is then retrieved using an index to the lookup table [10].

Lookup-table-based implementations are available in many libraries, including LibTomCrypt, mbed TLS, Nettle, and OpenSSL. However, AES can also be implemented without using lookup tables. For instance, OpenSSL defaults to AES-NI, i.e., AES encryption with hardware support using dedicated x86 instructions, and the AES implementation in NaCl is based on bitslicing, which implements the AES transformation rounds on the fly.

In our study, we consider the lookup-table-based AES implementations from LibTomCrypt, mbed TLS, Nettle, and OpenSSL for a key size of 128 bit, which implies that ten transformation rounds are performed [10]. The AES implementations in mbed TLS and Nettle AES use an S-Box and four 1 KB lookup tables. OpenSSL AES also uses four 1 KB lookup tables but no S-Box, while LibTomCrypt AES uses eight 1 KB lookup tables and no S-Box.

Caches. Caches are small and fast memories that store copies of selected memory entries to reduce the average memory access time of the Central Processing Unit (CPU). If the CPU accesses a memory entry that resides in the cache, it encounters a *cache hit*, and the entry is quickly read from the cache. Otherwise, the CPU encounters a *cache miss*, and the entry needs to be fetched first from the main memory to the cache, which is significantly slower.

In our study, we consider 4-way set-associative caches with 64 Byte line size and FIFO replacement. The chunks in which memory entries can be loaded into the cache are called *memory blocks*. Memory blocks are cached in *cache lines* of the same size as memory blocks, namely the *line size*. The *associativity* of a cache defines how many cache lines form one *cache set*. A given memory block is mapped to one specific cache set but can be cached in any of the cache lines in this cache set. A cache with associativity k is called k-way set-associative. If a memory block shall be cached into a cache set that is full, then another memory block is evicted from the cache set according to a replacement strategy, e.g., to evict the least recently cached memory block (*FIFO*).

Cache side-channel attacks. A side-channel attack recovers information about inputs to a program from characteristics of program runs. In 2002, Page [33] showed that the interaction between a program and the cache is such a characteristics, i.e., one that can be used to mount a side-channel attack. Such attacks are known as *cache side-channel attacks*. Since table lookups in lookup-table-based AES implementations depend on the secret key, they are prone to different kinds of attacks: *Time-based attacks* [5] recover the secret key from measurements of the the overall execution time; *access-based attacks* [15,32] recover the secret key from the cache state after termination; and *trace-based attacks* [1] recover the key from sequences of cache hits and misses.

3   Our Approach

We analyze AES implementations wrt. potential cache side channel's based on information theory and static analysis. The static-analysis tool that we employ is an extension of CacheAudit [12] that we developed for this research project. Our extensions increase the tool's coverage of the x86 machine language and improve the tool's precision wrt. its treatment of processor flags. These changes were crucial for analyzing the four AES implementations, without having to modify their off-the-shelf source code, and they might be beneficial for others.

We describe our approach to side-channel analysis in Sect. 3.1, illustrate it using mbed TLS AES as an example in Sect. 3.2, and sketch our conceptual and technical extensions of CacheAudit in Sect. 3.3.

3.1   Static Bounds on Cache Side Channels

A common approach for quantifying the information leaks of a program is to compute (upper bounds on) the number of observations that an adversary can make. This number comes with different interpretations in terms of security, such as lower bounds for the expected number of guesses required for recovering a secret [26] or upper bounds on the probability for correctly guessing the secret in one shot [38]. Moreover, this number can be obtained by combining off-the-shelf static analysis with model counting techniques [4,29]. The computation of this number has been implemented based on abstract interpretation [23], bounded model checking [16], and symbolic execution [36].

The CacheAudit static analyzer [12] leverages this basic idea for quantifying cache side channels of x86 executables, based on abstract interpretation. Given an x86 executable, CacheAudit computes bounds wrt. the three adversary models discussed in Sect. 2. Namely,

- for *access-based* attackers (denoted acc), CacheAudit computes a set O^{acc} that contains all possible states of the cache after termination. Here, cache states are represented as tuples of sequences of memory blocks, where each sequence is of bounded length and represents the content of one cache set.
- for *trace-based* attackers (denoted tr), CacheAudit computes a set $O^{\text{tr}} \subseteq \{hit, miss\}^*$ that contains all possible traces of cache hits and misses that can occur in an execution.
- for *time-based* attackers (denoted time), CacheAudit computes a set $O^{\text{time}} \subseteq \mathbb{N}$ that contains the possible execution times that can occur.

In addition, CacheAudit computes a set O^{accd} that contains a representation of cache states as tuples of integers, where each integer represents the amount of blocks loaded in a particular cache set. This corresponds to the possible observations of a fourth attacker, the *blurred access-based* attacker (denoted accd). This attacker is similar to acc, in the sense that it shares the cache with the victim, but it does not share the memory with the victim.

Bounds on the information (in bits) leaked to the four adversaries are given by $\log_2 |O^a|$ for $a \in \{\text{acc}, \text{tr}, \text{time}, \text{accd}\}$.

3.2   Analysis of AES from mbed TLS

We illustrate our approach using the AES implementation from mbed TLS (previously known as PolarSSL). This library is used, e.g., in the implementation of OpenVPN [31] and of Internet-of-Things products [2].

Table 1. Bounds for mbed TLS on leakage and entropy under acc

Cache [KB]	2	4	8	16	32	64	128
Leakage [bit] $\leq$	92.6	114.5	91.8	71.2	69.6	69.6	69.0
Entropy [bit] $\geq$	163.4	141.5	164.2	184.8	186.4	186.4	187

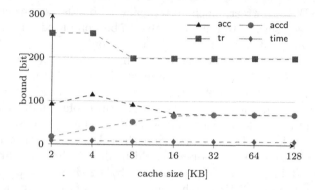

Fig. 1. Leakage bounds for mbed TLS AES encryption

Computation of bounds for mbed TLS *under acc.* The leakage bounds computed by our extension of CacheAudit for mbed TLS under acc for different cache sizes are listed in Table 1.[1] Table 1 also contains lower bounds on the remaining min-entropy of the 256 secret bits (key and message) after a side-channel observation. In the remainder of the article, we only explicate leakage bounds because the entropy can be easily computed. It equals 256 bit minus the leakage bounds.

Note that the acc leakage bounds converge to 69 bit, starting between the cache sizes 16 KB and 32 KB. This could be due to the fact that at least 17 KB of cache are required for an injective mapping from memory blocks (dominated by 4.25 KB lookup tables) to cache sets. Once the cache is so big that each cache set can contain at most one memory block, an attacker under acc is able to infer exactly which blocks are accessed by mbed TLS AES. In practice, a convergence of leakage bounds with growing cache sizes implies that leakage bounds will remain valid when processors with larger caches become available in the future.

Exploration of other attacker models. The leakage bounds that we obtain for mbed TLS AES, using all four attacker models, are depicted in Fig. 1.[2]

We observe that the leakage bounds for all attacker models converge with increasing cache size. This suggests that the leakage bounds for the mbed TLS AES implementation are robust against future hardware with larger caches, not only with respect to acc, but also for the attacker models accd, tr, and time.

---

[1] We round all leakage bounds up to one decimal place and truncate them to the maximum leakage of 256 bit (128 bit message and 128 bit key) throughout the article.

[2] To support the reader in reading such diagrams, we connect the leakage bounds computed for adjacent cache sizes and the same attacker model by dashed lines.

The leakage bounds for acc and accd converge to the same value, namely 69 bit. This could be due to the fact that an attacker under accd (like under acc) can infer exactly which memory blocks are cached – given that the mapping from memory blocks to cache sets is injective. In practice, this means that, for a system running mbed TLS AES, reducing the attack surface from acc to accd does not lead to better leakage bounds – given that the system has a cache of more than 16 KB. In contrast, much better leakage bounds can be achieved when reducing the attack surface to time (e.g., the 7.7 bit computed for a cache size of 128 KB correspond to 3% of the key and message only).

Before convergence, the leakage bounds computed for tr and time (marked by - ■- and - ♦- , respectively) decrease with increasing cache size. We will get back to this point in Sect. 4. In contrast, the leakage bounds for accd (marked by - ●-) increase with increasing cache size. Interestingly, the evolution of leakage bounds for acc (marked by - ▲-) follows a different pattern. These bounds increase, until a peak is reached for 4 KB cache size, and then decrease, until they stabilize. The peak observable in the acc bounds could be due to the exact fit of memory blocks with mbed TLS AES data (dominated by 4.25 KB lookup tables) into a cache with size around 4.25 KB. If the memory blocks fit exactly into the cache, the most information can be conveyed through the ordering of memory blocks, so that the potential leakage to an attacker under acc is maximized.

Note that our quantitative analysis of mbed TLS AES not only allows us to observe the influence of implementation-level design decisions on the interplay between cache size, attack surface, and leakage bounds. It also enables us to speculate about the practical consequences in an informed manner and, hence, to shed more light on the effects of such design choices. In Sect. 4, we study the influence of implementation-level design choices on the interplay between cache size, attack surface, and leakage bounds for three further off-the-shelf AES implementations. Moreover, we compare the effects of implementation-level design choices across all four AES implementations.

Details on our analysis setup. In our analysis of mbed TLS AES, we considered the sequential composition of the key expansion function mbedtls_aes__setkey_enc with the encryption function mbedtls_aes_encrypt from the file aes.c of mbed TLS version 2.2.1, configured to use hard-coded tables (option MBEDTLS_AES_ROM_TABLES) and to not use hardware support (option MBEDTLS_PADLOCK_C). We compiled to a 32 bit x86 binary without additional code for overflow protection (option -fno-stack-protector).

We configured the AES implementation to use a key size of 128 bit. Note that this choice complies with the recommendation of the US National Institute of Standards and Technology. They recommend a security strength of at least 128 bit to protect sensitive data in unclassified applications beyond the year 2031 [13, Sect. 5.6.2]. For simplicity, we configured the message size in the AES implementation also to 128 bit. We configured CacheAudit to assume a four-way set-associative cache with 64Byte line size. This cache configuration is used, e.g., for the level 2 cache in the current Intel micro-architecture Skylake

[17, Table 2–4]. We used FIFO replacement and varied the cache size from 2 KB to 128 KB.

Remark 1. A previous version (1.3.7) of mbed TLS AES was already analyzed in [11] (with focus on key size 128 bit) and in [12] (with focus on key size 256 bit). Like our analysis, [12] considered encryption jointly with key generation, while [11] considered encryption only. In [11,12], mbed TLS AES was transformed before the analysis to meet the x86 sublanguage supported by the analysis tool. As usual, a code transformation was chosen that preserves the code's semantics.

We extended the analysis tool to support the analysis of mbed TLS AES without code transformations. The reader might wonder how our results for the off-the-shelf binaries for Version 2.2.1 compare to the ones in [11,12] for the transformed code snippets of mbed TLS (Version 1.3.7). In brief, our results are rather similar (including the convergence of the bounds for acc and accd from a cache size of 16 KB). This similarity shows that both the evolution of mbed TLS versions and the application of code transformations in [11,12] did not have substantial effects (neither positive nor negative) on the leakage bounds.

3.3   Tool Support

From the beginning of our study, we wanted to analyze off-the-shelf AES implementations in their original form (i.e., without code transformations like the one discussed at the end of Sect. 3.2). To make this possible, support for additional x86 instructions was needed in CacheAudit. We have added such support. We extended the x86 parser and the abstract x86 semantics in CacheAudit for the instructions listed in Table 2. Now, CacheAudit supports all instructions that occur in the relevant code snippets from the off-the-shelf binaries of LibTomCrypt, mbed TLS, Nettle, and OpenSSL AES.

Table 2. Extended language coverage in CacheAudit

Type	New instructions
Arithmetic	2D (Sub), 18 (Sbb), 19 (Sbb), 11 (Adc), F7/6 (Div), 3C (Cmp)
Logic	08 (Or), 30 (Xor), 84 (Test), A9 (Test), F6/0 (Test)
Bitstring	0FA4 (Shld), 0FA5 (Shld), 0FAC (Shrd), 0FAD (Shrd)
Stack	07 (Pop)
Jump	7C, 0F8C, 7D, 0F8D, 70, 0F80, 71, 0F81, 78, 0F88, 79, 0F89, 7E, 0F8E, 7F, 0F8F (all Jcc)
Move	0F48 (Cmovs)

Some of the binaries contain jump instructions that branch on the sign flag or the overflow flag, which both were previously not supported by CacheAudit.

For instance, the conditional jump instruction Jnle (opcode 0F8F) occurs in the binary of mbed TLS AES encryption, and the conditional jump instruction Jl (opcode 0F8C) occurs in the binary of LibTomCrypt AES decryption. Jnle branches on the previously supported zero flag and the previously unsupported sign flag. Jl branches on both previously unsupported flags, i.e., the sign flag and the overflow flag. In abstract interpretation, both branches of a conditional need to be considered if the abstraction is too imprecise to determine which branch must be chosen. This can lead to substantial imprecision of analysis results. To avoid such imprecision, we conceptually revised the abstraction employed by CacheAudit and modified the implementation of CacheAudit to support this abstraction. The new abstraction represents the states of the sign and overflow flag on the abstract level with high precision. To implement this abstraction, we refined the data structure for representing flags on the abstract level and adapted the implementation of the abstract semantics of all x86 instructions.

The resulting, extended CacheAudit version enabled us to analyze the off-the-shelf binaries for mbed TLS AES, with the results described in Sect. 3.2. The extended version of CacheAudit is also the basis for our systematic study of cache side channels across AES implementations reported in Sects. 4 and 5.

Remark 2. In our study, we focus on architectures with a single cache. We leave a thorough analysis of multiple cache levels to future work. In particular, the effects of different cache inclusion policies deserve to be studied in detail.

While we focus on the FIFO cache replacement strategy throughout this article, we also investigated other replacement strategies, namely LRU (least recently used) and PLRU (Pseudo-LRU). We observed that the replacement strategies influence the concrete leakage bounds. The cache sizes at which the leakage bounds stabilize also vary across the replacement strategies. Interestingly, the leakage bounds for 128 KB cache size are identical for all three replacement strategies. We leave a more extensive investigation of replacement strategies for future work.

4   Leakage Across AES Implementations

The technique of lookup tables that store precomputed round transformations is supported by popular libraries like OpenSSL and mbed TLS. We investigate four such implementations, namely LibTomCrypt, mbed TLS, Nettle and OpenSSL AES. All four implementations use four 1 KB lookup tables with 32 bit entries to store the precomputed transformations for the first nine AES rounds. The implementation of the last AES round, which uses a different transformation, differs across the implementations. OpenSSL AES reuses the existing four lookup tables for the last AES round, while mbed TLS and Nettle AES use an additional 0.25 KB S-Box with 8 bit entries, and LibTomCrypt AES uses four additional 1 KB lookup tables with 32 bit entries. In this section, we study the effects of this design choice on the cache-side-channel leakage. We investigate how the different implementations of the last round compare in terms of

– security guarantees against cache side channels and
– the interplay between cache sizes and security guarantees.

To this end, we compute leakage bounds on the AES implementations from LibTomCrypt, mbed TLS, Nettle, and OpenSSL (see Table 3 for the exact functions that we analyze), with the experimental setup described in Sect. 3.2.

Table 3. AES implementations for which leakage bounds were computed

Library	Configuration	Analyzed functions
LibTomCrypt 1.17	`ENCRYPT_ONLY,` `LTC_NO_ASM,ARGTYPE`	`rijndael_enc_setup,` `rijndael_enc_ecb_encrypt` (`aes.c`)
mbed TLS 2.2.1	`MBEDTLS_AES_ROM-` `_TABLES`, removed `MBEDTLS_PADLOCK_C`	`mbedtls_aes_setkey_enc,` `mbedtls_aes_encrypt` (`aes.c`)
Nettle 3.2	default	`aes128_set_encrypt_key` (`aes128-set-encrypt-key.c`), `aes128_encrypt` (`aes-encrypt.c`)
OpenSSL 1.0.1t	default	`private_AES_set_encrypt_key,` `AES_encrypt` (`aes_core.c`)

Our results suggest that using fewer additional lookup tables in the last round of AES leads to better security guarantees against attackers under acc and accd. Furthermore, our security guarantees for implementations with fewer additional tables are more robust against an increase of the cache size. They stabilize already at a smaller cache size. In the subsequent subsections, we discuss the influence of the lookup tables in the last AES round in detail.

4.1 Security Guarantees

To study the influence of the lookup tables in the last AES round on the height of leakage bounds, we focus on a fixed cache size of 128 KB.

The lookup tables in AES implementations have been considered with respect to access-based attackers by Osvik, Shamir, and Tromer [32]. They discuss the use of smaller lookup tables (e.g., one 1 KB lookup table or one 2 KB lookup table in the main rounds of AES) as a countermeasure to access-based attacks. They state that for certain access-based attackers "smaller tables necessitate more measurements by the attacker", i.e., reduce the leakage of one program run. The leakage bounds that we obtain for the access-based attacker models (listed in Table 4) confirm this. For both accd and acc, we obtain the lowest leakage bounds, namely 64 bit, for OpenSSL AES, which uses only 4 KB of lookup tables. The implementations from mbed TLS and Nettle AES, which use lookup tables with a total size of 4.25 KB, follow closely with leakage bounds of 69 bit. The leakage bounds for LibTomCrypt AES, which uses lookup tables with twice the

Table 4. acc/accd leakage bounds for 128 KB cache

	LibTomCrypt	mbed TLS	Nettle	OpenSSL
accd	129 bit	69 bit	69 bit	64 bit
acc	129 bit	69 bit	69 bit	64 bit

Table 5. time/trace leakage bounds for 128 KB cache

	LibTomCrypt	mbed TLS	Nettle	OpenSSL
time	7.7 bit	7.7 bit	7.7 bit	7.7 bit
tr	198 bit	199 bit	199 bit	196 bit

total size, namely 8 KB, are roughly twice as high, namely 129 bit. Interestingly, reducing the total size of lookup tables in one transformation round only, already has a positive effect on the leakage bounds. LibTomCrypt AES and mbed TLS AES use lookup tables of the same total size in the first nine rounds, but differ in the total size of lookup tables used in the last round. While mbed TLS AES uses a single additional S-Box of 0.25 KB in the last round, LibTomCrypt AES, which has significantly higher leakage bounds, uses four additional lookup tables that each require 1 KB.

The influence of lookup tables in AES implementations on time- and trace-based attackers has been studied by Page [34]. He recommends the use of S-Boxes with 8 bit entries, instead of lookup tables with 32 bit entries. Page argues that, the smaller table entries are, the more table entries share the same cache line. Consequently, for smaller table entries, cache hits and misses reveal less information. Tiri, Aciiçmez, Neve, and Andersen [39] confirm this for two time-based attacks in a practical evaluation of variants of OpenSSL AES. They compare an attack on OpenSSL AES, which reuses the 1 KB lookup tables with 32 bit entries in the last round, to an attack on a variant of OpenSSL AES that uses an S-Box with 8 bit entries in the last round. The latter attack requires more attacker measurements than the former. Our leakage bounds for the attacker models time and tr are listed in Table 5. We observe that the leakage bounds are very similar across the different implementations. In particular, the bounds for mbed TLS and Nettle, which use S-Boxes with 8 bit entries in the last round, are not lower than the bounds for LibTomCrypt and OpenSSL, which use tables with 32 bit entries in the last round. Note that, in our approach, we approximate the possible observations about cache hits, but not the value that an individual observed cache hit has for the attacker. This difference between our approach and the one in [39] might be the reason for the difference in the findings.

In summary, our study suggests that the use of fewer additional lookup tables in the last round of AES leads to better leakage guarantees against attackers under acc and accd. While a more fine-grained approach would be needed to study the effectiveness of smaller table entries as a countermeasure against trace-

and time-based attackers, the leakage bounds are precise enough to confirm that smaller lookup tables are effective against access-based attackers.

4.2   Interplay of Cache Size and Security Guarantees

The leakage bounds that we obtain for varying cache sizes for the attacker models accd and acc are depicted in Fig. 2c and d.[3] For all four AES implementations the leakage bounds stabilize with increasing cache size. The cache size from which they stabilize differs across the implementations. This could be due to the minimum amount of cache sets that is needed for an injective mapping from memory blocks to cache sets. For LibTomCrypt, which uses 4 KB of additional tables in the last AES round, additional 15 KB of 4-way set-associative cache are needed, compared to mbed TLS AES, which uses only 0.25 KB of additional tables in the last AES round. Note that, it is of practical relevance that the leakage bounds for acc and accd stabilize at the observed points. If leakage bounds are computed for a stabilization point, they are robust against increasing cache sizes, and cache sizes tend to grow with technological improvements. In our analysis, the stabilization point is reached, once the mapping from memory blocks to cache sets is injective.

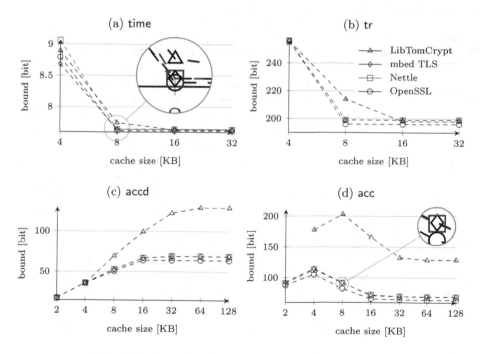

Fig. 2. Leakage bounds wrt. the four attacker models

---

[3] For LibTomCrypt AES and 2 KB cache size, the analysis ran out of memory.

The leakage bounds that we obtain for the attacker models time and tr are depicted in Fig. 2a and b. We observe that the tr leakage bounds for all four AES implementations decrease and then stabilize to roughly 200 bit with increasing cache size. The bounds for mbed TLS, Nettle, and OpenSSL are stable starting between cache size 4 KB and 8 KB. The bounds for LibTomCrypt are stable starting between cache size 8 KB and 16 KB. Note that, for all four implementations, the cache sizes at which the bounds stabilize correspond to the amount of data used by the implementations (dominated by the lookup tables). Since the AES implementations perform 200 accesses to lookup tables during one key expansion and encryption, a leakage of 200 bit corresponds to a leakage of 1 bit (hit or miss) per access to a lookup table. The additional leakage before stabilization could be due to secret-dependent eviction of other local variables. Once all memory blocks fit into the cache, local variables are not evicted any more. In practice, a smaller total size of additional lookup tables in the last round of AES leads to more robustness of our tr and time leakage bounds against changes in the cache size.

Overall, our study suggests that the decision how many additional lookup tables are used in the last round of AES has an influence on the robustness of the security guarantees for all four attacker models with respect to future hardware. A smaller total size of additional tables leads to implementations that are robust starting from a smaller cache size.

5 Hardening Across AES Implementations

Hardening techniques aim to reduce the side-channel leakage of implementations. The preloading hardening technique is tailored specifically to lookup-table-based implementations of AES. It preloads all memory blocks that belong to lookup tables into the cache, before running the actual implementation. Cache locking [27] locks memory blocks in cache lines. Locked memory blocks cannot be evicted from the cache. If lookup tables are preloaded and then locked in the cache, their presence in the cache is independent of secret information[4].

Does the implementation of the last AES round in a lookup-table-based implementation influence the effectiveness of preloading as a hardening technique? To address this question, we compute leakage bounds for preloading in multiple lookup-table-based AES implementations. These implementations differ in the techniques used to implement the last round of AES. More concretely, we analyze the implementations from LibTomCrypt (last round with four 1 KB lookup tables), mbed TLS and Nettle (last round with one 0.25 KB S-Box), and OpenSSL (last round without additional lookup tables), to which we manually added preloading. Throughout this section, we assume that no other processes affect the cache content.[5]

---

[4] Without cache locking, the preloaded table entries might be evicted from the cache by other processes [21,22].

[5] This can be realized using static cache locking if the cache size exceeds the total size of tables. One could consider dynamic cache locking [27] if the cache is too small.

In Table 6, each line corresponds to one AES implementation with preloading. The symbol ✓ marks the cache sizes for which we obtain the leakage bound 0 bit. The table is the same under all four attacker models acc, accd, tr, and time.

Table 6. Preloading effectiveness for acc/accd/tr/time

Cache Size [KB]	4	8	16	32	64	128
LibTomCrypt			✓	✓	✓	✓
Nettle		✓	✓	✓	✓	✓
OpenSSL		✓	✓	✓	✓	✓
mbed TLS		✓	✓	✓	✓	✓

We observe that the leakage bounds for LibTomCrypt stabilize to 0 bit for caches greater than 8 KB and the leakage bounds for the other AES implementations stabilize to 0 bit for caches greater than 4 KB. This could be due to the cache size required to hold all lookup table entries and additional variables of an AES implementation. When no lookup-table entry can be evicted from the cache, the cache trace and the final cache state are constant for any secret key and message. To rule out evictions, OpenSSL AES requires at least 4 KB cache for its 4 KB lookup tables. The AES implementations from mbed TLS and Nettle require roughly 0.25 KB additional cache for the additional S-Box that they use in the last AES round. LibTomCrypt AES requires at least 4 KB of additional cache for its additional 4 KB of lookup tables in the last round. In practice, this suggests that the use of fewer additional lookup tables in the last round of AES not only makes preloading more efficient (because fewer blocks need to be preloaded), but also makes preloading effective on more systems.

Furthermore, for each AES implementation and cache size, we either obtained the leakage bound 0 bit for all attacker models or for none of the attacker models. This could be because the final cache state and the cache trace can depend on secret information if and only if preloaded table entries might be evicted from the cache. In practice this suggests that, if preloading is used, no additional effort has to be spent to reduce the attack surface of an AES implementation from tr to a more restricted attacker model.

Overall, our study suggests that preloading is effective against acc, accd, tr and time for lookup-table-based AES implementations whose data fits into the cache entirely.

Remark 3. It is also possible to avoid cache-side-channel leakage by implementing AES without lookup tables. Instead of precomputing the round transformations, they can be computed on the fly, e.g., using bitslicing. We analyze the bitsliced AES implementation from the library NaCl[6] [6]. We obtain the leakage bound 0 bit for all four attacker models and all six cache sizes.

---

[6] The sequential composition of the functions `crypto_stream_beforenm` (`beforenm.c`) and `crypto_stream_xor_afternm` (`xor_afternm.c`) from NaCl in version 20110221.

6 Related Work

Cache attacks on AES. AES implementations have been attacked using different techniques to exploit cache-side-channel vulnerabilities.

Bernstein's time-based attack on OpenSSL AES [5] exploited that a given byte of the AES key can be characterized by the running times it induces on different messages. Information about an unknown key was obtained by comparing the duration of multiple sample AES runs with this key against previously measured running times for known keys. The attacker model time captures the observations from one sample AES run, where the actual running time is approximated based on the numbers of cache hits and cache misses. Acıiçmez and Koç presented trace-based attacks on OpenSSL AES [1]. The underlying samples of cache traces were generated by instrumenting OpenSSL AES to store all access indices. The attacker model tr captures the observations from one such sample.

Osvik, Shamir, and Tromer mounted access-based cache attacks on OpenSSL AES using two techniques [32]. In EVICT+TIME, the attacker clears a cache set after running AES and times a subsequent encryption. In PRIME+PROBE, the attacker fills the cache with his data and times his own accesses to his data in a cache set after an encryption. Both techniques allow an attacker to determine whether a given cache set was used. This scenario is generalized by the attacker model accd, under which attackers can observe the fill-degree of all cache sets.

An asynchronous access-based attack on AES was mounted by Gullasch, Bangerter, and Krenn [15] with a technique later extended to FLUSH+RELOAD [42]. These attacks motivated the attacker model acc, which is weaker because it captures a synchronous attacker, who can only observe the final cache state.

While cache side-channel attacks [1,5,15,18,19,32,40] have often targeted OpenSSL, recently the Java library Bouncy Castle was also attacked through a cache side channel [25]. A detailed survey of microarchitectural side-channel attacks is provided by Ge, Yarom, Cock, and Heiser [14].

Hardening techniques for AES. Preloading is a code-based technique to counter cache side channels in lookup-table-based implementations. The cache-locking technique, mentioned in Sect. 6, is supported by multiple commercial processors [27]. Multiple other code-based, hardware-based, and operating-system-based countermeasures exist. A survey of countermeasures is provided in [14].

Already in 2003, Page considered a variety of code-based countermeasures against trace- and time-based cache side channels, including preloading and lookup tables with smaller entries [34]. As countermeasures against access-based cache side channels, Osvik, Shamir, and Tromer suggested different possibilities to avoid memory accesses [32]. As alternatives to avoiding memory accesses, they discussed, e.g., the use of smaller lookup tables. Brickell et al. suggested to harden AES implementations against cache side channels by permuting the lookup tables during the algorithm and by using one compact lookup table that can be preloaded before each AES round [7]. Crane et al. proposed a randomization of the control flow and the execution characteristics of binaries [9].

On the operating system level, Page considered restricting access to precise timing information, randomizing the duration of memory accesses, and out-of-order execution of memory accesses [34]. On the hypervisor level, STEALTH-MEM [20] counters cache side-channels by avoiding that different VMs evict each other's cache lines. Hardware-based countermeasures include larger cache lines, physical shielding of devices [34], and special cache architectures [35, 41].

Leakage across implementations. To our knowledge, ours is the first systematic study of cache-side-channel leakage across off-the-shelf AES implementations.

Different variants of one specific AES implementation have been investigated by Tiri, Acıiçmez, Neve, and Andersen [39]. They propose an analytical model for time-based cache attacks that predicts the number of required running time samples for key recovery. They validate the model with respect to three variants of OpenSSL AES (5 KB, 4.25 KB, and 4 KB lookup tables), two specific approximations of the attacker model time, and two different cache line sizes. To this end, they mount attacks with an attacker who can directly access the number of cache misses. In their predictions as well as in their attacks, the 4.25 KB variant requires more samples than the 5 KB variant. While Tiri, Acıiçmez, Neve, and Andersen consider only OpenSSL AES, we investigate cache-side-channel leakage across multiple AES implementations. Furthermore, while Tiri et al. focus on time-based attacks, our study also covers access- and trace-based attacks.

Variants of mbed TLS AES 1.3.7 with/without preloading and varying key sizes (128 bit, 192 bit, 256 bit) have been analyzed by Doychev, Köpf, Mauborgne, and Reinecke [12]. They observed that, under FIFO replacement, preloading is effective against acc, accd, tr, and time for the cache sizes large enough to hold all AES lookup tables. They also observed a positive effect of larger cache sizes on their leakage bounds for accd, tr, and time as well as a negative effect on their bounds for acc. They describe that the acc leakage bounds converge to the same value as the accd leakage bounds because each cache set can contain at most one lookup table block at the point of convergence. Our study shows that the observations from [12] carry over to a newer version of mbed TLS. Moreover, we show that these observations are also valid for three further AES implementations.

7 Conclusion

We conducted a systematic study of cache side channels in off-the-shelf AES implementations, namely OpenSSL, LibTomCrypt, mbed TLS, and Nettle AES. Our goal was to better understand the influence of implementation details on upper bounds for the cache-side-channel leakage of AES implementations.

Our findings suggest that the total size of lookup tables in an AES implementation plays an important role for the leakage bounds on cache side channels. The use of a dedicated S-Box in the last round of AES, for instance, can be avoided by masking entries of the lookup tables used in the first rounds of AES.

An interesting direction for future work will be to study the influence of multiple cache levels and of cache inclusion policies. We hope that the approach used for AES in this article will also be adopted by others to enable the analytic study of cache side channels in a broad range of cryptographic implementations.

Acknowledgements. We thank Clémentine Maurice and the anonymous reviewers for helpful comments. We also thank Artem Starostin for inspiring discussions in the initial phase of this project and Xucheng Yin for his contributions to CacheAudit. This work has been funded by the DFG as part of the project Secure Refinement of Cryptographic Algorithms (E3) within the CRC 1119 CROSSING and was supported by Ramón y Cajal grant RYC-2014-16766, Spanish projects TIN2012-39391-C04-01 StrongSoft and TIN2015-70713-R DEDETIS, and Madrid regional project S2013/ICE-2731 N-GREENS.

References

1. Acıiçmez, O., Koç, Ç.K.: Trace-driven cache attacks on AES (short paper). In: Ning, P., Qing, S., Li, N. (eds.) ICICS 2006. LNCS, vol. 4307, pp. 112–121. Springer, Heidelberg (2006). doi:10.1007/11935308_9
2. A.R.M Ltd.: ARM buys Leading IoT Security Company Offspark as it Expands its mbed Platform (2015). https://www.arm.com/about/newsroom/arm-buys-leading-iot-security-company-offspark-as-it-expands-its-mbed-platform.php. Accessed 11 Feb 2017
3. A.R.M Ltd.: mbed TLS (Version 2.2.1-gpl) (2016). https://tls.mbed.org/download/mbedtls-2.2.1-gpl.tgz. Accessed 28 Jul 2016
4. Backes, M., Köpf, B., Rybalchenko, A.: Automatic discovery and quantification of information leaks. In: S&P, pp. 141–153 (2009)
5. Bernstein, D.J.: Cache-timing attacks on AES. Technical report, University of Illinois at Chicago (2005)
6. Bernstein, D.J., Lange, T., Schwabe, P.: The security impact of a new cryptographic library. In: Hevia, A., Neven, G. (eds.) LATINCRYPT 2012. LNCS, vol. 7533, pp. 159–176. Springer, Heidelberg (2012). doi:10.1007/978-3-642-33481-8_9
7. Brickell, E., Graunke, G., Neve, M., Seifert, J.: Software mitigations to hedge AES against cache-based software side channel vulnerabilities. IACR Cryptology ePrint Archive, pp. 1–17 (2006)
8. Committee on National Security Systems: CNSS Policy No. 15: National Information Assurance Policy on the Use of Public Standards for the Secure Sharing of Information Among National Security Systems (2016). https://www.cnss.gov/CNSS/openDoc.cfm?1858/J1y8IPFvRRvn+ZZBw==. Accessed 29 Dec 2016
9. Crane, S., Homescu, A., Brunthaler, S., Larsen, P., Franz, M.: Thwarting cache side-channel attacks through dynamic software diversity. In: NDSS (2015)
10. Daemen, J., Rijmen, V.: AES submission document on Rijndael, Version 2 (1999). http://csrc.nist.gov/archive/aes/rijndael/Rijndael.pdf
11. Doychev, G., Feld, D., Köpf, B., Mauborgne, L., Reineke, J.: CacheAudit: a tool for the static analysis of cache side channels. In: USENIX Security, pp. 431–446 (2013)
12. Doychev, G., Köpf, B., Mauborgne, L., Reineke, J.: Cacheaudit: a tool for the static analysis of cache side channels. ACM Trans. Inf. Syst. Secur. **18**, 4:1–4:32 (2015)
13. Barker, E.: Nist special publication 800–57 part 1, revision 4: Recommendation for key management - part 1: General (2016). http://nvlpubs.nist.gov/nistpubs/SpecialPublications/NIST.SP.800-57pt1r4.pdf

14. Ge, Q., Yarom, Y., Cock, D., Heiser, G.: A survey of microarchitectural timing attacks and countermeasures on contemporary hardware. J. Cryptogr. Eng., 1–27 (2016)
15. Gullasch, D., Bangerter, E., Krenn, S.: Cache games - bringing access-based cache attacks on AES to practice. In: S&P, pp. 490–505 (2011)
16. Heusser, J., Malacaria, P.: Quantifying information leaks in software. In: ACSAC, pp. 261–269 (2010)
17. Corporation, I.: Intel® 64 and IA-32 Architectures Optimization Reference Manual. Order Number: 248966–032 (2016)
18. Irazoqui, G., Eisenbarth, T., Sunar, B.: S$A: a shared cache attack that works across cores and defies VM sandboxing - and its application to AES. In: S& P, pp. 591–604 (2015)
19. Irazoqui, G., Inci, M.S., Eisenbarth, T., Sunar, B.: Wait a minute! a fast, cross-VM attack on AES. In: Stavrou, A., Bos, H., Portokalidis, G. (eds.) RAID 2014. LNCS, vol. 8688, pp. 299–319. Springer, Cham (2014). doi:10.1007/978-3-319-11379-1_15
20. Kim, T., Peinado, M., Mainar-Ruiz, G.: STEALTHMEM: system-level protection against cache-based side channel attacks in the cloud. In: USENIX Security, pp. 189–204 (2012)
21. Kong, J., Aciiçmez, O., Seifert, J.P., Zhou, H.: Deconstructing new cache designs for thwarting software cache-based side channel attacks. In: CSAW, pp. 25–34 (2008)
22. Kong, J., Aciiçmez, O., Seifert, J.P., Zhou, H.: Hardware-software integrated approaches to defend against software cache-based side channel attacks. In: HPCA, pp. 393–404 (2009)
23. Köpf, B., Rybalchenko, A.: Approximation and randomization for quantitative information-flow analysis. In: CSF, pp. 3–14 (2010)
24. Käsper, E., Schwabe, P.: Faster and timing-attack resistant AES-GCM. In: Clavier, C., Gaj, K. (eds.) CHES 2009. LNCS, vol. 5747, pp. 1–17. Springer, Heidelberg (2009). doi:10.1007/978-3-642-04138-9_1
25. Lipp, M., Gruss, D., Spreitzer, R., Maurice, C., Mangard, S.: ARMageddon: cache attacks on mobile devices. In: USENIX Security, pp. 549–564 (2016)
26. Massey, J.L.: Guessing and entropy. In: ISIT, p. 204 (1994)
27. Mittal, S.: A survey of techniques for cache locking. ACM Trans. Des. Automat. Electron. Syst., 49:1–49:24 (2016)
28. Möller, N.: Nettle (Version 3.2) (2016). https://ftp.gnu.org/gnu/nettle/nettle-3.2.tar.gz. Accessed 28 Jul 2016
29. Newsome, J., McCamant, S., Song, D.: Measuring channel capacity to distinguish undue influence. In: PLAS, pp. 73–85 (2009)
30. OpenSSL Software Foundation: OpenSSL (Version 1.0.1t) (2016). https://www.openssl.org/source/openssl-1.0.1t.tar.gz. Accessed 28 Jul 2016
31. OpenVPN Technologies, Inc. HOWTO (2017). https://openvpn.net/index.php/open-source/documentation/howto.html. Accessed 16 Feb 2017
32. Osvik, D.A., Shamir, A., Tromer, E.: Cache attacks and countermeasures: the case of AES. In: Pointcheval, D. (ed.) CT-RSA 2006. LNCS, vol. 3860, pp. 1–20. Springer, Heidelberg (2006). doi:10.1007/11605805_1
33. Page, D.: Theoretical Use of Cache Memory as a Cryptanalytic Side-Channel. IACR Cryptology ePrint Archive, pp. 1–23 (2002)
34. Page, D.: Defending Against Cache-Based Side-Channel Attacks. Information Security Technical Report, pp. 30–44 (2003)
35. Page, D.: Partitioned cache architecture as a side-channel defence mechanism. IACR Cryptology ePrint Archive, pp. 1–14 (2005)

36. Pasareanu, C.S., Phan, Q., Malacaria, P.: Multi-run side-channel analysis using symbolic execution and max-SMT. In: CSF, pp. 387–400 (2016)
37. libtom projects: LibTomCrypt (Version 1.17) (2010). https://github.com/libtom/libtomcrypt/archive/1.17.tar.gz. Accessed 28 Jul 2016
38. Smith, G.: On the foundations of quantitative information flow. In: FOSSACS, pp. 288–302 (2009)
39. Tiri, K., Acıiçmez, O., Neve, M., Andersen, F.: An analytical model for time-driven cache attacks. In: Biryukov, A. (ed.) FSE 2007. LNCS, vol. 4593, pp. 399–413. Springer, Heidelberg (2007). doi:10.1007/978-3-540-74619-5_25
40. Tromer, E., Osvik, D.A., Shamir, A.: Efficient cache attacks on AES, and countermeasures. J. Cryptology **23**(1), 37–71 (2010)
41. Wang, Z., Lee, R.B.: A novel cache architecture with enhanced performance and security. In: MICRO, pp. 83–93 (2008)
42. Yarom, Y., Falkner, K.: FLUSH+RELOAD: a high resolution, low noise, L3 cache side-channel attack. In: USENIX Security, pp. 719–732 (2014)

Idea: A Unifying Theory for Evaluation Systems

Giampaolo Bella[1]([⊠]) and Rosario Giustolisi[2]

[1] Dipartimento di Matematica e Informatica, Università di Catania, Catania, Italy
giamp@dmi.unict.it
[2] IT University of Copenhagen, Copenhagen, Denmark
rosg@itu.dk

Abstract. Secure systems for voting, exams, auctions and conference paper management are theorised to address the same problem, that of secure evaluations. In support of such a unifying theory comes a model for *Secure Evaluation Systems* (SES), which offers innovative common grounds to understand all four groups. For example, all rest on *submissions*, respectively votes, test answers, bids and papers, which are to be *evaluated* and ultimately ranked. A taxonomy for all groups is advanced to provide a comparative understanding of the various systems. The taxonomy is built according to the type of submissions and the type of evaluation.

The uniformity of the security requirements across all groups offers additional validation, and this is an innovative finding in the direction, currently unexplored, of a common system design. Still, the requirements may variously shape up. For example, while voter privacy is normally required forever, anonymity of the submissions is required until after the marking/evaluation phase for the test answers of an exam, for the (sealed) bids of an auction, and for the papers submitted to a conference.

1 Introduction

There are at least four groups of secure systems that are widely used at present. These are respectively for *voting, exams, auctions* and *conference paper management.* Each group has been extensively studied so far. To advance an example system per group, we mention Helios for voting [1], Remark! for exams [2], the protocol presented by Curtis et al. for auctions [3] and Confichair for conference paper management [4].

This idea paper unfolds our theory that all groups can be unified at an abstract level. The theory is supported by three main pillars. One is a formal model for *Secure Evaluation Systems* (SES), whose main elements are the submitters, the authorities, the submissions and an evaluation function (Sect. 2). The model is a tuple that can be instantiated over each group or a specific system, thus offering a benchmark for a contrastive assessment of the various systems.

Another pillar in support of our unifying theory is a taxonomy for the groups of systems based upon the type of submissions and the type of evaluation (Sect. 3). For example, the taxonomy supports the claim that exam systems and

© Springer International Publishing AG 2017
E. Bodden et al. (Eds.): ESSoS 2017, LNCS 10379, pp. 231–239, 2017.
DOI: 10.1007/978-3-319-62105-0_15

conference systems are very similar, although only exams may seek submissions of type ordered choice, namely a ranked list.

The third pillar is a requirement elicitation process across the four groups of systems (Sect. 4). It is found that all systems have in common various flavours of authentication, non-repudiation, fairness and privacy. In particular, receipt-freeness and coercion-resistance, traditionally spelled out for voting, are interpreted for the first time for exams, indicating the impossibility for an examinee to prove the ownership of her test until after the marking, even with the collaboration of a coercing examining authority. By contrast, after the marking terminates, the system should allow the examinee to publicly leverage the mark for her test.

2   A Model for Secure Evaluation Systems

Secure Multi-Party Computation (SMPC) is a widely studied area of cryptography aimed at the distributed, privacy preserving computation of a function [5]. It means that all participating players will provide inputs that are needed to compute the function, whose output may be made public; however, the computation must not reveal anything about the inputs, hence preserve the privacy of the players. This model can be reviewed to emphasise the details of secure evaluation systems. It is useful to further detail our four groups of secure systems.

Voting system is a method for making a decision or expressing an opinion, usually following discussions, debates or election campaigns. The submissions consist of a set of preferences (votes) over some options (candidate, decisions, etc.). The evaluation consists of a tallyng algorithm that outputs a ranking of candidates (or a winning candidate).

Exam system is a method for evaluating candidates according to their knowledge or skill. The submissions consist of a set of tests over some options (open-ended questions, multiple-questions, etc.). The evaluation consists of a marking algorithm that outputs a ranking of tests (or a winning test).

Auction system is a method for buying and selling goods or services by offering them up for bidding, then taking the bids, and finally selling to the winning bidder. The submissions consist of a set of offers (bids) over some options (goods, prices, etc.). The evaluation consists of an algorithm that outputs a ranking of bids (or a winning bid).

Conference system is a method for managing the papers to be presented at a conference and often published in a book of proceedings. The submissions consist of a set of papers, which are often anonymised. The evaluation consist of an algorithm that outputs a ranking of papers (or a winning paper).

This description underlines clear similarities among all groups, such as that they all aim at producing a ranking. However, the evaluation used for the raking is inherently different. While there is no notion of "correctness" of a vote in democracy, there clearly is such a notion for test answers. Also, while all bids are potentially correct once they are in the right format, correctness of a research paper also is meaningful.

An informal definition can be given to identify the subject matter.

Definition 1 (SES — Informal). *A Secure Evaluation System is a SMPC system that computes a function termed* evaluation function *securely. Its players can be partitioned as* submitters, *who* contribute *submissions, and* authorities, *who* contribute *administration.*

A formal model can then be built to capture a SES abstractly. The model rests on a set S of *submitters* a set s of *submissions* and a set A of *authorities*. The players treat the submissions by means of a set T of *tasks*, such as sending the submissions or entering data in a computer. The specific list of tasks is normally understood as the protocol definition underlying the system. The tasks may express important features of a SES, for example as an electronic protocol if the tasks occur over computing devices, or as a face-to-face protocol if the tasks take place traditionally, *de visu*. Both submitters and authorities may misbehave to obtain an advantage maliciously. This admits a threat model, namely a set of malicious tasks T_t.

The evaluation function f, which may be jointly computed by the players, should satisfy a set R_f of functional requirements. The privacy preservation prerequisite can be generalised as a set R_s of security and privacy.

A SES can thus be formalised as a tuple.

Definition 2 (SES — Formal). *A Secure Evaluation System, at the formal level, is a tuple* $SES = \langle S, A, s, T, T_t, f, R_f, R_s \rangle$ *such that:*

- S *is a set of* submitters;
- A *is a set of* authorities;
- s *is a set of* submissions;
- T *is a set of* tasks, *which the players carry out;*
- T_t *is a* threat model;
- f *is an* evaluation function, *which the players may jointly compute;*
- R_f *is a set of* functional requirements;
- R_s *is a set of* security requirements.

The model can be easily instantiated over a target secure system of our four chosen groups. We instantiate it over the groups themselves, building a table that expresses an inclusion relation, Table 1. Therefore, the table is incomplete because it only provides a limited set of examples, but offers a compact, unifying workbench. This highlights a minor ambiguity in the terminology, that a candidate in voting is someone who can be voted for, while a candidate in exam is someone who is examined.

It must be emphasised that all groups of systems are aimed at computing a ranking. This underlines the competitive nature of the problems that all systems address. Also the R_s line is limited, providing just one obvious security requirement per group, but a more comprehensive analysis will follow (Sect. 4).

Table 1. An incomplete demonstration of the SES formal model

⊆	Voting	Exam	Auction	Conference
S	Voters	Candidates (examinees)	Bidders	Authors
A	Talliers, officials	Invigilators, examiners	Auctioneer	Program chair
s	Votes	Test answers	Bids	Research papers
T	Vote casting	Answering questions	Bidding	Paper writing
T_t	Voting twice	Over-marking	Bid alteration	De-anonymisation
f	Candidate ranking	Test ranking	Bid ranking	Paper ranking
R_f	Efficiency	Efficiency	Efficiency	Efficiency
R_s	Voter privacy	Anonymous marking	Bid sealing	Anonymous reviewer

3   A Taxonomy for Secure Evaluation Systems

We build a taxonomy based upon the types of submissions and the type of evaluation. Submissions can be of three types.

3.1   Types of Submissions

Single-choice submission allows the submitter to select one of the possible options. In voting, this submission type reflects Single-Mark Ballot type where each voter chooses one candidate. In exams, it reflects both open-ended tests and those multiple-choice tests that only demand one answer. In auctions, it reflects Dutch and Sealed first-price auction types where each bidder may only put in one bid. In conferences, this type of submissions is the standard one.

Check-All-That-Applies (CATA) submission allows the submitter to select more than one of the possible options, precisely all those that the submitter deems appropriate. In voting, this reflects Approvals ballot type where each voter can select any number of candidates of her choice. In exams, it reflects tests with more than one correct answer. In auctions, it reflects English auction types where bidders can submit multiple bids to get the standing bid. In conferences, it may be interpreted as the submission of more than one paper by the same author list.

Ordered-choice submission allows the submitter to order the options according to a stated criterion. In voting, this submission type reects Rank and Score ballot types where each voter produces a hierarchy of the candidates. In exams, it reects scale format tests, where submissions are based on a rating scale. In auctions, it reects Combinatorial auction type where each bidder can place bids on combinations of discrete items. In conferences, this type of submissions does not seem to be used.

3.2   Types of Evaluation

The tasks for evaluating the submissions managed through a SES may, in turn, be carried out in three alternative ways, depending on who performs them (while meeting the requirements in R_s):

Authority evaluation prescribes the submissions to be evaluated by a set of dedicated authorities.

Peer evaluation sees the evaluation of the submissions being performed by a set of peers of the submitter's. Also in this case, anonymity may contribute to the submitter's trust in the peers for the sake of evaluation; for example, the submissions might be anonymised. Additionally, the evaluation may extend, as prescribed by R_f of the specific protocol, to the answers of a subset or all of the submitters, as we shall see below.

Self evaluation limits the evaluation to be carried out by the individual submitter, namely each individual can perform the evaluation that meets the requirements stated in R_f. Soundness and fairness of such an evaluation are not obvious so will have to derive from the specific tasks of the system.

3.3   Taxonomy

With all the details provided above, a taxonomy can be built for secure evaluation systems. The taxonomy is in Table 2: a cell mentions a group of secure systems when we are aware that there exists at least one system in the group that exhibits the specific combination of submission and evaluation types that the cell pinpoints.

Authority evaluation. Most SES's feature an authority that takes care of the evaluation process. All democracies elect holders of offices by voting systems that have tallying authorities. This applies to single-choice, CATA, and ordered-choice types of submissions. In electronic voting, some systems have been proposed to distribute the trust among different authorities. For example, one such system is Helios [1]. Similarly, in most classic auctions, the auctioneer is the authority who declares the winning bid. E-bay is a popular example of electronic auction with a CATA type of submission. The auction system by Curtis et al. [3] fits any submission type. In entrance examinations, authorities normally produce the list of admitted candidate. Some effort to distribute the trust on such authorities

Table 2. A taxonomy for secure evaluation systems

		Evaluation		
		Authority	Peer	Self
Submission	**Single-choice**	Voting auction exam conf.	Exam conf.	Voting auction
	CATA	Voting auction exam conf.	Exam conf.	Voting
	Ordered-choice	Voting auction exam	Exam	

has been discussed in a recent proposal of a secure exam system [2]. Notably, the latter fits any submission type. In Easychair, the program chair acts as authority and decides the list of accepted papers. Easychair accepts submissions of more than one paper by the same author list, hence supports both single-choice and CATA submission types.

Peer evaluation. Peer evaluation is peculiar to conferences and exams. For example, in MOOCs homeworks are peer-reviewed. To our knowledge, neither voting nor auction systems have been proposed so far with this feature.

Self evaluation. Kiayias and Yung [6] introduced the notion of self-tallying voting for single-choice submission type, in which the result can be tallied and verified by anybody. Hao et al. [7] proposed a different system that supports an approval ballot type, hence a CATA submission. No exam systems today support ordered-choice with self evaluation. Recent works on smart contract technology, such as AuctionHouse [8] seems to lead to auctions with self-declaration of winning bids enforced by the use of blockchains. To our knowledge, there is no work on exam with self-evaluation, although the use of smart contracts may favour the construction of such a kind of systems.

4   Requirement Elicitation for Secure Evaluation Systems

We now wonder whether it is also possible to find similarities among the SES multi-objective security goals. More specifically, given any security goal of a group of SES systems, can we find a similar interpretation in each of the other groups? History of secure systems tell us that it is unfeasible to list and freeze all the security goals of a system because people's needs may change over time, hence the system's requirements tend to change as well. However, while we may not reach a definitive answer to our question, we may find a temporary answer by considering the main requirements that are popular nowadays. In our analysis, we focus on classic authentication, non-repudiation, fairness, and privacy goals.

Authentication. Data origin Authentication naturally maps to the authentication of the submissions of a SES system. Data origin authentication is a common goal with the same interpretation in voting, exams, auctions, and conferences. It is normally expected that any evaluation algorithm considers only inputs submitted by eligible parties: only ballots cast by eligible voters should be recorded in a voting system; only test answers originated with eligible candidates should be marked in an exam; only bids put by registered bidders should be considered in an auction; only papers by registered authors should be considered as valid submissions to a conference.

In the same way, data origin authentication is also expected for authenticating the outcome of the evaluation in each of the systems. It means that the rankings in all four groups of systems are generated by the corresponding set of official authorities. Note that data origin authentication does not imply the *correctness* of the evaluation, which means that the outcome derives by correct execution of the evaluation function. Data origin authentication guarantees that such a function is fed with all and only eligible submissions. However, correctness of the evaluation is a desired goal for each of our systems, and has a similar interpretation across each of them.

Non-repudiation. An interpretation of non-repudiation [9] is the impossibility for submitters to deny their participation. In voting, it means that a voter cannot deny to have participated in an election. The same clearly applies to exams with candidates, to auctions with bidders and to conferences with papers. However, auctions support an additional interpretation in which non-repudiation may signify the impossibility for a bidder to claim that she did not submit the winning bid. A similar interpretation is hard to find in voting, in which the very opposite is actually desirable, namely that a voter cannot prove the way she voted (receipt freeness). We observe that in exams a test should eventually be linked to the corresponding author in order to assign a mark to each examinee, hence non-repudiation applies to exams.

Another instantiation of non-repudiation regards the reception of submissions. This interpretation applies to voting, exams, auctions and conferences, so that no authority can successfully deny having received valid submissions.

Fairness. As regards submissions, fairness means that choices are submitted independently from other submissions. In voting, it means that no voter can be influenced by votes already cast. In most auction types, submitted offers should not influence subsequent offers. However, this interpretation of fairness obviously does not apply for English auctions, in which bidders submit new offers to displace the standing bid. From a bidding strategy point of view, if we consider the submission of a bidder as the final bid she wishes to offer for an auction, we can see our fairness interpretation in English auctions as well. Fairness is of utmost importance in exams and means that candidates should answer their test based on their knowledge and skills. An additional fairness goal exists for exam and can be named *marking fairness*: it prescribes that tests should be marked independently from the identity of their authors. Note that marks are not the outcome of exam's function evaluation but they rather are inputs to the function to calculate the rank of the tests. Marks can be associated to weights in voting and auctions, in which votes or bids have different weights. Such interpretation, however, requires weights to depend on the identity of the submitters. Thus, an interpretation similar to marking fairness is hard to find in voting and auctions. By contrast, fairness in conferences abides by the same interpretation as for exams.

Privacy. Privacy goals have seen many interpretations. If we look at the privacy of the submission, the interpretation in voting is that the system does not reveal how a voter voted. The same applies to the pairs examinee/test, bidder/bid and author/paper. Note that this definition is strongly related to the definition of fairness discussed above, and the same considerations made about English auctions apply here. Voting systems normally require vote privacy to hold even after the evaluation. The winning bid is normally revealed in auctions, still the identity of the bidder may not be disclosed. The same applies for exams in which the right to publicly disclose the link of a test with its author is left to the examinee. By contrast, this link is routinely disclosed in conferences, where the author is normally required to attend and present the accepted paper. Further differences among those systems find a place in specific definitions of privacy. Strong privacy definitions in voting state that a voter cannot prove the way she voted (*receipt-freeness*) even if the voter collaborates with the coercer (*coercion-resistance*) [10]. Similar strong privacy definitions are less meaningful in auctions since winning bids are normally announced publicly. Also information revealed through other channels, such as who is the (new) owner of the auctioned good or service, would disclose if a bidder sent a winning or a losing offer. In exams, receipt-freeness and coercion-resistance are meaningful through the marking phase and can be seen as stronger definitions of marking fairness. In particular, receipt-freeness and coercion-resistance are two detailed instances of *anonymous marking*, in which tests are marked while ignoring their authors. They signify that an examinee should not be able to prove the ownership of her test until after the marking (receipt-freeness) even if the examinee collaborates with the coercer, e.g. the examiner (coercion-resistance). However, the possibility of a covert channel between examinee and examiner should be ruled out. Privacy over conferences can be interpreted much the same way as with exams.

Although we found many similar security goal interpretations among SES systems, there may still be differences in other clusters, such as verifiability and accountability [11]. The requirement elicitation needs to be expanded also over such clusters to fully substantiate a putative claim that all systems state the same security requirements.

5   Conclusions

Secure systems for voting, exams, auctions and conferences have never been analysed comparatively before. Our unifying theory claims that this is possible, and our supporting model confirms their similarities. Our taxonomy favours a comparative understanding of the various systems. The traditional security requirements of authentication, non-repudiation, fairness and privacy apply to all four groups. The next step is to focus on either one of the three introduced pillars, i.e., formal model, taxonomy, or requirement elicitation, and to study it thoroughly. For example, it would be interesting to study those group of systems, such as surveys, that normally do not produce a ranking.

A readily-exploitable value of this work is a deep understanding of the security requirements of each system; this is made possible precisely by their argumentation across the various groups. An additional value is that it may inspire a combination of the research efforts that are currently spent in each individual group towards solving more effectively than before what seems to be a same problem, that of secure evaluation.

Acknowledgement. This work is supported in part by DemTech grant 10-092309 from the Danish Council for Strategic Research, Programme Commission on Strategic Growth Technologies.

References

1. Adida, B.: Helios: Web-based open-audit voting. In: Proceedings of the 17th Conference on Security Symposium, USENIX Symposium (2008)
2. Giustolisi, R., Lenzini, G., Ryan, P.Y.A.: *Remark!*: a secure protocol for remote exams. In: Christianson, B., Malcolm, J., Matyáš, V., Švenda, P., Stajano, F., Anderson, J. (eds.) Security Protocols 2014. LNCS, vol. 8809, pp. 38–48. Springer, Cham (2014). doi:10.1007/978-3-319-12400-1_5
3. Curtis, B., Pieprzyk, J., Seruga, J.: An efficient eauction protocol. In: Proceedings of the Second International Conference on Availability, Reliability and Security (ARES), pp. 417–421. IEEE Computer Society (2007)
4. Arapinis, M., Bursuc, S., Ryan, M.: Privacy supporting cloud computing: ConfiChair, a case study. In: Degano, P., Guttman, J.D. (eds.) POST 2012. LNCS, vol. 7215, pp. 89–108. Springer, Heidelberg (2012). doi:10.1007/978-3-642-28641-4_6
5. Yao, A.C.: Protocols for secure computations. In: Proceedings of the 23rd Annual Symposium on Foundations of Computer Science (SFCS), pp. 160–164, IEEE (1982)
6. Kiayias, A., Yung, M.: Self-tallying elections and perfect ballot secrecy. In: Naccache, D., Paillier, P. (eds.) PKC 2002. LNCS, vol. 2274, pp. 141–158. Springer, Heidelberg (2002). doi:10.1007/3-540-45664-3_10
7. Hao, F., Kreeger, M.N., Randell, B., Clarke, D., Shahandashti, S.F., Lee, P.H.J.: Every vote counts: ensuring integrity in large-scale electronic voting. USENIX J. Election Technol. Syst. **2**, 1–25 (2014)
8. Petkanics, D., Tang, E.: Auctionhouse. http://auctionhouse.dappbench.com/ (2016). Accessed 16 Jan 2017
9. Kremer, S., Markowitch, O., Zhou, J.: An intensive survey of fair non-repudiation protocols. Comput. Commun. **25**, 1606–1621 (2002)
10. Delaune, S., Kremer, S., Ryan, M.: Coercion-resistance and receipt-freeness in electronic voting. In: 19th IEEE Computer Security Foundations Workshop (CSFW 2006), pp. 12–42(2006)
11. Küsters, R., Truderung, T., Vogt, A.: Accountability: Definition and relationship to verifiability. In: Proceedings of the 17th ACM Conference on Computer and Communications Security, CCS 2010, pp. 526–535. ACM, New York (2010)

Author Index

Alm, Cecilia O. 70

Baldwin, Carliss 53
Baudry, Benoit 97
Beato, Filipe 19
Bella, Giampaolo 231
Beni, Emad Heydari 19
Bielova, Nataliia 115
Bogaerts, Jasper 1
Bos, Herbert 177

Cojocar, Lucian 177
Coull, Natalie 133

De Cock, Danny 19
De Meo, Federico 196
Doolan, Lee 53

Fellner, Richard 161
Ferguson, Robert Ian 133

Giustolisi, Rosario 231
Gruss, Daniel 161

Hammer, Christian 87

Joosen, Wouter 1, 19

Koo, Hyungjoon 143
Köpf, Boris 213
Kroes, Taddeus 177

Lagaisse, Bert 1, 19
Lagerström, Robert 53
Laperdrix, Pierre 97
Le, Anhtuan 36

Li, Forrest 143
Lipp, Moritz 161

MacCormack, Alan 53
Mangard, Stefan 161
Mantel, Heiko 213
Maurice, Clémentine 161
Meneely, Andrew 70
Meyers, Benjamin S. 70
Mishra, Vikas 97
Monrose, Fabian 143
Morton, Micah 143
Munaiah, Nuthan 70
Murukannaiah, Pradeep K. 70

Nafees, Tayyaba 133

Polychronakis, Michalis 143
Prud'hommeaux, Emily 70

Rashid, Awais 36
Rezk, Tamara 115
Roedig, Utz 36

Sampson, Adam 133
Schwarz, Michael 161
Snow, Kevin Z. 143
Somé, Dolière Francis 115
Sturtevant, Dan 53

Viganò, Luca 196

Weber, Alexandra 213
Welearegai, Gebrehiwet Biyane 87
Wolff, Josephine 70

Yu, Yang 70

Zhang, Ren 19

Printed in the United States
By Bookmasters